AMERICA'S
NATIONAL
MONUMENTS

DEVELOPMENT OF WESTERN RESOURCES

The Development of Western Resources is an interdisciplinary series focusing on the use and misuse of resources in the American West. Written for a broad readership of humanists, social scientists, and resource specialists, the books in this series emphasize both historical and contemporary perspectives as they explore the interplay between resource exploitation and economic, social, and political experiences.

John G. Clark, University of Kansas, General Editor

AMERICA'S
NATIONAL
MONUMENTS

The Politics of
Preservation

Hal Rothman

University Press of Kansas

First published as *Preserving Different Pasts:*
The American National Monuments.
© 1989 by the Board of Trustees of the University of Illinois

This paperback edition is published by the University Press of Kansas by
arrangement with the University of Illinois Press. All rights reserved.

Library of Congress Cataloging-in-Publication Data

Rothman, Hal, 1958–
    [Preserving different pasts]
    America's national monuments / Hal Rothman.
       p.   cm.
    Originally published: Urbana: University of Illinois Press, c1989.
    ISBN 0-7006-0672-6 (paperback ; alk. paper)
    1. National monuments—United States. 2. Monuments—
United States—Conservation and restoration.   I. Title.
E159.R68   1994
363.6'9'0973–dc20   93-43439

British Library Cataloguing in Publication Data is available.

Printed in the United States of America
10   9   8   7   6   5   4   3   2

The paper used in this publication meets the minimum requirements of
the American National Standard for Permanence of Paper for Printed
Library Materials Z39.48-1984.

For my parents,
Neal and Rozann,

And in memory of
Lisa Eller Bruhn

Contents

Acknowledgments

I WOULD LIKE TO THANK the many people who helped me during the course of researching and writing this book. At the University of Texas at Austin, William H. Goetzmann taught me about the American West, while Alfred W. Crosby Jr. enlightened me about things environmental. Robert Abzug, Suzanne Shelton Buckley, and William Scheik all read the manuscript and offered their suggestions. At an early stage, Robert M. Crunden helped me to see the larger implications of the work. Dwight Pitcaithley's comments led me to see a number of issues more clearly. Alfred Runte's precise criticisms and sometimes acerbic insights have played an important role in shaping the focus of this book. Robert Righter, Kenneth Helphand, and Sally K. Fairfax each read all or part of the manuscript and their comments also improved it. Barry Mackintosh, the Bureau Historian of the National Park Service, offered the benefits of his experience. Melody Webb, the Southwest Regional Historian of the Park Service provided me with a frequent sounding board for ideas. Former Chief Historian Robert M. Utley generously gave me a couple of hours on the telephone one afternoon to help me unravel the intricacies of the Park Service during the New Deal. Richard Crawford and Bill Creech of the National Archives taught me to negotiate the perils of Record Group 79, the Records of the National Park Service.

The Eastern National Park and Monument Association gave me the Ronald F. Lee Graduate Research Fellowship during 1984-85. This grant provided immeasurably valuable support as I struggled to complete the manuscript. During my extended stays in the Washington, D.C., area, Rita and Julian Simon and their family, John Medina, and my cousins Sam and Barbara Rothman and their family all extended gracious hospitality to me.

An author's first book is an ordeal, a process that often seems to go forward slowly but backward rapidly. I was fortunate to be surrounded by an extraordinary group of people at the University of Texas at Austin who provided both intellectual stimulation and social support. Martin and Heather Catto Kohout, Rick Bruhn and the late Lisa Eller Bruhn, Tony and Lisa Gaxiola, Rick McCaslin, Peter Fish, Suzanne Seifert, Barry Webb, and Rob Lewis all provided commentary and perspective. The students in my Parks and Monuments in American Culture class at the University of New Mexico also helped broaden my perspective. My friends in Santa Fe—Joe Lenihan and Quincie Hopkins, David Shapiro and Jennifer Dixon, Jon and Virginia Robicheau, Mark Altschuler, and Rory Gauthier—repeatedly reminded me that what I was doing really was important. Robin Winks was a role model and source of inspiration during his stay in New Mexico. Barbara Greene Chamberlain contributed her editorial skills in the final stages of the manuscript, and Carole S. Appel of the University of Illinois Press continually encouraged me. My parents, Neal and Rozann Rothman, believed in me when I had doubts. To all of these people, I am grateful. Any errors, shortcomings, or omissions that remain are strictly my own.

Introduction

THIS IS THE STORY of the American national monuments and the way in which they became an important part of the American preservation movement. The evolution of the monument category reveals the gradual awakening of government officials and the public to the importance of a broadly based approach to federal preservation, while the areas preserved mirror the changing values of American society. The lessons it shows are less those of participatory democracy than of individual perceptions of social obligation, less those of the moment than of the future. Although everyone recognizes the national parks as American treasures, the national monuments are evidence of the story of federal preservation from inside the government—the vision of a few that has become a generally held social objective.

The law that allowed this "inside" form of preservation, An Act for Preservation of American Antiquities, more commonly known as the Antiquities Act of 1906, has been undervalued, ignored, and discounted by both contemporary observers and historians. The Antiquities Act, in fact, is the most important piece of preservation legislation ever enacted by the United States government. Although its title suggests significance only in archaeological matters, in practice the law became the cornerstone of preservation in the federal system. Without it, there would have been little flexibility in the preservation process, and many areas of significance would have been destroyed long before Congress passed legislation to protect them.

The passage of the Antiquities Act created a mechanism through which federal officials, interested professionals, and other special-interest groups could achieve preservation goals without waiting on popular or congressional consensus. The law provided for the establishment of national monuments by executive proclamation, creating a system to ensure preservation in ways that individual national park bills could not. This gave the preservation constituency a special voice in the process of selecting and designating national monuments.

The Antiquities Act preserved much more than archaeological areas. The law is the tool by means of which the broadest category of park areas ever created has been established. It allows the president of the United States to permanently reserve public lands with significant prehistoric, historic, or natural features. There are few statuatory limits upon this power; the only restrictive clause in the law limits the monuments to "the smallest area compatible" with their management. This has given federal administrators a flexibility that no other piece of legislation has allowed.

Ironically, there are no intrinsic features that separate the national monuments from the national parks. The difference is in mode of establishment; Congress must pass bills authorizing new national parks, whereas the president can proclaim national monuments with the stroke of a pen. As a result areas with identical features may be found in both categories simultaneously. But the term *national park* has acquired a clear meaning to Americans of the twentieth century, whereas *national monument* has not. The federal agencies that have adminstered the park system—prior to 1916 the General Land Office of the Department of the Interior and after that date the National Park Service—have sanctioned this informal distinction. As a result the two types of areas have developed in distinctly different fashions. National monuments have proliferated since 1906, while the number of parks has increased relatively slowly.

The Antiquities Act has the flexibility that it does as a result of the time in which it became law. The bill passed Congress in 1906, at the height of the Progressive era. That year was also the year of archaeology in Congress, the one moment in American history when archaeological ruins were important enough to merit the actions of national legislators. The establishment of Mesa Verde National Park, the only national park established purely for its archaeological value, followed the passage of the Antiquities Act by less than one month. This interest in preservation of archaeological sites in the Southwest was closely linked to the issues of the time: the closing of the westward frontier and an awakening to the idea that Americans could exhaust the natural attributes of the continent, xenophobia that held that the American West had natural and cultural attributes as spectacular as those of Europe, and the Progressive-era desire for scientific management and centralized authority over the resources of the nation. The window opened, Congress passed the Antiquities Act, and as quickly as issues of archaeological preservation came to the fore, they faded from the position they held in 1906.

The Antiquities Act of 1906 typifies the legislation that emanated from the administration of Theodore Roosevelt, and as a result its limits are similar to those of most of the bills passed during the Progressive era. With its passage, the Act codified established government practice by centralizing power in a group of people presumed to have the best interests of the public in mind. This notion of an elite in the know that should take responsibility for the direction of American society gained credence as a response to the excesses of the private sector during the last quarter of the nineteenth century. A result of the impetus for middle-class reform, the Antiquities Act embodied the middle-class values of 1906, at once its saving grace and its downfall. A product of the move to apply government regulations and scientific principles to natural and cultural resources of the continent, the Act also contained the assumption that the public would obey its dictates simply because it was the law. In this respect the Antiquities Act and its legacy are important parts of the transition from the unrestricted ethos of the nineteenth-century West to the more structured and regulated world that replaced it.

The evolution of the monument category provides one of the clearest pictures of the changing values of American preservation. Because it could be applied to much more than archaeological sites, the Antiquities Act remained useful as the accepted ideas of what constituted an important part of the American past changed. The law was malleable, allowing the differentiation between public and federal visions of the past while providing for both the eccentric view of national significance and a consensus within the federal system. As a result, the Antiquities Act allowed the preservation of different pasts—archaeological, natural, historical, as well as differing aspects of each of these categories. Its amorphous nature gave it a significance that belies its narrow title.

From the beginning, the ease of proclamation and the sheer number of national monuments made the category seem less important than the national parks. While new national parks generally represented a consensus of preservation values, the monuments became a dreamland for those with preservation-oriented agendas. The Antiquities Act offered advocates an easy way to accelerate the preservation process, resulting in a category of areas linked more by nomenclature than by content. The emphasis of administrators was on the national parks, leaving the national monuments to grow unchecked. Little of the enthusiasm and boosterism surrounding the national parks was used in promoting the national monuments.

The initial applications of the Antiquities Act were largely in the West, the location of the vast majority of public land in the United States. Because the area east of the Mississippi River had long been settled, the West became the stage upon which this Progressive impulse was implemented. The fate of archaeological ruins in the Southwest concerned congressional sponsors of the Act, and federal bureaus shared this attitude. With the new law, the federal government gained another way to regulate land in less-settled regions of the nation. But the unrestricted power that the Antiquities Act offered meant that its confinement to the West was a temporary condition. From archaeological and western roots, the monument category evolved to include large natural areas, historic places, and nearly every other type of place that had preservation value.

As a result of the ease with which a national monument could be proclaimed, the category served a variety of functions for federal agencies. It began as a storehouse of places preserved for no distinct purpose, gradually growing to include many areas that federal officials sought as national parks, but for which they could not find sufficient support in Congress. Instead of waiting for passage of a bill, federal officials could lobby for a national monument. Because this required only the signature of the president, it was easy to achieve. Yet this way-station status hurt the development of the monuments, particularly after the advent of the National Park Service in 1916. Some of the most spectacular park areas—the Grand Canyon, Zion Canyon, the Olympic Mountains, the Petrified Forest, and Chaco Canyon— were once national monuments; all received new designations with congressional approval at a later date.

During the 1920s, when the National Park Service shaped the public image of the park system, the national monuments were largely ignored. In the fifteen years that followed the establishment of the agency in 1916, the national parks became the focus of American travelers. But this distinction did not include the national monuments; except for those in the Southwest, administered by a dedicated iconoclast, the national monuments were largely left out of the development of the park system.

Only with the advent of the New Deal in the 1930s did the monuments become an important part of the park system. The money that federal relief programs pumped into the economy also reached the park system. Civilian Conservation Corps camps were a major source of labor for park projects, and their existence gave high-level Park Service administrators new options. No longer did they have to select areas for development. With the added money from relief programs, there was enough for most of the areas that had the potential to attract visitors.

But the influx of New Deal money changed the park system. Before 1933, "preservation" meant the reservation of areas from settlement or commercial use. After the New Deal, tourist development became an important part of the responsibilities of the Park Service. No longer were areas established and not developed; the construction of facilities for visitors became a primary concern for an agency that to a large extent measured its success in visitation statistics. By the 1950s, the Park Service had spent more than thirty-five years accommodating visitors. Reaching the level of visitation that agency officials sought required continued development of facilities.

This emphasis made the Antiquities Act of 1906 less important than it had been prior to 1933. The law offered no way to fund the development of monuments. It allowed only establishment. In a time when executive fiat did not match the exuberance of the first decade of the twentieth century and funding of park areas required the approval of congressional committees, the advantages that the Antiquities Act offered lost much of their significance. The law became a last resort in cases when rapid presidential action was the only way to attract the attention of Congress.

The evolution in the use of the Antiquities Act mirrors the changing nature of American preservation. At the turn of the century, the simple reservation of threatened areas was the primary objective of advocates of preservation. As the Park Service developed its agenda

in the competitive arena of the Washington bureaucracy, its needs
changed. A wider range of areas, most of which were not new discoveries of remote places, entered the park system. Fortunately for
park proponents, the Antiquities Act was amorphous enough to serve
their needs. But with the advent of widespread federal funding for
park development, this law and its Progressive-era assumptions became insufficient to meet the new needs of the agency. As a result,
the Antiquities Act was used less frequently. Reserved for special
circumstances, it became less a part of the continuous process of the
growth of the park system.

Since 1906 the expectations of the public and of the federal agencies
responsible for preservation have changed dramatically. As the national park system grew, it embodied more and different types of park
areas, and the monument category became the place where the General Land Office and the National Park Service experimented with
new concepts. Types of areas that more recently have been transferred
to the national park category entered the park system as national
monuments. The monument category helped broaden the federal
vision of preservation. The range of possibilities allowed by the Antiquities Act has made the national monuments the focus of the attention of special-interest groups with agendas that differ from those
of federal agencies.

The Antiquities Act and the national monuments became less significant to the goals of the Park Service after the New Deal financed
the development of the park system. The New Deal introduced new
kinds of areas to the park system and developed them, and after 1945,
both the public and the Park Service regarded development instead
of the reservation of an area as the paramount consideration of the
system. While the Antiquities Act allows for the establishment of areas,
it offers no provisions for funding, and as Congress exerted greater
control over the operations of the park system, the Antiquities Act
has been used less and less frequently. It has been reserved for emergency situations, urgent cases in which there are no other options
similar to the circumstances under which a number of the early monuments were proclaimed.

The real achievement of the Antiquities Act of 1906 was that it
allowed the establishment of a system of preservation without the
approval of Congress. Prior to its existence there had been few mechanisms through which the federal government could permanently and

easily preserve the public domain. While the system that the law established did not solve all questions of preservation, it was significantly better than no system at all. The Antiquities Act of 1906 laid the basis for further federal legislation to preserve the cultural resources of the public domain; seventy-three years after the passage of the law, Congress took the next step in that direction with the passage of the Archaeological Resources Protection Act of 1979.

The Antiquities Act has been a critical factor in the formation of the national park system as we know it today. Without it, many areas of outstanding natural and cultural significance would have been lost as a result of congressional inertia and indifference. Its significance lies foremost in its contribution to the development of the park system as a broadly based entity. Throughout the twentieth century, the modern federal vision for the preservation of areas of prehistoric, historic, and natural significance has been shaped by the provisions of the Antiquities Act of 1906. The national monuments are the basis of the modern park system, the raw material with which the boundaries of federal preservation have been established.

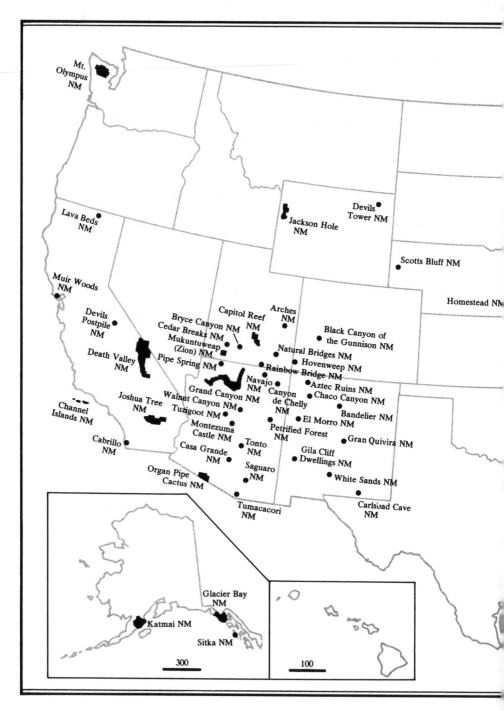

Mt.
Olympus
NM

Devils
Tower NM

Lava Beds
NM

Jackson Hole
NM

Scotts Bluff NM

Muir Woods
NM

Homestead NM

Devils
Postpile
NM

Bryce Canyon NM

Capitol Reef
NM

Arches
NM

Cedar Breaks NM

Black Canyon of
the Gunnison NM

Mukuntuweap
(Zion) NM

Death Valley
NM

Pipe Spring NM

Natural Bridges NM

Hovenweep NM

Rainbow Bridge NM

Navajo
NM

Aztec Ruins NM

Joshua Tree
NM

Walnut Canyon NM

Grand Canyon NM

Canyon
de Chelly
NM

Chaco Canyon NM

Channel
Islands NM

Tuzigoot NM

Bandelier NM

El Morro NM

Montezuma
Castle NM

Petrified Forest
NM

Gran Quivira NM

Cabrillo
NM

Tonto
NM

Casa Grande
NM

Gila Cliff
Dwellings NM

Saguaro
NM

Organ Pipe
Cactus NM

White Sands NM

Tumacacori
NM

Carlsbad Cave
NM

Glacier Bay
NM

Katmai NM

Sitka NM

300

100

Location of Selected National Monuments

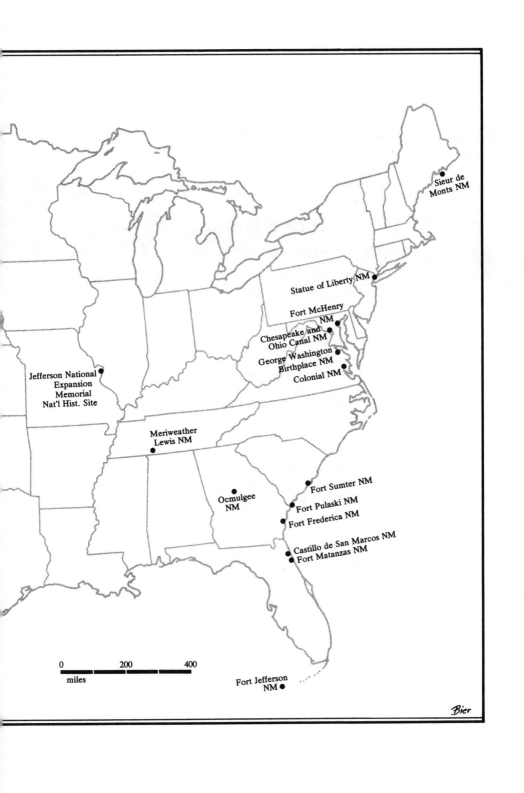

Sieur de
Monts NM

Statue of Liberty NM

Fort McHenry
NM

Chesapeake and
Ohio Canal NM

George Washington
Birthplace NM

Colonial NM

Jefferson National
Expansion
Memorial
Nat'l Hist. Site

Meriweather
Lewis NM

Fort Sumter NM

Ocmulgee
NM

Fort Pulaski NM

Fort Frederica NM

Castillo de San Marcos NM

Fort Matanzas NM

0   200   400

miles

Fort Jefferson
NM ●

Bier

Abbreviations

APVA	Association for the Preservation of Virginia Antiquities
AT&SF	Atchison, Topeka, and Santa Fe Railroad
BIA	Bureau of Indian Affairs
CCC	Civilian Conservation Corps
CCNPF	Coordinating Committee on National Parks and Forests
CWA	Civil Works Administration
D&RG	Denver and Rio Grande Western Railroad
FERA	Federal Emergency Relief Administration
GLO	General Land Office
NA, RG 79	National Archives, Record Group 79, Records of the National Park Service
NPS	National Park Service
PWA	Public Works Administration
USFS	United States Forest Service
USGS	United States Geological Survey
WPA	Works Progress Administration

AMERICA'S
NATIONAL
MONUMENTS

1

The Sequoia Stone Dish Incident

ON 25 AUGUST 1904 CAPT. GEORGE F. HAMILTON of the United States Army, the acting superintendent of both Sequoia and General Grant National Parks in California, informed Secretary of the Interior Ethan A. Hitchcock that a laborer "in an unfrequented part of the park, found a [prehistoric] stone dish, apparently roughly gouged out of a piece of soft stone, the dimensions being approximately, 12 × 7 × 5 inches."[1] According to the captain, this was not the first artifact found within the boundaries of Sequoia National Park. Because he expected that others might find "Indian relics," Hamilton requested guidelines for handling this and other similar cases.

The Department of the Interior immediately responded. Since the 1890s preserving prehistory had been a concern of the federal government, and by 1904 officials at the department had the makings of a policy in place. On Hitchcock's behalf, Acting Secretary Thomas Ryan expressed an interest in the situation. He instructed Hamilton to require the man who found the dish, J. F. Seabright, to turn it over to the superintendent. "Do not permit tourists," his telegram continued, "to remove Indian relics or other objects of interest found on Government lands."[2] Ryan believed that his action was essential if the government was to safeguard prehistoric ruins in the public domain.

The discovery of the stone dish in Sequoia also excited the interest of cultural institutions affiliated with the federal government. On 3 September 1904 Ryan asked the acting secretary of the Smithsonian Institution, Richard Rathbun, if Hamilton's description of the dish intrigued him. Interested, Rathbun asked to have the dish forwarded to the Smithsonian for examination.[3] When others in cultural circles in Washington, D.C., heard of the discovery, they added their perspective. The acting commissioner of the Bureau of Ethnology, William Harris, thought that the dish belonged in the National Museum. He also recommended the passage of legislation that would require individuals to obtain authorization to comb government lands for relics of any kind. Charles D. Walcott of the U.S. Geological Survey concurred, suggesting that the secretary of the Smithsonian Institution and the head of the Bureau of Ethnology were the logical people to administer a system of permits. W. A. Richards, the commissioner of the General Land Office, also agreed and indicated that anyone removing artifacts from the public domain could be charged with trespassing.[4] All these, however, were stopgap measures. Clearly the government needed a comprehensive system.

There was a larger question that also required consideration. Hamilton had wondered whether people could legally keep artifacts that they found within the boundaries of the park. In response to this query, Rathbun informed the secretary of the interior that letting the public take what they wished from public land was a flawed policy. Allowing people to carry away artifacts "piecemeal" affected scientific efforts to understand prehistory, and he suggested that collecting the pieces only gratified the curiosity of visitors "in a small way." Rathbun "did not know that any specific law exists that would cover this subject, but it would seem elementary that objects found in the public domain should remain the property of the United States, and may not be appropriated by private persons."[5]

Contrary to Rathbun's expectations, resolving the question was anything but elementary. The government had no way to prove that it owned the artifact, and Seabright clearly stated in two interviews with Forest Ranger Ernest Britten, the officer of the Department of the Interior responsible for national parks in California, that he did not intend to give it up. In the first interview, Seabright intimated that he no longer had possession of the bowl. In the second, on 23 September 1904, Britten asked Seabright for the artifact point-blank and the latter "refused to deliver the dish. He stated that the government would be compelled to prove their right to [it] before he would deliver same." Seabright's recalcitrance continued. On 10 October Seabright acknowledged receipt of three letters from Captain Hamilton pertaining to the matter and referred the superintendent to Ranger Britten, refusing to answer any further questions.[6]

By late January 1905 Britten was in a quandary. He could not decide on a proper course of action. Seabright refused to succumb to pressure, and without legal authorization, Britten could not compel him to turn over the artifact. He believed that the man had the dish and that an itinerant laborer like Seabright would soon depart, taking the artifact with him. The situation became urgent. Britten pleaded with his superior: "If the Hon. Secretary of the Interior, can suggest any means by which Seabright can be forced to return the dish, I most urgently recommend that it be applied, for the reason that the taking of this dish is widely known, and if allowed to remain in Seabright's possession, similar cases will follow. . . . [I]f any action is to be taken it should be at once."[7]

In actuality, there was nothing that the secretary of the interior could do. Keeping artifacts was technically illegal, but there was no statute that empowered Britten to seize the dish, to arrest Seabright, or even to prevent Seabright from leaving California. The Department of the Interior could only give orders to Seabright to return the dish. If Seabright chose not to comply, there was little that the combined might of the Department of the Interior, the Smithsonian Institution, and the Bureau of Ethnology could do.

"The matter of [the] 'stone dish,' taken from the Sequoia Park," as federal officials came to call the incident, pointed out a critical gap in the laws governing publicly owned land in the United States.[8] Existing laws covered the land and its mineral and water rights, but the federal government had no law that prevented people from walking off with material treasures that they discovered. This oversight, so clearly illustrated in the incident at Sequoia National Park, required immediate rectification. For too long the government had been forced to tolerate this situation. As more people settled in the West, federal officials recognized that this sort of incident would become more common. If the situation persisted, private citizens might appropriate the physical evidence of the prehistoric past on the North American continent at the very moment when American scientists were beginning to explore its ruins systematically. If allowed to become dispersed in private collections all over the world, further knowledge of this heritage would be lost before the general public was aware of the extent of the cultures that preceded Europeans in the Americas.

At the time, the preservation of archaeological resources by the federal government was a new concept. Before the turn of the twentieth century, only a few Americans expressed any scientific interest in the pre-European past of North America; a few American professional archaeologists were describing ancient monuments in the Ohio and Mississippi river valleys, but most were trained in Europe and concentrated their work upon European and Middle Eastern sites. Government surveys of the West reported the existence of massive prehistoric structures among their many findings, and although these were of interest to antiquarians, the value of archaeological treasures paled when compared to the potential of western mineral, agricultural, and timber resources. Although the government supported the early archaeological surveys carried out by agencies such as the Bureau of Ethnology, federal officials did not see the preservation of archaeological areas as a responsibility of the federal government or its institutions.

The Sequoia stone dish incident was just one of many times that the need for legislation regulating the collecting of archaeological artifacts had come to the attention of the Department of the Interior. In 1904 Congress considered three separate preservationist bills, one of which the department had put forward, but failed to vote on any of them. Despite increasing federal bureaucratic recognition of the need for governmental regulation and control of archaeological ruins upon the public domain, there was not enough support to pass any legislation. A number of issues prevented consensus. Eastern and western regional interests came into conflict over this issue, as they did over so many natural resource questions. As experts from different fields offered their input, the range of viewpoints on preservation seemed to preclude compromise.

Notes

1. Capt. George F. Hamilton to the secretary of the interior, 25 August 1904, National Archives, Records Group 79 (hereafter given as NA, RG 79), Records of the National Park Service, Series 1, Records Relating to National Parks and Monuments 1872-1916, Letters Received by the Office of the Secretary of the Interior Relating to National Parks 1872-1907, Tray 165. All subsequent citations in this chapter are to documents in Tray 165.

2. Telegram, Interior Department to Superintendent G. F. Hamilton, 1 September 1904.

3. Richard Rathbun to the secretary of the interior, 8 September 1904.

4. Charles D. Walcott to the secretary of the interior, 14 October 1904; W. A. Richards to the secretary of the interior, 11 October 1904.

5. Hamilton to secretary, 25 August 1904; Rathbun to secretary, 8 September 1904.

6. Ernest Britten to the secretary of the interior, 3 February 1905. At the time, the Department of the Interior managed the forest reserves [national forests], a reality that changed with the establishment of the United States Forest Service (USFS) in 1905.

7. Ibid.

8. Rathbun to secretary, 8 September 1904

2

Pothunters and Professors

B Y 1904 ARCHAEOLOGICAL PRESERVATION had become a point of
confluence for a number of trends in the American social climate.
Historic preservation by local groups, exploration of the West and
discovery of prehistoric structures throughout the Southwest, and
greater government control over public land through the implementation of laws centralizing power in the executive branch all played
an important role in establishing social underpinnings for federal
action. From these disparate actions came the impetus for legislation
to protect archaeological ruins.

Historic preservation in the United States began as the province of
elite social groups with the desire to protect historic structures. Abra-
ham and Judah Touro, who helped finance the upkeep of the Touro
Synagogue in Newport, Rhode Island; Uriah Levy, who purchased
Jefferson's home at Monticello in 1836; and the Mount Vernon Ladies
Association, chartered by the Virginia legislature in 1856 to accept
title to Mount Vernon and spearheaded by a woman from a plantation
in upcountry South Carolina, Ann Pamela Cunningham, typified the
people and organizations responsible for early preservation. When
such people had the ability to finance the purchase of the places they
believed important, they often took personal initiative to ensure the
safety of historic properties. More often, they tried to save historic
buildings by raising a public hue and cry that led to action either by
an organization of concerned citizens or by the state or local government. Before the Civil War, most efforts were unsuccessful, preserving

in at least two noteworthy cases only the doors of the structures in question. But the emergence of a small group who publicly avowed the importance of preserving historic places planted the seeds for the intellectual climate in which preservation became important.[1]

Social, cultural, and economic catalysts spurred the preservation movement after the end of the Civil War. The war itself tore deeply into the American psyche, and the construction of memorials to important people on both sides of the conflict as well as local memorials to war dead became significant. Yet the heroes of the Civil War were partisan figures, intrinsically linked to one side or the other. The leaders from the generation of the Revolutionary War transcended the barriers of internecine conflict. George Washington, John Adams, Thomas Jefferson, and their peers seemed more representative of an all-encompassing view of the heritage of the United States than were the leaders of the Civil War. The industrialization of the North during the war led to an economic revolution at its close, and as Americans began to make fortunes in developing industries, more capital in circulation created additional opportunities for preserving historic places.

The regionalization of preservation arose within this climate of postwar change. Different kinds of historic places were preserved in each geographic region, with the cultural needs of the various sectors in mind. New England, the middle Atlantic region, and the South all developed distinct styles of preservation. The economic capabilities of each area and its cultural need for a link with its past provided an important impetus in determining the nature of preservation in differing locales.

In the words of the most important scholar of American historic preservation, New England became the "home of militant private preservation organizations." More individual homes were preserved by these groups than by groups in the other two regions in which historic preservation became a force. Most of these houses became museums commemorating important local figures, a practice the same scholar called "ancestor worship." Such places had a largely local focus, glorifying early inhabitants of the Northeast and appealing to local pride.[2]

The middle Atlantic region provided the best overall situation for historic preservation. Whereas New England preserved monuments recognizing localized themes, preservation in the middle Atlantic states took on broader realms. Historic preservation in this region focused upon the early national period in American history, with a particular emphasis on buildings and places associated with the Revolutionary War. Many battlefields from the Revolutionary War were located between the Hudson River valley and the Potomac River, and the area north of Philadelphia possessed a large urban population that expressed interest in preservation. Advocates of preservation in this region usually sought the support of local and state government.

Preservation in the South had a flavor all its own. Southern advocates sought to preserve places associated with famous people from the region. They formed organizations, and because of the desperate economic situation in the South for a generation following the Civil War, they often had to rely upon state governments for funding. After the founding of the Association for the Preservation of Virginia Antiquities (APVA) in the spring of 1888, preservation efforts in the South accelerated, and the efforts of the organization included preserving places of significance to both the Confederacy and the United States.

American women played a major role in local efforts at preservation. The two most important local groups, the Mount Vernon Ladies Association and the APVA, were both founded and dominated by women. At Mount Vernon, Ann Pamela Cunningham's dedication was responsible for the preservation and protection of Mount Vernon. She relied on women in the South to spread information and to raise money, and she singlehandedly convinced the Washington family that the Mount Vernon Ladies Association had the best interests of the family and the property in mind. Mary J. Galt founded the APVA; she was responsible for interest in preserving Jamestown and for the preservation of the home of Mary Washington, George Washington's mother, in Fredericksburg Virginia. The social efforts of women in the nineteenth century were confined to domestic and moral areas, and efforts to preserve the achievements of the past were among the many types of activities they carved out in a world that increasingly confined educated women to the home.

Toward the end of the century, the desire to preserve physical remnants of the past spread beyond the East Coast. During the 1880s, efforts to preserve the increasingly romanticized Spanish presence began in California and New Mexico. Some influential westerners sought the trappings of civilization, which at the end of the nineteenth century included concepts like historical societies and historic preservation. In 1881 the New Mexico Historical Society unsuccessfully tried to locate itself in the seventeenth-century Palace of the Governors in Santa Fe; after some artful maneuvering by L. Bradford Prince, a lawyer who headed the New Mexico Historical Society and who later became governor of the territory, the Department of the Interior granted the historical society two rooms in the palace in 1885. During Prince's term as governor, he used the palace as his official residence. Almost simultaneously, work to preserve the chain of Spanish missions in southern California began in earnest. Catholic priests raised money for the preservation of the San Carlos Borromeo Mission in Carmel, while in the 1880s, the Catholic church reopened Mission San Miguel near Pasa Roblés. Soon an array of social organizations became interested in preservation in California.[3]

But even with all of this activity, at the end of the nineteenth century historic preservation remained a piecemeal process that was the province of local organizations and, on occasion, state government. Its focus was largely regional, and local and state interests determined its concerns. Congress or some bureau in the federal government sometimes expressed interest in the plans of local groups, but their interest was fleeting. Preservation remained the realm of those who sought the role of guarding patriotic feelings. The federal government was busy with tasks more suited to a nation that saw its best years in its future.

Among the obligations that the federal government laid out for itself at the end of the nineteenth century was a growing concern for the state of American land. The census of 1890 showed Americans that the frontier had closed, and this perception inspired anxiety about the future of the nation.[4] No longer constantly expanding westward, the nation instead began to fill in the gaps created by its seemingly random growth. Simultaneously, a rush to conserve the natural resources of the American West began, as it became apparent that a nation unlikely to grow into any more territory needed to establish regulations for the use of the land and resources it already possessed. More efficient use of resources required different values than those that had characterized the largely haphazard exploitation of the West during the nineteenth century. Fortunately for the advocates of conservation, in 1890 the public domain still contained vast areas of land, and early in the decade, many people in the Department of the Interior sought a way to protect lands from abusive practices.

Section 24 of the General Revision Act of 1891 was the first result. In the pattern of federal land legislation that stretched back to the Homestead Act of 1862, which allowed people who paid a filing fee, improved the tract, and lived upon it for five years to own 160 acres of land in the West, the Act of 1891 allowed the president the discretionary power to reserve forest lands in the public domain from the claims of citizens. In 1889 the law committee of the American Forestry Association conceived of the measure and the following year transmitted it to President Benjamin Harrison's secretary of the interior, Gen. John W. Noble. Noble added the section concerning the reservation of forest lands in areas called *forest reserves* to the bill. It was added as a rider to the bill, prompting later historians to suggest that Congress was not clearly aware of the significance of the clause.[5]

Both Benjamin Harrison and his successor, Grover Cleveland, made use of the provisions of the bill, and in 1897 Cleveland's actions were responsible for the passage of a clause that granted money to the forest reserves. During the remainder of his term, Harrison proclaimed more than 13 million acres of forest reserves. Cleveland followed with an additional 5 million acres and then stopped until Congress provided funding to protect the reserved land. But forestry advocates such as Bernhard E. Fernow, the chief of the Division of Forestry in the Department of Agriculture, and Wolcott Gibbs, the president of the National Academy of Sciences, prevailed upon Cleveland to proclaim an additional 20 million acres of forest reserve on George Washington's birthdate in 1897. Cleveland did so, and in the furor that resulted, westerners headed by Sen. Richard Pettigrew of South Dakota supported an amendment to the Sundry Civil Appropriations Bill for 1897 that allowed for management of the forest reserves as well as for a process through which homesteaders within the new reserves could exchange their claims for others elsewhere in the public domain. The management of federal forests had become a responsibility of the federal government.[6]

The earliest federal efforts at archaeological preservation developed from the same cultural sources as did regional attempts to preserve historic places and the increased federal desire to manage its natural resources. The cultural impulse to protect American prehistory was a logical extension of the actions of local groups interested in their own pasts, and the chain of federal laws governing land indicated the broadening of the obligations of government agencies. The constituencies for archaeological preservation and local historic preservation were different only in degree of emphasis. The same kinds of groups that supported historic preservation on the East Coast became critical advocates of efforts to preserve the prehistoric ruins of the Southwest. From the very beginning, these groups sought legislation that granted powers similar to those of the General Land Revision Act of 1891.

Throughout the nineteenth century, prehistoric ruins in the Southwest had attracted the attention of American explorers on federal surveys, and as the scientific bent of such efforts became more important, more observers of the West commented upon the ruins of prehistoric civilizations. Army Lt. James H. Simpson was a member of Col. John M. Washington's puntative expedition against the Navajos with specific instructions to find out all he could about the Old Spanish Trail from Santa Fe across the Upper Colorado to Los Angeles. In 1849 Simpson added his name to the historic and prehistoric inscriptions at Inscription Rock (El Morro National Monument) in western New Mexico. Simpson's report described El Morro and Chaco Canyon and elicited much surprise among government officials. In 1874 William Henry Jackson, the photographer on the survey headed by renowned scientist Ferdinand V. Hayden, took photographs of ruins in the Mesa Verde area of southwestern Colorado. Jackson made models of the ruins he had seen for the exhibit of the Department of the Interior at the Philadelphia Centennial in 1876. The sophistication of the ruins astonished observers, and gradually a small but influential minority became peripherally interested in the fate of American prehistory.[7]

The founding of the Bureau of American Ethnology in 1879 (changed to Bureau of Ethnology in 1894) also contributed to growing interest in American prehistory. Under the guidance of Maj. John Wesley Powell, the one-armed Civil War veteran who went down the Colorado River on a raft and became the preeminent power in federal science, the Bureau sponsored numerous projects in the West and Southwest. Interested individuals also contributed to exploration of the region. Mary Hemenway, an affluent Bostonian, financed the work of Frank Hamilton Cushing, the erratic and frequently ill genius of the Bureau, at Zuñi Pueblo. Others followed her lead.[8]

Privileged and educated easterners were the first to recognize the value of American prehistory. In 1882 Sen. George F. Hoar of Massachusetts presented a petition to the Senate from the New England Historic Genealogical Society. The antiquarians sought a general designation for prehistoric ruins in the Southwest that made them distinct from the rest of the public domain. This proposal died in congressional committee, deemed impractical by eastern and western members alike. Reaching national consensus apparently required more than the desire of elite organizations.

But in 1889 the persistence of advocates and a change in their tactics led to the creation of the first national reservation from the public domain. On 4 February 1889 Hoar presented another petition to the Senate from easterners interested in the preservation of prehistoric remains. This petition asked that the Casa Grande ruins, in Pima County, Arizona, be designated a national reservation, reserved for its cultural value. Many prominent Bostonians, including Oliver Wendell Holmes, Anna Cabot Lodge, R. Charlotte Dana, Mary Hemenway, Edward Everett Hale, Francis Parkman, and the governor of Massachusetts, Oliver Ames, signed the petition. Congress quickly acted upon it, passing legislation that appropriated funds for the repair and upkeep of Casa Grande and allowing the president to permanently set aside the land on which the ruins stood. Three years later, on 22 June 1892, Benjamin Harrison officially sanctioned the action when he established the Casa Grande Ruins Reservation.[9]

But Casa Grande was an unusual case, from which little precedent could be drawn. The petition that established it only requested the reservation of the 160-acre quarter section that contained the four-story adobe ruin. Unlike its earlier counterpart in 1882, the petition offered no provisions for American antiquities in general. The bill had many prominent and influential supporters and it asked only for a small, one-time appropriation, which probably explains why it passed. Preservationists were interested in it because Casa Grande was a link between prehistory and the written past. It was a testimony to the architectural and engineering skill of its builders. Father Eusebio Kino, a Spanish missionary, wrote of it in 1694, and other Spaniards who traversed the region had also described it. Europeans had seen Casa Grande before the nineteenth century, an idea that fascinated the American antiquarians who supported the bill.

In 1890 Americans in general were not yet prepared to think in terms of a need to preserve prehistory on any great scale. Yellowstone National Park had become reality, and Yosemite was undergoing the transformation from state to national park; federal preservation of scenic wonderlands was becoming accepted practice. Any specific case that piqued the interest of prominent and affluent Americans had a good chance to be the subject of protective legislation, but action to protect unspecified ancient sites in the West was liable to meet with opposition.

The difference between the perspectives of easterners, government officials, and settlers in the West generated this resistance. The easterner's definition of the past encompassed land still active in the present of the western settlers, and frequently the withdrawal of public land meant impositions upon homesteaders. To many southwestern settlers, the lands containing prehistoric ruins had more immediate uses; in that arid region, settlers coveted land with water, and the majority of prehistoric sites were located near sources of water. The survival of homesteads and ranches depended upon access to water, and giving up their livelihood to reassure anxious antiquarians made little sense to people struggling for subsistence. With no obvious economic advantages in the age before mass tourism, preservation meant little to settlers, many of whom had recently battled what they incorrectly thought were the descendants of the cliff dwellers. Some westerners argued with disdain that these relics of an ancient civilization were only houses, and abandoned ones at that. As eastern society began to mythologize its past, the practical perspective of westerners put them at odds with emerging public sentiment.

One important development in the East at this time was the professionalization of a variety of fields, particularly medicine and the sciences, which had begun during the late nineteenth century. By the 1880s, it was no longer possible to become a doctor by simply hanging out a shingle; the fledgling group that later became the American Medical Association required credentials for its members, preferably from the new medical school at Johns Hopkins University. As the range of scientific knowledge expanded, similar transformations took place in other scientific disciplines; many specializations developed that explored new areas of inquiry.

Among these offshoots was the science of anthropology, which crystallized into a scientific discipline in the 1890s. To the practitioners of the new discipline, Indian culture past and present was of great interest. The recent recognition that the American Southwest contained archaeological ruins and the subsequent setting aside of Casa Grande were milestones in the emergence of the field. By the end of the 1890s, the American Association for the Advancement of Science began to consider official sanction for the field of anthropology.

Training in the discipline also developed during the decade. Franz Boas, a Jewish emigre from Germany, taught anthropology at Clark University in Worcester, Massachusetts, which in 1892, granted the first Ph.D. in anthropology in the United States. When he moved to Columbia University in 1899, Boas developed the first comprehensive anthropology program in the United States. Perhaps the most eminent anthropologist in America at the turn of the century, Boas saw that tangible field achievements would hasten the coming of respectability for the new science and he encouraged interest in American subjects. Meanwhile American archaeologists, long preoccupied with European and Middle Eastern antiquities, began to develop training programs, with Harvard University and its Peabody Museum appearing in the forefront. They too discovered and became interested in southwestern sites.

As they defined their discipline, anthropologists and archaeologists became concerned with unauthorized excavation of archaeological sites. Training in the two fields developed, but reports of excavations by everyone from dentists to cowboys circulated among the professional community. Scientists began to worry over the fate of unattended ruins on both federal and private land. The Southwest was their crucible, from which peer acceptance of their discipline had to emerge. They believed that they held the key to unlock the secrets of prehistoric life, but if pothunters were allowed to comb the ruins for artifacts, overturning walls and destroying the evidence of the past, then the future of anthropology and archaeology as important sciences could not be realized.

The excavation of southwestern ruins actually predated the rise of anthropology as a science. A rush to excavate began in 1882, after Senate Public Lands Committee member Preston B. Plumb told the groups who favored the first preservation legislation that they should beat other vandals to the ruins. Plumb pointed out that reputable institutions were rushing to make collections for their museums as quickly as vandals were destroying the sites.[10] During the 1880s and

1890s, federally sanctioned excavators included Victor and Cosmos Mindeleff, Dr. J. W. Fewkes, and Dr. Walter Hough, who published accounts of their fieldwork in the annual reports of the Bureau of American Ethnology. At the same time, Adolph F. A. Bandelier and Charles Lummis, noted southwestern explorers, both ventured into the commercial market with actual and fictionalized stories about the Southwest.[11] Gradually, the public discovered another kind of American past, and officials of the General Land Office in the Department of the Interior became interested in prehistoric structures and relics.

At the end of the 1890s, changing cultural conditions throughout the nation, the development of the new sciences, and the magnitude of the task of preserving prehistoric remains combined to propel the federal government into the business of preservation. As the century closed, the American government began to broaden its agenda to include a more extensive array of obligations than ever before. Social change directed by the federal government began to play a more important role in shaping policy, and a spirit of reform labeled *Progressivism* entered American political and social discourse. Sparked by the images of realist artists such as Robert Henri, John Sloan, and the rest of their group known as The Eight or the Ash Can school, and put into practice by activists like Jane Addams at Hull House, the principles of social reform took root in American society. The confluence of science and reform had a particularly powerful impact upon the management of natural resources, and the input of scientists in this field laid the basis for the eventual entrance of federal agencies into the preservation of prehistory.

Following the lead of the nineteenth-century scientist par excellence, John Wesley Powell, the federal government laid plans to manage natural resources. With government encouragement, scientists began to apply their skills and ideals to create a coherent federal resource policy.[12] Influential people like Bernhard Fernow in forestry and W J McGee, a close associate of Powell's at the Bureau of Ethnology and the man who coined the famous conservation phrase "the greatest good for the greatest number," favored the systematic organization of resources in accordance with newly recognized scientific principles. They sought to protect scarce resources from depletion while conserving the more abundant ones for future use.[13] If the closing of the frontier told Americans they would not be expanding into new territory, modern science gave the nation a way to counter the anxiety created by its loss. Conservation allowed for the planning of the future through goals of increased efficiency and equitable distribution.

But westerners feared the intrusion of scientists and scientific dogma in their lives. Most particularly, they worried about the potential consequences that the less-developed West would face at the hands of government bureaucrats and their professional advisors in Washington, D.C.[14] Their needs were unique, westerners felt, and many times the involvement of federal officials insensitive to or unaware of conditions in the West created more problems than it solved. Federal officials already had too much power, westerners such as Colorado senator Henry D. Teller and congressman John F. Shafroth argued, and many sympathized with their point of view.

Federal actions after 1897 did little to allay western suspicions. President Cleveland's proclamation of extensive forest reserves that year became the catalyst for increased mistrust, and as a rule, westerners generally opposed bills that granted the federal government additional power over federal lands. Even the Reclamation Act of 1902, which provided funding for the reclamation of arid land in the West for agricultural purposes, met with strong resistance from western congressmen. They were wary of the strings they felt certain were attached to any exercise of centralized power.[15] From a western perspective, decisions affecting the future of western land too often came from the Atlantic seaboard.

Western sentiment against the exercise of federal power was strong, and so was the distaste for easterners who offered book knowledge as a substitute for years of actual experience in the West. Those in the West saw these people, their fortunes already secure, as hypocrites, pontificating about conservation to others who still inhabited a world of potential abundance. Westerners were also reluctant to share their source of wealth with the established East. They could not understand why the West should mortgage its present for the future of the rest of the nation. Traditional American individualism was at odds with the new techniques of management promulgated by scientific experts and their institutional backers.

This political dichotomy between the old individualism and the new public policy trapped advocates of the preservation of prehistoric ruins. The focal point of western resentment was the federal policy of withdrawing land in the public domain from homestead claims. As long as a tract was withdrawn, it remained the property of the federal government. No one could enter claims of ownership upon it, and prospecting, grazing, and farming necessitated government permission. To western farmers and ranchers, withdrawal seemed an arbitrary policy designed to deny them their living. This posed a real problem for supporters of legislation designed to protect and preserve the remains of prehistoric Indian civilizations in the Southwest.[16] Preserving the unique but obscure heritage of the region required the withdrawal of lands that contained tangible ruins. More often than not, these lands also included resources that had commercial value.

Little middle ground existed between the two points of view. The land that archaeologists and anthropologists wanted to use to piece together the ethnological and social history of the pre-Columbian Americas was the same land from which some settler earned a living. Scientists were often insensitive to the needs of the settlers, and the overview that science sought was foreign to people concerned foremost with their own survival. Each side misunderstood the motives of the other. Preservation and development seemed incompatible; progress toward the protection of antiquities frequently became impaled upon this question.

The upsurge of interest in contemporary and prehistoric Indian cultures resulted from the public sense that the Indian, like the frontier, was a relic of the past worth preserving. The World's Columbian Exposition of 1893 in Chicago housed the most comprehensive display of American Indian artifacts ever assembled. Under the direction of such rising talents as Franz Boas and William Henry Holmes, who trained during the 1870s on the F. V. Hayden surveys, the exhibition surpassed even the Columbian Historical Exposition of 1892 in Madrid, noted as the most important collection of artifacts assembled to that point. The exhibition ignited a general interest in the southwestern relics, furthering the development of public interest in Indian cultures.

Among those who worked at the Indian exhibit in Chicago was a man against whom the collective power of the Department of the Interior and the newly established anthropological discipline would soon be exerted. The state of Colorado hired Richard Wetherill, a rancher from Mancos, Colorado, to answer questions about the collections of artifacts he and his brothers had taken from ruins in southwestern Colorado and southern Utah. When Wetherill arrived in

Chicago, he possessed not only astounding artifacts of American prehistory, but considerable knowledge and field experience as well.[17]

Wetherill's personal history was typical of the lives of many who
settled the West, except that he stumbled across something extraordinary in the ruins of the Mesa Verde region. The eldest son of a
wandering family that had come to Colorado in search of silver, Wetherill took responsibility for his family's less-than-lucrative Alamo
Ranch near Mancos, Colorado, during the 1880s. Wetherill and his
brothers drove their cattle through the steep canyons of southwestern
Colorado. They were peripherally aware of the many cliff dwellings
that dotted their pastures, but it was not until 1887 that one of the
brothers, Al Wetherill, discovered the first major ruin (now called
Sandal House) in what is now Mesa Verde National Park. A year later,
while hunting for stray cattle, Richard and his brother-in-law, Charlie
Mason, discovered Cliff Palace, the most spectacular of the Mesa Verde
ruins. Excited, the men rapidly uncovered additional ruins, and Richard Wetherill found himself involved in more than a hobby. The "lost
civilization" that he thought he had discovered consumed him.[18]

The Alamo Ranch rarely provided an ample living for the Wetherill
clan, and Richard Wetherill took advantage of his growing archaeological knowledge to support his family. In 1890 the Denver Historical
Society offered to purchase the mummy of a child that Clayton Wetherill and Charlie Mason had discovered at Mesa Verde, and Richard
Wetherill accepted its offer of $3,000. The Wetherills then began
excavating "in a more businesslike manner," and in 1892 they assembled an extensive collection of artifacts with the visiting Gustav Nordenskiold of Sweden. By 1894 Richard Wetherill was a seasoned relic
hunter with extensive experience in the field. He had developed his
own cottage industry and placed advertisements in the local paper
offering curios and artifacts for sale.[19] There was a better living in
purveying the relics of a lost civilization than ranching could provide
in the Mancos region.

An individualist, Wetherill was a nineteenth-century person in an
area increasingly crowded with twentieth-century scientists who had
something to prove. He did as many westerners did, going about his
business in a region that he believed was beyond the interest and reach
of federal officials. But as the collections he made began to attract the
attention of anthropologists at universities and museums, Wetherill's
name became notorious. When the collection the Wetherills made

with Nordenskiold appeared in Sweden, American scientists howled. Wetherill offended their professional pride and they became nationalistic as they publicly castigated him. Simply put, his presence at southwestern sites threatened the fledgling profession of anthropology, and his work with foreigners gave the anthropologists an avenue to attack him. A dramatic powerplay evolved, with Richard Wetherill at its center. He became anathema to American anthropologists, epitomizing chaos in the world of order they sought to create.

Wetherill was outside the institutional structure of American science. Unlike the military surveyors, the first Americans to explore the ruins, and the anthropologists who followed them, Wetherill was not accountable to anyone. As anthropologists strove for professional status, credentials such as field experience with the United States Geological Survey (USGS) or academic training became necessary entry cards to their discourse. Wetherill ignored such developments. He was not a member of the cadre of professionalizing anthropologists, and many of them regarded people like him as pothunters, no better than criminals.

Wetherill also knew the location of more ruins than anyone else at that time, and his knowledge made him an essential contact for anyone hoping to find undisturbed sites in Arizona, New Mexico, Utah, and Colorado. He attracted considerable attention among potential excavators, and by the mid-1890s the Alamo Ranch became the meeting place for people interested in excavating ruins in the Southwest. Many travelers came to see the Mesa Verde ruins and to talk to Wetherill about the possibility of future expeditions to more remote places.

Among the expeditions Wetherill organized was one financed by two brothers, Talbot and Frederic Hyde. Heirs to the Babbitt soap fortune, the Hydes met Wetherill at the Columbian Exposition in Chicago and became interested in Indian artifacts. They went to Mancos, and in the winter of 1893 the three formed a partnership. Their first expedition to Grand Gulch, Utah, uncovered many artifacts, and the Hydes donated their collection to the American Museum of Natural History in New York.[20] In the process, Wetherill's name became more familiar to those interested in American antiquities.

Wetherill's connection, via the Hyde brothers, to the American Museum of Natural History gave that institution the upper hand in the rapidly expanding field of American antiquities. At the turn of the century, prehistoric artifacts were the most important results of excavation. Cultural institutions and private collectors engaged in fierce competition for these spoils. To load their halls with full museum cases, institutions cavalierly sponsored scientists who tore through southwestern archaeological sites in search of artifacts. Wetherill often served as point man. His vast knowledge guaranteed the success of expeditions in which he was involved. Others did not fare as well, and competitors attacked Wetherill for his success because his sponsors were often beyond reproach.

The partisan nature of anthropological politicking helped account for the general disavowal of his discovery of the Basketmakers, the ancestors of the people who built the cliff dwellings. Although George H. Pepper of the American Museum of Natural History and Dr. T. Mitchell Prudden, a medical doctor with strong ties to institutional anthropology, reported Wetherill's find in scholarly and commercial articles, others dismissed it as a hoax. The self-affirmed anthropological and archaeological clique again felt threatened; without any formal training, Wetherill was altering their intellectual terrain. If his discovery gained credence, it could have dire consequences for establishing professionals.

In part as a response to their perception of this blatant challenge, institutional anthropologists in the late 1890s began to organize an appeal for legislation designed to prevent people like Richard Wetherill from digging up the ruins of prehistoric civilizations. Anthropologists needed exclusive access to sites to acquire professional respectability, if they were to avoid the challenge represented by Wetherill's work. They sought legal remedies to protect their territory from intrusion.

But the anthropologists faced western resentment of their good intentions. People scratching out a frontier existence regarded the anthropologists as aristocrats, representatives of an eastern elite in a highly specialized field that seemed superfluous. From a western perspective, they were out of touch with the key value of the times— constant progress towards a civilized West. With little support in the West and only sporadic interest on the part of the government, those who favored preservation of prehistoric ruins were in a difficult position. Achieving their desired results looked to be a very complicated proposition.

Eastern academics and scientists were a powerful force, and they took their efforts to the legislative arena. As representatives of a growing professional community just beginning to assert itself, American scientists believed that the preservation of American antiquities was an issue that demanded their input. In early 1900, at the behest of the American Association for the Advancement of Science and the Archaeological Institute of America, Rep. Jonathan Dolliver of Iowa introduced H.R. 8066, a measure designed to afford protection to American antiquities scattered around the Southwest.[21]

Dolliver's proposal followed earlier patterns of American land legislation and reflected the values of the scientific community. It granted the president almost unlimited power to create reservations "in the same manner and form as now provided by law and regulation for forestry reservations." The reservations could include almost anything of public interest, including historic and prehistoric places and natural or scenic areas. Most important, the bill did not restrict the size of the reservations. A much broader bill than Senator Hoar's petition in 1882, H.R. 8066 granted powers that many in the West feared.[22]

Westerners immediately rejected the concept. The next day, Rep. John F. Shafroth of Colorado introduced a bill to counter Dolliver's proposal of strong central power. H.R. 8195 focused on punishing vandals who disturbed ruins on public property, not on reserving lands on which there were known ruins. The House Public Lands Committee quickly put it aside. Yet Shafroth's proposal clearly made his point: executive interference in questions concerning the public domain had to be checked. The bill was a gesture, its rapid introduction an indicator of the seriousness of the issue to western representatives. Pursuing a worthwhile end, advocates of preservation had again imposed on the rights of individual western settlers.

His point clear to the preservationists, Shafroth tried to negotiate a compromise. On 7 March 1900, a few weeks after his initial bill, he offered a less extreme measure, H.R. 9245, which allowed the USGS to survey areas containing prehistoric ruins. It granted the secretary of the interior the power to proclaim reservations limited to a maximum of 320 acres. Shafroth's perspective typified the western view: Preserving antiquities was a good concept, but safeguarding regional interests required concrete limitations on the power granted by legislation. The restriction to 320 acres effectively prevented a chief executive from hampering the ability of western farming and ranching interests to prosper. Cropped as it was, H.R. 8195 allowed the president no powers he might use capriciously.

All three bills went to the House Committee on Public Lands, where they became entangled in Washington politics. Committee chairman John F. Lacey of Iowa, the author of many pieces of conservation-oriented legislation, passed them on to Secretary of the Interior Ethan A. Hitchcock, who gave them to Binger Hermann, the commissioner of the General Land Office (GLO). Hermann was a strong advocate of preservation legislation. He inspected the bills, found them lacking, and responded by proposing his own draft, which the House Public Lands Committee coolly received.[23]

The question of preservation became deeply entangled in the issue of the administration of public lands, and the first signs of official interest in preserving southwestern ruins clearly revealed conflicting perspectives on the issue. Western congressmen wanted to solve the questions of their region without interference from national policy-makers. Federal bureaucrats seemed far too willing to sacrifice potentially valuable western land for their peculiar sense of the overall good of the nation. Dolliver and other supporters of preservation and conservation regarded recalcitrance on this type of issue as evidence of individual greed and ignorance of the problems of the future. With no consensus among the proponents, all the bills, including Hermann's proposal, H. R. 10451, died in Congress. Unpopular with Western congressmen, the protection of aboriginal ruins appeared to be a classic special-interest issue.

Nearly three thousand miles away, westerners developed new interest in the archaeological ruins that intruded upon their economic lives. On 30 April and 1 May 1900, the Santa Fe *New Mexican* reported that the Hyde Exploring Expedition, under the direction of Richard Wetherill, was excavating ruins in Chaco Canyon, located in the northwestern corner of the New Mexico territory. In an inflammatory tone, the *New Mexican* insinuated that the expedition was merely a raid on the ruins by professional pothunters.

The *New Mexican* did not initiate the public reaction to the excavation at Chaco Canyon. Earlier in the spring of 1900, Edgar L. Hewett, the president of New Mexico Normal University in Las Vegas, New Mexico, and at that time an amateur archaeologist who staked an informal claim to the thousands of pueblo ruins on the Pajarito Plateau northwest of Santa Fe, complained to the surveyor general of the General Land Office about the work at Chaco Canyon. The GLO took note of the complaint but did little. When Hewett convinced the newspaper to publish its report on the excavation, Washington dispatched Special Agent Max Pracht from Santa Fe to the Chaco basin. Unhappy at being sent to a remote corner of the New Mexico territory, Pracht went unwillingly and seems to have made only a cursory attempt to understand the situation. Nevertheless, in May 1900 he sent his report to the commissioner of the GLO.[24]

Pracht indicated that he thought the excavation was a responsible, professional operation. Prof. Frederic W. Putnam of the American Museum of Natural History, an important name in American archaeology, was the nominal head, and at the time of Pracht's visit, George H. Pepper, one of Putnam's former students and the author of an article about the Basketmakers, supervised the excavating. Richard Wetherill led a band of Navajo laborers who did much of the actual digging. Pracht believed that the artifacts the men found were being "used in a legitimate way as a scientific collection. The result of the work of these scientific men ... cannot but rebound [sic] to the immediate benefit of ethnological and historical bodies the world over."[25]

Pracht had few options, and he suggested that his superiors handle the question. He knew of no law that specifically prevented excavation of public land, and indeed none existed. Pracht thought that the secretary of the interior should contact Putnam and ask the professor to withdraw his crew or request a presidential order that forbade the work. The status quo was clearly intolerable. Either the ruins had to be left alone, or a system had to be developed that protected the ruins from depredation and destruction of all kinds.[26]

Pracht had no complaints about the Hyde Exploring Expedition as long as someone like Pepper, with scientific credentials, oversaw the work, and it appeared that the interests of science were served. He hoped to thwart those intending to make a fast profit in selling antiquities. The General Land Office in Washington, D.C., had little to go on other than the report. Its officials concurred with Pracht's findings and informed Putnam that a complaint had been filed.

Not everyone accepted Pracht's verdict on the Chaco Canyon excavations. Edgar L. Hewett particularly remained unconvinced, and on 17 November 1900 the Santa Fe Archaeological Society, upon which he was an important influence, requested that Secretary Hitchcock put an end to the "depredations" at Chaco Canyon.[27] Responding to the pressure, Commissioner Hermann secured an order requiring the excavation in the Chaco region to cease. He sent the order to Putnam and planned another inspection of the area, for which he selected Special Agent Stephen J. Holsinger.

The cessation order was a necessary gesture. Disturbing reports about activities in Chaco Canyon continued to filter back to Washington. On 18 January 1901 Special Agent S. S. Mathers of the GLO office in Santa Fe informed Commissioner Hermann that the delegate to the New Mexico legislature and the county clerk of San Juan County, where the ruins were located, visited him. They reported that although the Hyde brothers had stopped excavating, Richard Wetherill had continued. Their most damaging contention was that Wetherill and his men had found a very valuable piece of turquoise, which they had sold for $1,200. Mathers also reported the existence of the Hyde Exploring Expedition trading post with stock worth more than $80,000. Mathers contended that Wetherill and the Hydes had made the entire sum since beginning their work in the Chaco region.[28]

These were devastating accusations made by responsible representatives of San Juan County, and in Washington, D.C., it appeared that Pracht had been deceived. Apparently unaware that Holsinger had already been sent from Phoenix, Mathers offered to go to Chaco Canyon. "This thing ought to be stoped [sic]," he declared, "and what is taken from these ruins ought to be sent to the Smithsonian Institute."[29] The entire situation had become a serious problem for Commissioner Hermann. Mathers's report clouded an already murky picture. Hermann's men could not agree whether responsible scientists or pothunters were excavating the ruins.

Holsinger was one of the most dependable people that the GLO employed in the West. He had extensive experience in settling land claim disputes, a reputation for being fair, and an air that made him formidable. Holsinger went to Chaco Canyon to settle the dispute by judging the facts. Along with many that followed him, he was dragged into a situation with no clear right and wrong and, in the end, made judgments based as much on conviction as on discernible fact.

Holsinger's inspection at the Chaco Canyon produced the first truly close look at the activities of Richard Wetherill and the Hyde Exploring Expedition. Holsinger arrived at Chaco Canyon on the evening of 23 April 1901, and by the time he left nearly a month later, he knew as much of the excavations as did any of the participants. On 5 December 1901 Holsinger filed his report to the commissioner of the GLO. In it he examined the situation from many points of view. His investigation resulted in a document that juxtaposed the values of the nineteenth-century frontier and those of twentieth-century regulatory bureaucracy.

Wetherill's motivation particularly intrigued Holsinger, and in his search for clues, he untangled the story of the Hyde Exploring Expedition. According to Holsinger, Wetherill realized that he had found an area with considerable significance for southwestern archaeology, and from which he could make possibly the most important collection of prehistoric artifacts yet discovered. "To make this stupendous collection entire," Holsinger wrote, "became his one ambition."[30] Wetherill's project required capital he did not have, but his acquaintances from the Chicago Exposition, the Hyde brothers, could easily afford the investment. The Hyde Exploring Expedition was the result.

The Hydes and Wetherill went to great lengths to convince Holsinger that they had reputable intentions. The men and their Navajo laborers excavated in the summers following 1896, and they estimated that they found 50,000 pieces of turquoise, 10,000 vases or pieces of pottery, 5,000 stone implements, 1,000 wood and bone implements, a few baubles, fourteen skeletons, a few copper bells, and a jewelled frog in Pueblo Bonito, the largest individual ruin. The Hydes, to whom the terms of the partnership gave the collection, reported that they donated everything to the American Museum of Natural History, "not a single specimen having been retained, not even a souvenir by any member of the company or their families." In a sworn affidavit, Talbot Hyde told Holsinger that along with the collection, the brothers gave the museum "many other valuable artifacts purchased from Wetherill, who secured them in Colorado and Utah."[31]

From the perspective of the GLO, the evidence posed numerous problems. Foremost was the question of ownership of artifacts found on the public domain. Because mineral, timber, and other rights on such land belonged to the government, it seemed a simple extension of law that artifacts and anything else remained federal property. If that was the case, then the expedition was guilty of violations of federal law. In short, from the stance of the government, their investment in the Hyde Exploring Expedition gave the Hyde brothers no right to collect artifacts or to donate them to anyone. The issue of the sale of what was ostensibly federal property also appeared. If the Hydes purchased other artifacts from the public domain from Wetherill, the government might be able to prosecute. Holsinger's report revealed that Wetherill's cottage industry and his ability to produce artifacts from all over the Southwest posed an even greater threat to the ability of the GLO to administer its domain than GLO officials had previously realized.

Fact and impression had become closely intertwined, and the situation made Commissioner Hermann's job difficult. The Hyde Expedition trading post at Chaco Canyon contributed to the well-being of destitute Navajo Indians in the area, but the economics of the trade in modern Native American goods was a side issue. The primary concern of the GLO was the disposition of what appeared to be one of the most important relics of the prehistory of the North American continent. If Chaco Canyon resembled Holsinger's description, it deserved some kind of protection from careless depredation, and Hermann believed that accredited anthropologists should be responsible for excavating the ruins. But short of a special act of Congress, similar to the one drawn up to protect Casa Grande, no means to accomplish this existed.

The need for rules and regulations to govern activities in places like the Chaco Canyon clearly emerged from the otherwise confused situation. Government officials increasingly believed that they had to do something to protect ruins from random excavation, but without a law that specifically defined artifacts on public land as federal property, they had no place from which to begin. Holsinger could not prove that the string of Hyde trading posts were marketing relics from the ruins, but neither was there evidence to allay his suspicions. At the conclusion of Holsinger's investigation, it seemed that the Hyde Exploring Expedition would continue its activities. Another existing law, however, offered the GLO a way to stop Wetherill.

The government used the Homestead Act of 1862 as its means to regulate Wetherill's activities. The homestead claims filed by Wetherill and Frederic Hyde were an obvious target for concerned federal officials. Both filed claims on quarter sections that contained ruins, locations they were not homesteading in the traditional sense. Instead of farming, Holsinger wrote, Wetherill "occupied and used [the land] for the purposes of trade," a practice that did not allow an individual to receive a perfected patent. Even so, Wetherill and the Hydes "took frequent occasion . . . to avow goo[d] faith and disclaim any intent to defraud the Government or in removing relics from public."[32] But

Wetherill's claims of good intention did not sway GLO officials in Washington, D.C. In March 1902 the General Land Office suspended his homestead claim because he had not planted sufficient acreage in crops to satisfy the requirements of the Homestead Act. Simultaneously, the temporary cessation order against the Hyde Exploring Expedition became permanent.[33]

Preempting homestead claims in the Chaco Canyon on superficial grounds hailed the beginning of a new era in the disposition of the public domain. Spurred by Progressive reforms in other areas of resource preservation, the GLO came to see preservation as a significant goal. The Department of the Interior began to express a position toward government land in the Southwest that was closely allied with President Theodore Roosevelt, who ascended to the White House after the assassination of William McKinley in 1901, and his belief in centralized power.

Despite its isolation, Chaco Canyon was obviously a national treasure, and an active Department of the Interior took a strong stance to protect it. The issue was no longer whether the participants in the Hyde Exploring Expedition were vandals or responsible archaeologists. Holsinger did not complain about their methods; instead he questioned whether individuals had the right to appropriate a shared resource for their own gain. Although of a different character than forests or minerals, the ruins were certainly prone to damage.

Chaco Canyon was not an isolated example, nor was the government singling out Wetherill for castigation. After 1902 the GLO stepped up its efforts all over the public domain. Before then, the bureau routinely granted requests to excavate to respectable citizens, usually anyone who could find a congressman to ask on their behalf. But by 1902 the outcry was sufficient to stem this practice, and GLO officials felt a much stronger commitment to protecting archaeological areas. After 1902 they refused requests to excavate from people without scientific credentials. Even ostensibly responsible citizens were asked to refrain from unsupervised digging, and no matter to what lengths their congressmen went, permission to excavate was rarely granted.[34] A value system different from any that Richard Wetherill understood began to govern the decisions of the GLO.

The suspension of his homestead claim was a message to the individualist from Mancos. His era of self-taught people was being brought to a close by trained, accredited institutional professionals.

People like Wetherill could no longer consider the public domain of twentieth-century America their private territory. Like it or not, a strong central government was starting to manage resources, regulating and legislating land use in the United States. This meant that prehistoric ruins were no longer going to be the de facto property of the first person to stumble over them.

According to Holsinger, Wetherill chose not to cease his activities in the Chaco Canyon. On 15 May 1902 the agent again wrote the commissioner of the GLO about the actions of Wetherill and one of his brothers, who continued to excavate near Pueblo Bonito. Richard Wetherill denied the allegations, claiming that his brother acted alone, but Holsinger believed that both men were selling the newly found artifacts.[35] Wetherill also told visitors to Chaco Canyon that the excavation belonged to the Hyde Exploring Expedition, a fact that particularly galled Holsinger. "The work is the purest vandalism," he insisted. "The more I know of Richard Wetherill, the more I am convinced that he is a man without principle."[36]

Holsinger's objections to Wetherill increasingly became personal. He had given Wetherill grudging respect on his first trip to the Chaco Canyon. Holsinger had not impugned Wetherill's or the Hydes' statements, preferring instead to believe their sworn testimony. But even after the cessation order, Wetherill continued to excavate; worse than that in Holsinger's eyes, he lied about his activities and incriminated the Hydes, who had chosen to obey the regulations. Wetherill forfeited the right to have his word honored, and Holsinger came to regard him in a different light. "He boasted to me that he was known as the 'vandal of the Southwest,'" Holsinger wrote, "which at the time I did not accept seriously but have since learned was a matter of some pride with this man."[37] Wetherill's behavior offended Holsinger's sense of decency and convinced the GLO agent that the man deserved to be treated like a criminal.

Wetherill was the consummate representative of the attitudes of nineteenth-century Americans, accustomed to doing as he chose without being bothered by rules and regulations. Firm in his convictions to the point of self-righteousness and stubborn to a fault when compelled to obey the directives of others, Wetherill believed he had as much right to the artifacts that he found as did the government. He felt unjustly deprived of his way to earn a living. Washington, D.C., was a long way from the San Juan River basin, and Wetherill knew the Chaco area from first-hand experience. To give an order was one thing, to enforce it another, and Wetherill felt no remorse as he continued to dig. Perhaps realizing his days in the field were numbered, he set out to "take all that I can get in the next four years."[38]

Holsinger was equally determined to put an end to Wetherill's activities. He continued to keep a close eye on his suspect and stepped up his attacks on other southwestern pothunters. In November 1902 Holsinger arrested four Mexicans in Arizona whom he caught trafficking in illegal artifacts. He hoped that the arrests might deter Wetherill, but by December 1902 he was convinced that Wetherill would not stop excavating. "I have understood upon reliable information that he has openly boasted that he would pay no attention to the warning notices given by me in the name of the Interior Department, G.L.O.," Holsinger wrote to his superiors, "and that he defies anyone to prevent his despoiling said ruins."[39]

By this point, Holsinger recognized Wetherill as a direct challenge to the ability of the government to enforce the law in the West, and his quest for justice took on broader connotations. Wetherill's success led others to emulate his behavior, and Holsinger feared that people in the West would not respect the law. Further investigation into Wetherill's affairs became a high priority. "Wetherill has the reputation of being a 'bad man,'" Holsinger insisted. "My acquaintance with him convinced me that he at least wants to be a proverbially bad man. It is important . . . that he be made an object lesson for others who would follow his example if given the least encouragement."[40] In Holsinger's opinion, no less than the ability to properly administer the public domain was at stake. A symbol of the lawless frontier past, Wetherill challenged the federal government to a confrontation. If he could catch Richard Wetherill in the act, Holsinger would make an example of this individualist pothunter as he had of the four Mexicans he had caught in Arizona.

The conflict between Wetherill and the General Land Office further emphasized the need for legislation defining what could be done with relics found on the public domain. Wetherill was an extreme case, but many westerners shared his sentiments about public land; laws that did not specifically apply to a situation were not enough to restrain those who had come to see the public domain as their own. But the Chaco Canyon episode became an important turning point. It placed GLO employees in the West firmly in the pro-legislation camp. Pracht,

Holsinger, and their counterparts dealt with questions about the public domain on a daily basis. To Holsinger, Wetherill was exactly the kind of person who had to be tamed before the West could become an orderly, law-abiding place. To its employees in the outposts of the nation, the federal government was a powerful entity and the one best suited to bring the West into the twentieth century. From the perspective of the Department of the Interior, people like Richard Wetherill were symbols of a past that needed to be forgotten.

More than a scofflaw, Richard Wetherill was a man out of his time. He grew to adulthood in a world where the individual reigned supreme and people made their own rules. The West he knew was an open place, where people had the option to do as they pleased without interference from government. But that time had passed, and Wetherill could not adapt. The idea of a regulated society confounded him, and he could not adjust to federal agencies that exerted power over land thousands of miles from Washington, D.C. He continued to act as if no laws applied to his situation.

The clash of values between Wetherill and Holsinger was indicative of the future. The cessation order represented new and decisive action by the federal government, and its ramifications stretched to Congress and beyond. Wetherill's name became synonymous with vandalism, and his presence galvanized supporters of legislation to preserve American prehistory. Twentieth-century congressmen, their elitist archaeological and anthropological associates, and concerned citizens all responded to what the name Wetherill represented, and some came to see stopping him as their singular goal. From the battle over Chaco Canyon, and many others like it, came the drive for legislation to protect American prehistory.

NOTES

1. Charles B. Hosmer, Jr., *Presence of the Past: A History of the Preservation Movement in the United States Before Williamsburg* (New York: G. P Putnam's Sons, 1965), 21-29. Hosmer's book and its later companion two-volume set, *Preservation Comes of Age: From Williamsburg to the National Trust 1926-1949* (Charlottesville: University of Virginia Press, 1981) are the authoritative sources on the history of American preservation.

2. Hosmer, *Presence of the Past*, 102-3.

3. Ibid., 123-32; for more about the romanticization of California, see

Leonard Pitt, *The Decline of the Californios* (Berkeley: University of California Press, 1971), 285-91.

4. Roderick Nash, *Wilderness and the American Mind*, 3d ed. (New Haven: Yale University Press, 1982), 141-60.

5. Harold K. Steen, *The United States Forest Service: A History* (Seattle: University of Washington Press, 1976), 5-6. Steen cites Samuel Trask Dana, the dean of forest historians, for the view that Congress did not understand the implications of Section 24 of the General Revision Act of 1891.

6. Ibid., 29, 36.

7. William H. Goetzmann, *Exploration and Empire: The Explorer and the Scientist in the Winning of the American West* (New York: Alfred A. Knopf, 1966), 274-76, 324-26, 523-26.

8. Curtis M. Hinsley, Jr., *Savages and Scientists: The Smithsonian Institution and the Development of American Anthropology 1846-1910* (Washington: Smithsonian Institution Press, 1981), 200-204; Ronald F. Lee, *The Antiquities Act of 1906* (Washington, DC: National Park Service, 1971), 16.

9. John Ise, *Our National Park Policy: A Critical History* (Baltimore: The Johns Hopkins Press, 1961), 147-48, 158; Lee, *Antiquities Act*, 10.

10. Ise, *Our National Park Policy*, 144.

11. For details of the Mindeleff's work, see *13th Annual Report of the Bureau of American Ethnology for the Years 1891-1892* (Washington, DC: Government Printing Office, 1892), 289-319, which covers the excavations at Casa Grande. Adolph Bandelier's novel, *The Delightmakers* (1890; reprint, New York: Harcourt Brace Jovanovich, 1971), is one example of a work that brought attention to the prehistoric Southwest.

12. Samuel P. Hays, *Conservation and the Gospel of Efficiency: The Progressive Conservation Movement 1890-1920* (Cambridge, MA: Harvard University Press, 1959), 2.

13. For a more efficient view of this position, see J. Leonard Bates, "Fulfilling American Democracy: The Conservation Movement 1907-1921," *Mississippi Valley Historical Review* 44 (June 1957), 29-57.

14. See G. Edward White, *The Eastern Establishment and the Western Experience: The West of Frederick Remington, Theodore Roosevelt, and Owen Wister* (New Haven: Yale University Press, 1968), for an interesting discussion of the East-West dialectic that White believes characterized the late nineteenth and early twentieth century.

15. Lee, *Antiquities Act*, 44; Hays, *Conservation and the Gospel of Efficiency*, 13.

16. According to Hays, *Conservation and the Gospel of Efficiency*, 13, "the very word 'withdrawal' aroused Western farmers to a fighting pitch."

17. Frank McNitt, *Richard Wetherill: Anasazi* (Albuquerque: University of New Mexico Press, 1957), 56-57.

18. Ibid., 22-23, 27.

19. Ibid., 31, 35-37; see also Florence C. Lister and Robert F. Lister, *Earl Morris and Southwestern Archaeology* (Albuquerque: University of New Mexico Press, 1968), 2, 8-9, 32, 42.

20. McNitt, *Richard Wetherill*, 62-74.

21. Lee, *Antiquities Act*, 47-77, details the legislative battles that preceded the Antiquities Act.

22. H.R. 8066, 56th Cong., 1st sess., discussed in Ise, *Our National Park Policy*, 149.

23. Lee, *Antiquities Act*, 47-50.

24. McNitt, *Richard Wetherill*, 188.

25. Max Pracht, "Report to the Commissioner of the General Land Office," 16 May 1900, NA, RG 79, Series 1, Records Relating to National Parks and Monuments 1872-1916, Letters Received by the Office of the Secretary of the Interior Relating to National Parks 1872-1907, Tray 166. All subsequent citations to letters and reports in this chapter are to documents in Tray 166.

26. Ibid.

27. Lee, *Antiquities Act*, 36. Former New Mexico territorial governor J. Bradford Prince used the term *depredations*.

28. S. S. Mathers to the commissioner of the General Land Office, 18 January 1901.

29. Ibid.

30. Stephen J. Holsinger to the commissioner of the General Land Office, 5 December 1901, 69, 81, 83. The Holsinger report has three separate sets of pagination; I will cite only the first from here on. Holsinger's assertions were incorrect. Lt. James H. Simpson's expedition visited the ruins and excavated there in 1849. See William H. Goetzmann, *Exploration and Empire*, 326-27.

31. Holsinger to commissioner, 5 December 1901, 71.

32. Ibid., 74-75.

33. McNitt, *Richard Wetherill*, 202.

34. Among others, Congressman Irving Wanger of New York asked that a constituent of his, a dentist, be granted a permit to dig archaeological sites in Arizona to make a collection for the University of Pennsylvania. Although neither GLO commissioner Binger Hermann nor the young and inexperienced Frank Pinkley objected, William Henry Holmes at the Bureau of Ethnology protested vigorously. The permit was flatly denied. Wanger's letter requesting the favor is in NA, RG 79, Series 1, Records Relating to National Parks and Monuments 1872-1916, Letters Received, Tray 166.

35. Stephen J. Holsinger to the commissioner of the General Land Office, 15 May 1902.

36. Ibid.

37. Ibid.

38. Richard Wetherill to Talbot Hyde, 26 January 1903. See McNitt, *Richard Wetherill*, 203-15, for another interpretation. He suggests that the new manager of the Hyde Exploring Expedition conspired against Wetherill.

39. Stephen J. Holsinger to the commissioner of the General Land Office, 18 December 1902.

40. Ibid.

3

The Antiquities Act

THE SPECTRE OF RICHARD WETHERILL may well have been the most important catalyst in galvanizing support for legislation to protect southwestern antiquities, but the passage of such a law required the cooperation of a number of disparate elements in the American arena. The situation at Chaco Canyon fueled advocates and gave them a sense of urgency about their work. But each faction of preservationists had an agenda of its own, and as Holsinger's vigilance made Wetherill's excavation into a symbol instead of an actual threat, the Department of the Interior, professional archaeologists and anthropologists, and western legislators all sought to create a law that protected their own interests as well as the antiquities.

Richard Wetherill provided American preservation with a fragile consensus. The GLO and its special agents advocated preservation because they saw him as a hindrance to the process of bringing law and order to the West; anthropologists wanted the government to act in order to protect their domain and to enhance their status with other scientists; and the only real objection western congressmen had was to a law that granted arbitrary power to the president without congressional approval. The people with the interest and the power to orchestrate the passage of a law to protect antiquities agreed in principle; finding a compromise that served the range of interests was a more complicated problem.

Theodore Roosevelt's ascendance to the White House helped elevate conservation to the upper levels of the American social agenda, and archaeological preservation was only one beneficiary. Roosevelt advocated a watchful bureaucracy with the power to enforce concepts of fairness and justice. Policymakers became important under Roosevelt, and they strove to implement social programs throughout the nation. With the support of the same people who engineered Progressive-era policies directed towards natural resources, antiquities legislation acquired a new significance. It also became part of the drive to centralize power in the hands of the qualified few.

At the turn of the century, anthropologists and archaeologists took the lead in creating a climate in which the government would favor the preservation of antiquities. In the exuberance that followed the Spanish-American War of 1898, they sought to give American archaeology the intellectual status of European and Middle Eastern antiquities, while simultaneously bemoaning the lack of care American areas received. Initially the cry came from individuals, but soon professional organizations such as the Archaeological Institute of America made their presence felt. One of the leading organizations in this battle was the Records of the Past Exploration Society.

The Records of the Past Exploration Society had the credentials to make a noticeable impact on the American archaeological scene. In 1900 the Reverend Henry Mason Baum, the long-time editor of the *American Church Review* and an amateur archaeologist who excavated biblical sites in the Middle East, founded the organization. Its membership included institutional professionals, degreed academics, respected church leaders like Baum, and other interested people of means, most with some field experience in archaeology. Headquartered in Washington, D.C., Records of the Past avidly worked for preservation.

The *Records of the Past* journal was one of its most successful means of attracting attention. Under Baum's experienced tutelage, it acquired a good reputation among professionals and interested laypeople. Its authors included eminent archaeologists and institutional professionals such as Dr. Arthur Stoddard Cooley of the American School of Classical Studies at Athens, Prof. William C. Mills, the curator of the Ohio State Archaeological and Historical Society, and Albert T. Clay, the assistant curator of Babylonian antiquities at the University of Pennsylvania. These men were acknowledged experts, and their experience in European, Egyptian, and Babylonian archaeology lent considerable status to the organization.

In a stance typical of the early years of the twentieth century, Baum and his peers had patriotic objectives for the prehistoric ruins of the Southwest. The first issue of the *Records of the Past* journal, published in January 1902, clearly articulated their program. Baum's editorial emphasized "the marvelous prehistoric ruins of our own country," suggesting that Americans were "apt to ignore the wonders at our own door in contemplation of the ruins in the valley of the Nile."[1] He favorably compared the human experience in the Americas with that of Europe and the Middle East. An America equal to the Old World in terms of an historic past could shed some of its cultural insecurities.[2]

Yet the elitism of the educated class placed limits on the effectiveness of the Records of the Past society. Baum stressed the importance of preservation, but in the long run, his perspective obstructed the results he desired. "It is almost unanimously conceded by those entitled to an opinion on the subject," Baum wrote, "that Congress should enact a law for the protection of the antiquities of our own country." Arrogant and lacking concern for competing interests, Baum and his "entitled" friends presented the guidelines that they thought were necessary to protect American antiquities. These included placing control of the excavations in prehistoric ruins in the hands of the secretary of the interior, a general prohibition on the sale of aboriginal artifacts, appropriations for the upkeep and maintenance of the various sites, and penalties for violations of any of the regulations.[3]

Baum's attitude typified that of Progressive-era scientists and professionals. To these people, science and government were tools with which to tame the wilder forces in society. Strong central government served as the regulator, the great equalizer, that ensured fair competition and wise use of resources. The qualified few would manage American society for the good of all. Disparate elements opposed such ideas, but to scientists and professionals of the early twentieth century, these dissenters were the very people responsible for the depletion of timber and mineral resources that compelled regulation. As irreplaceable as more utilitarian resources, archaeological sites also required protection and regulation. Although imbued with the belief that their cause was just, Baum and his friends were only peripherally aware of the need to compromise to achieve their goals.

Baum's condescending attitude toward people outside the scientific community became a major barrier. He and his friends were neophytes in the political arena, where connections and contacts were more important than the righteousness of a cause. They often approached the wrong people in federal agencies, and to many in Congress, the leaders of Records of the Past sounded too shrill when they expressed their point of view. Many of the archaeologists spoke more to each other than to the public or Congress, and although they made solid arguments, their tone was patronizing to people who were not part of the inner circle of the Records of the Past society.

Although he worked tirelessly, Baum frequently alienated potential allies. In January 1902 Baum announced that "everyone . . . must feel humiliated over the failure of this Government to protect the ruins within its territorial limits." Baum's polemic made him few friends at the Department of the Interior. Given a vast domain and limited resources, the GLO did the best it could, and Commissioner Binger Hermann believed that the attack was unwarranted. Baum fared even less well with the few sympathetic westerners. In June 1902 he offended western supporters of preservation. Unaware of the role of the Santa Fe *New Mexican* in bringing Richard Wetherill's activities to public attention, Baum announced "that the newspapers of our Southwest are taking up to some extent the cause of the . . . prehistoric records."[4] Edgar L. Hewett and others in the forefront of preservation in the West felt both ignored and usurped. Differences of opinion within the preservation coalition became public.

During the summer of 1902, the Records of the Past society sponsored an expedition to the Southwest. Baum led the party, which stopped at most of the significant ruins known to American scientists. Flushed with his new experiences, Baum made judgments on the archaeological sites he saw. He declared the Canyon de Chelly, Mesa Verde, and Chaco Canyon regions suitable for national parks status, but the ruins of the Pajarito Plateau, where Hewett worked, failed to impress Baum.[5] Others, including the commissioner of the GLO, had advocated park status for the region, and with no label other than national park for reserved areas, Baum's suggestion that the plateau lacked significance seemed inexplicable. Again Baum's priorities strained the preservation alliance.

During his visit to Chaco Canyon, Baum encountered Richard Wetherill, who lived near Pueblo Bonito even though the GLO had suspended his homestead claim, and the individualist ethic that characterized the frontier directly confronted the institutional mentality that dominated the East.[6] No account of their meeting survives, but it must have been contentious. Wetherill personified everything to which Baum objected, whereas Baum's self-righteousness and lack of sensitivity to other points of view must have galled the stone-faced westerner. Baum regarded Wetherill as a profiteering renegade, and from Wetherill's point of view, Baum's moral issue was his livelihood. Baum and Wetherill were the opposite ends of the spectrum when it came to the preservation of archaeological ruins.

After seeing the realities of preservation in the West, Baum's resolve was strengthened. From then on, he worked frantically. Faced with the immensity and urgency of his endeavor, Baum stepped up efforts to initiate legislation and also arranged practical activities in the field. In April 1903 Baum learned that unauthorized people were preparing to excavate in the Canyon de Chelly area the following summer. Assuming the potential excavators to be on the level of Richard Wetherill, Baum requested that the secretary of the interior provide a custodian to guard the ruins.[7] The ruins were on the Navajo Indian reservation, and the Bureau of Indian Affairs acted quickly. On 8 May 1903 Charles C. Day became the caretaker of Canyon de Chelly. The excavations were prevented; Baum's watchful vigilance began to pay dividends.

The campaign to initiate preservation legislation also picked up speed. During the winter of 1903-4, Baum and his associates drafted a bill that protected antiquities upon public land. In the spring of 1904 they approached Congressman William Rodenberg of Illinois, and on 2 March 1904 he introduced the bill in the House of Representatives. Rodenberg sent copies of the draft to archaeologists, anthropologists, and university presidents all over the country. Their comments were unilaterally favorable. Conspicuous by their absence, however, were such western archaeologists as Hewett and Byron L. Cummings of the University of Utah. Perhaps unaware of their existence, Rodenberg had not asked them to comment.

As the Senate Public Lands Committee met on 20 April to consider the companion bill (S. 5603) proposed by Sen. Henry Cabot Lodge of Massachusetts, the chances of passage looked excellent. There were bills on the floor of both Houses of Congress; the president of almost every important university, archaeological association, and historical society had written to express support for the measure, and few in Congress opposed it. It seemed that everyone agreed upon the bill, and Baum must have been pleased with the results of his work. He

knew that other bills on the floor of Congress embodied similar concepts, but none had the widespread support that backed the Lodge-
Rodenberg bill.[8]

Baum had rushed his legislation every step of the way, and the time
had come to work out the details. The Senate Public Lands Committee
hearing centered around the merits of the various bills. Each offered
different administrative provisions, but on one point, all agreed. The
"legislation should at this time be preservative rather than administrative. It should not attempt to deal with the things that may arise
in the future," University of Michigan archaeologist Dr. Francis Kelsey, the secretary of the Archaeological Institute of America, told the
committee, "but should meet immediate contingencies to preserve
what we have."[9] The spectre of Richard Wetherill, to whom Baum
alluded in his testimony, provided cause enough for the urgency.

Such a short-sighted approach postponed decisions on the real issues
facing advocates of preservation. It failed to take into account the
rivalries among archaeologists and their organizations. Despite agreement upon the principle of preservation, each of the bills on the floor
of Congress proposed a plan for administering archaeological areas
that assigned responsibility to a government agency, institution, or
professional organization. All the measures had vociferous proponents, and self-interest and merit became confused.

In early 1904, if all that preservation advocates wanted was legislation which allowed them to preserve ruins in the Southwest, any of
the bills on the floor of Congress would have fulfilled their ends. The
administrative program of each became the point of contention. The
Lodge-Rodenberg bill made the secretary of the interior responsible
for antiquities on public land, granting him the power to issue excavation permits to responsible "incorporated" groups. Its major competitor was a bill that William Henry Holmes of the Bureau of Ethnology
had written. Sen. Shelby Cullom of Illinois, a regent of the Smithsonian
Institution, sponsored it in the Senate, while Rep. Robert Hitt, also
of Illinois, introduced it in the House of Representatives. The measure
resembled the Lodge bill, except that Holmes replaced the secretary
of the interior with the secretary of the Smithsonian. Bernard S.
Rodey, the territorial delegate from New Mexico, also introduced a
measure similar to Holmes's, but it drew less attention.[10]

From Baum's point of view, material treasures, not the locations
that contained them, offered the great prize of American archaeology.

In his eyes, collections for museums became the objective for scientists, and he saw his peers as participants in a race to find prehistoric relics and ship them east. Typical of his era, he perceived equality among an exclusive group of accredited contestants. Only people like Richard Wetherill were excluded. As a result, Baum objected to the Cullom-Hitt bill. He thought it a partisan measure that gave the Smithsonian Institution an unfair advantage in acquiring relics. If it passed, Baum felt, the Wetherills of the world would be replaced by an officially sanctioned system of favoritism. The bill "might well have said, no explorations except by the Smithsonian," Baum reported being told by an unidentified eminent archaeologist.[11] Despite public expressions to the contrary, administering archaeological ruins, not preservation itself, remained the key question.

Again Baum's attitude put him at odds with potential allies. After previously alienating the commissioner of the General Land Office, Baum now took on Holmes, the Bureau of Ethnology, and the Smithsonian. Committed to "equal privileges," Baum accused Holmes of favoritism.[12] Baum thought that both the Smithsonian and Rodey bills extended unfair advantages, and in front of the Senate Public Lands Committee, he vehemently attacked the bills. Invoking the authority of the professional community, Baum relied upon the array of letters that supported the Lodge-Rodenberg bill to show its superiority.

Unfamiliar with Washington politics and the interests of his competitors, Baum set himself a difficult course. He refused to consider the merit in other points of view, and a competitive situation emerged in which the various groups each tried to protect their own position. Baum's attacks on government agencies splintered the developing consensus. To the General Land Office and the Smithsonian Institution, he was an interloper who sought legislation to further his goals. In contrast, Baum presented himself as a crusading reformer, ensuring fair access to the fruits of American archaeology. Baum's credibility became an issue that overshadowed the preservation question.

A controversy was brewing, and the House of Representatives became the battleground. The Senate Public Lands Committee reported favorably upon the Lodge-Rodenberg bill, and on 26 April the full Senate passed it. Little time remained in the congressional session, and Baum sought unanimous consent for the measure. The subcommittee that assessed the bill for the House of Representatives supported his efforts, but the Smithsonian unequivocally opposed passage.

On the second to the last day of the legislative session, its representatives, headed by the assistant secretary of the Smithsonian, Richard
Rathbun, succeeded in a parliamentary maneuver to block the bill.
They persuaded Rep. De Alva S. Alexander of Buffalo, New York,
to oppose a voice vote that would have permitted immediate consideration of the bill. By the following morning, the last day of the
legislative session, Baum had shown Alexander the "animus of the
Smithsonian" and he refused to block consideration any longer.[13] The
Smithsonian operatives convinced another representative, Robert Adams of Philadelphia, to object. The session adjourned without hearing
the bill.

Baum regarded the efforts to block passage of his bill as an assault
on his efforts and he responded in kind. As the session ended on 28
April, he attacked Rathbun. After a consensus had been reached,
Rathbun "appear[ed] as a lobbyist to delay passage of the bill," Baum
accused. "The objections [you] offered . . . are trivial in the extreme."
In Baum's self-righteous opinion, Rathbun's actions pointed to grace-
less self-interest. Baum's vitriolic attack continued in the May 1904
issue of *Records of the Past*, where he printed his letter to Rathbun and
pointed a finger at the Smithsonian, holding it "responsible for all
injury done to antiquities on the Public Domain until the final passage
of the [Lodge-Rodenberg] Bill." The Department of the Interior had
done its best for the Lodge-Rodenberg bill, and Baum believed its
support would continue. The Smithsonian was his culprit.[14]

Personalities impeded the effort to enact legislation to preserve
American antiquities. Ironically, western intransigence was no longer
the problem; pro-preservation elements created their own obstacles
to passage. Baum's heavy-handedness fragmented the consensus. His
peers thought the public attack on Rathbun was inappropriate, and
support for Baum waned. Preservation advocates found themselves
in a stalemate. Although everyone agreed to leave unsettled the question of administering the reserved land until legislation was enacted,
their disagreements over the structure of this administration caused
the disintegration of the fragile alliance that favored preservation.

Washington, D.C., administrators and specialists fought the Lodge-
Rodenberg battles. Few of the participants in the fray had substantial
experience in the American Southwest. Baum had visited the region,
but his travels had not given him the ability to understand the concerns
of southwesterners. Many of the other supporters had little feel for

the region, which they believed was full of gila monsters and Apache
Indians. Even William Henry Holmes, who had developed into a first-
class geologist and anthropologist on the F. V. Hayden survey in 1872,
had been away from the Southwest for a long time.[15] It remained for
Edgar L. Hewett, a westerner with actual experience in prehistoric
ruins and close ties to the Department of the Interior and the House
Public Lands Committee, as well as the credentials to mix with archaeologists and anthropologists, to unite the disparate preservation
forces.

Hewett, already the primary cultural force in New Mexico, sat out
the Lodge-Rodenberg fiasco. He found himself obsessed with the
remains of aboriginal cultures, but his perspective differed greatly
from that of Richard Wetherill. He too staked out an area, the Pajarito
Plateau northwest of Santa Fe, but he cultivated GLO operatives and
local and territorial officials. In 1900 he alerted the Department of
the Interior about Wetherill's work at Chaco Canyon. At different
times during the summer of 1902, he showed the archaeology of
northern New Mexico to both Rep. John F. Lacey of Iowa, the chairman of the House Public Lands Committee, and Baum. By 1904
Hewett's ties to Lacey and W. A. Richards, the new commissioner of
the GLO, were firm. An adopted southwesterner, he understood the
concerns of people of the region and was as comfortable with the
specialists as with laymen. He was also instrumental in turning Santa
Fe into a cultural center. Yet at the time, Hewett's highest degree was
a Master of Arts in pedagogy, and on the national scene, it did not
qualify him as an expert.

Hewett understood what the future held, and he busily acquired
credentials to back up his fieldwork. An educator by training, Hewett
rose quickly in the Southwest. In 1898, at the age of thirty-three, he
became the first president of New Mexico Normal University in Las
Vegas, New Mexico. Archaeology also figured in his plans. Later that
year, he helped found the Archaeological Society of New Mexico in
Santa Fe. In 1901 he became both a fellow of the American Association
for the Advancement of Science and a lifetime member of the Archaeological Institute of America. In 1903, after political opponents
ousted him from his university post, Hewett began postgraduate work
in archaeology at the University of Geneva under Louis Waurin and
the noted Egyptologist Edouard Naville. He saw that an advanced

degree in archaeology could propel him in the direction he wanted to go.[16]

By mid-1904, support for antiquities legislation began to galvanize around Hewett. Despite the fact that he lacked formal archaeological credentials, the GLO and many professional archaeologists appreciated his efforts on behalf of southwestern antiquities. He dug extensively, but his educational credentials precluded putting him aside as a vandal, and his wide knowledge of the region and its peoples increased his importance. The archaeological profession needed Hewett as a counterpoint to Wetherill. Few in the West had closer connections to the federal government or as much field experience.

Hewett's institutional base blossomed in the aftermath of the Lodge-Rodenberg debacle. Professional archaeologists sought his opinion on southwestern issues. As if to rectify its earlier high-handedness, the Records of the Past society appointed Hewett as one of its consulting editors in January 1905.[17] Even more significant, the Department of the Interior sought his counsel. In the summer of 1904 Commissioner W. A. Richards of the GLO turned to Hewett for a report on all aspects of southwestern archeological areas. Hewett obliged.

Hewett's report provided the first comprehensive look at southwestern ruins. He identified three river basins that contained most of the known ruins and subdivided them into twenty districts. He also provided the first compilation of maps showing the approximate position of all known sites. Hewett also pointed out many ruins that had previously escaped attention. Hewett's report appeared objective and scientific, organized by fact rather than by opinion. It gave Commissioner Richards a better idea of the scope of preservation needs.

Increasingly sophisticated as a politician, Hewett did not favor the administration of southwestern archaeology by any specific group. The Department of the Interior seemed the logical choice for administration, but staunchly in favor of immediate action, Hewett downplayed his choice of authorities. He also avoided the sensitive question of how to handle collections made in the ruins. He had learned much from the Records of the Past fiasco, and instead of a prescribed program, Hewett offered a goal for the legislation: "All measures . . . should look towards the encouragement of research and the advancement of knowledge and not toward its restriction."[18]

Hewett was aware of the tension between eastern and western interests and he tried to offer solutions that satisfied the needs of both. In a letter he wrote on 14 September 1904, Hewett proposed archaeological reservations of limited area. "I believe the scientists and the country at large will favor," he informed Richards, "a simple measure authorizing the creation of . . . small groups of ruins, that demand permanent protection, and the establishment of a system of supervision of all ruins on the public domain and Indian reservations by the Department of [the] Interior." He suggested that Lacey's bill from 1900, reintroduced after the Lodge-Rodenberg failure, needed only one minor change to serve the purpose. Lacey had not considered archaeological areas that were not included in reservations, and Hewett believed that some protection for these areas was imperative.

Although Hewett did not want to end up in the Baum-like position of telling the GLO how to do its job, he did have choice comments about the Lodge-Rodenberg bill. Hewett showed that the hastily written bill seemed tailored to specific situations and that it did not serve the general interest of archaeologists. It would have forbidden the excavations conducted by many qualified excavators. The Lodge-Rodenberg bill allowed only an "incorporated public museum, university, college, scientific society or educational institution" to sponsor exploratory work in archaeological ruins. Hewett pointed out that this language excluded the Bureau of Ethnology, which was not incorporated, an entity created for the "sole purpose of doing archeological and ethnological work in this country."[19]

Nor did Hewett believe that the authors of the bill understood the process of archaeological investigation. The bill contained a clause that compelled any fieldwork to be "continuously" pursued until the secretary of the interior deemed it completed. This, Hewett said, made archaeology an expensive, time-consuming proposition dependent upon the whim of a government official. It would discourage even the most affluent institutions, for many excavations would take decades to complete. The Lodge-Rodenberg bill also made collecting artifacts in the public domain a misdemeanor. Hewett stressed that this failed to differentiate between archaeology and vandalism and made all excavators liable to prosecution, for "under strict construction, it prohibits the most harmless and commendable pursuits."[20]

According to Hewett, the Lodge-Rodenberg bill was a disaster. It seemed "merely [to] impose an unfortunate restriction upon existing powers." It confined archaeological reservations to a single section of land for each, an area Hewett believed too small. In 1904 temporary withdrawal by the secretary of the interior, upon which there were no restrictions, offered the primary tool to protect prehistory, and instead of rectifying the problems of archaeological preservation, the new bill merely restricted existing options. "In fact, the whole effect of this bill," opined Hewett, "is to place serious obstacles in the way of the advancement of Archeological Science."[21]

After taking Hewett's arguments into account, Commissioner Richards agreed that the Lodge-Rodenberg bill was a seriously flawed piece of legislation. Hewett's keen eye and interpretive sense detected severe problems in the bill that had been buried during the heated emotional conflicts earlier in the year. Seen in a new light, the bill did little for preservation and the advancement of knowledge that the existing de facto situation did not cover. Worse, it imposed new and, to Hewett, unnecessary restrictions upon qualified archaeologists. On 5 October 1904 Richards wrote the secretary of the interior to concur wholeheartedly with Hewett's suggestions.[22] Hewett now had the official sanction of the Department of the Interior behind his efforts.

In December 1904 the Lodge-Rodenberg bill was reintroduced in Congress, and the lukewarm reception it received led to a major realignment of preservation advocates. Although on 5 January 1905 the House Public Lands Committee reported favorably upon it, Congress adjourned before a vote could be taken, and the Lodge-Rodenberg bill died. Hewett's comments to Richards certainly cooled support at the Department of the Interior. Baum's attitude and presentation had alienated many of the supporters of preservation legislation, and when Hewett and the GLO found his bill seriously flawed, many were pleased. Baum's power base disintegrated following the demise of the bill, and a vacancy in the leadership of the movement to preserve American antiquities appeared. Hewett filled the void. A formidable man, he nonetheless offered the House Public Lands Committee a more palatable personality to support. It remained to be seen if Hewett could pull the fragmented groups together behind any one piece of legislation.

The Baum debacle forced preservation advocates to reconsider their objectives, and many favored compromise in order to achieve an early solution. Archaeologists and anthropologists toned down their actions considerably, and they soon followed the charismatic Hewett. Looking for some kind of conciliatory legislation, the American Anthropological Society appointed him to its committee to promote legislation in favor of preservation. In 1904 the committee had supported the Lodge-Rodenberg bill as the best available option, and its members prepared to reintroduce it when Congress reconvened in January 1906.[23] Hewett convinced them to do otherwise.

To a committee of the organization, he presented his previous objections and added a new one. The Forest Transfer Act of 1905 transferred the forest reserves (national forests) from the Department of the Interior to the Department of Agriculture. The transfer imposed a bifurcated system of administration upon southwestern archeological areas, for the new United States Forest Service (USFS) assumed responsibility for ruins on national forest land whereas the GLO still managed those that remained in the public domain. This made the Lodge-Rodenberg bill an archaic measure; it no longer addressed the issues facing all southwestern archaeological ruins. Hewett recognized the urgency long associated with preservation and did not want the change in administration to initiate interdepartmental strife in Washington, D.C. He suggested that the interior, agriculture, and war departments, the latter of which had jurisdiction over ruins on military land, separately administer antiquities on the lands for which each was responsible. Again Hewett effectively worked within the rules of federal politics, an endeavor at which earlier proponents of preservation had failed. Instead of favoring one department over another, Hewett proposed leaving each department in charge of its own ruins. Better a system with a number of responsible authorities than no system at all.

With Hewett's guidance, a new drive took form. At a joint meeting of the American Anthropological Association and the Archaeological Institute of America in Ithaca, New York, on 28 December 1905, Hewett presented a draft of his bill for the preservation of American antiquities. His measure preserved "the exact spirit" of the archaeologists' and anthropologists' draft of the previous year and covered issues of concern to the General Land Office, the Department of the Interior, and people in the West. The meeting unanimously endorsed Hewett's draft, and Hewett presented it to John Lacey, who introduced it in the House. Sen. Thomas Patterson of Colorado followed with an identical bill in the Senate.[24]

Hewett's bill, titled "An Act for the Preservation of American Antiquities," and which came to be known as the Antiquities Act, had broad appeal. It pleased scientists, academics, government officials, and concerned citizens. The bill rectified many of the problems that Hewett had previously called to Richards's attention. It avoided administrative questions beyond assigning departments to guard ruins on lands they already administered, something presumably within the scope of their responsibilities. It also included "objects of historic and scientific interest" among the features that could be protected. Hewett suggested that the president have the power to proclaim this new category of federal reservations—the national monuments—subject to the stricture that their size "should be limited to the proper care and management of the objects to be protected," a drastic change from the restrictive 320- or 640-acre areas previous measures allowed.[25]

Although the unchecked power that Hewett's bill granted to the president appeared to compromise western interests, the bill really only extended executive fiat into a new realm; it granted no extension of the nature of that power. The Forest Reserve Act of 1891 granted to the president the unlimited power to create forest reserves. During the late 1890s controversy swirled around uses of that law to reserve vast timbered areas. In contrast, most archaeological areas were minute, and although the language of the bill included more than archaeological areas, few recognized it as a threat to their interests. The agreed-upon imperative of preservation outweighed existing concerns.

Hewett was a persuasive advocate, and after powerful legislative support emerged for the bill, the Antiquities Act became law. Colorado senator Thomas Patterson's sponsorship of the bill in the Senate helped allay western fears. With Hewett's growing reputation to back him, Lacey handled similar suspicions in the House of Representatives. During discussion of the measure on the House floor, Rep. John Hall Stephens of Vernon, Texas, asked Lacey if the bill would permit anything like the powers of the Forest Reserve Act of 1891, "by which seventy to eighty million acres of land in the United States had been tied up." "The object is entirely different," Lacey responded, "it is to preserve these old objects of special interest and the Indian remains on the pueblos in the Southwest."[26] Lacey's response satisfied westerners, and the Antiquities Act passed in the House of Representatives.

On 8 June 1906 Theodore Roosevelt signed it into law. It seemed that the preservation of antiquities and private use of natural resources could coexist.

The situation deceived both Lacey and Stephens. The following year, Congress forbade the president to create additional forest reserves in western states without congressional approval, and the importance of the Antiquities Act increased.[27] It became the primary federal tool in urgent situations, and beginning with Theodore Roosevelt, it was used in ways that closely resembled uses of the Forest Reserve Act. Areas far larger than ever conceived were reserved under the auspices of the Act. As a result of the compromise Hewett arranged, the Antiquities Act became the way to protect public land in the United States quickly and effectively.

Hewett succeeded where other more prominent professionals had failed, for he had something to offer all the factions in the controversy. With a perspective that was part westerner, part scientist, and part government official, Hewett could clearly see the concerns of each. By seeking "in advance the approval not only of the committees of the [American Archaeological] Institute and of the Anthropological Association but also of the heads of the Government Departments concerned," Hewett deflected professional opposition to the bill.[28] His work with the organizations and the government brought him prestige among the people he sought as peers, and because he sought a Ph.D., he contradicted the inclination of scientists to regard excavating westerners as profiteering vandals. He had also helped blunt western opposition to another law granting unlimited presidential power over lands primarily located in western states.

Equal parts nineteenth- and twentieth-century person, Hewett provided the link that earlier attempts to pass legislation to protect American antiquities had lacked. Narrowly conceived, the earlier measures provoked controversy within a loose confederation of supporters. People who supported the idea of preservation had fought among themselves. In the right place at the right time, Hewett capitalized on the heightened sense of urgency inspired by the failure of the Lodge-Rodenberg bill. He consolidated supporters behind one proposal. He had close ties to all of the appropriate factions and his unique status as one of the few westerners with credentials and excavating experience enabled him to speak for the West of the future. Hewett replaced Richard Wetherill as an image of the West in the minds of scientists and government officials concerned with American antiquities.

The initiation of a movement to preserve human history and prehistory on the North American continent paralleled the drive to conserve other natural resources. It also embodied a cultural nationalism that required the forging of uneasy alliances between the East and the West and between science and government. The passage of the Antiquities Act was another step away from the individualistic, nineteenth-century ethic characterized by people like Richard Wetherill. Progressive sensibilities began to be applied to western land, to make rules for the greater good. To be a respected professional in twentieth-century America required credentials as well as field experience, and the cooperative ethic of the Progressive era temporarily subsumed the individualism of the frontier. The federal government determined to take a more active hand in the administration and disposition of the public domain, and if Richard Wetherill planned to harvest upon his homestead claim, he would have to plant crops. Hewett had orchestrated a solid fusion where others, with equally good intentions, had failed. As a result, it became possible to preserve American antiquities.

But the Antiquities Act left many issues unresolved. Because it was a hasty compromise, drawn up to placate various government agencies, the new law left administrative questions unsettled. Recognizing the immediate need for the law, Hewett followed the lead of earlier preservation advocates. He tabled questions of jurisdiction and administration so that the proclamation of worthy sites as national monuments could begin. The only administrative provision in the act was one that allowed each department to retain responsibility for lands proclaimed as national monuments. There were no provisions for funding of the national monuments, effectively inhibiting the establishment of any system of caretaking. Other crucial questions were left to be decided at a later date. The Antiquities Act had closed gaps in the law; in practice, effective preservation had yet to be achieved.

NOTES

1. Henry Mason Baum, "Records of the Past and American Antiquities," *Records of the Past* 1, pt. 1 (January 1902): 1.
2. For a discussion of the effects of cultural nationalism on the development

of American national parks, see Alfred Runte, *National Parks: The American Experience* (Lincoln: University of Nebraska Press, 1979), 71-73, 82-106.

3. Baum, "Records of the Past," 3.

4. Ibid., 4; anonymous (attributed to Baum), *Records of the Past* (June 1902): 127.

5. Henry Mason Baum, "Pueblo and Cliff Dwellers of the Southwest," *Records of the Past* 1, pt. 12 (December 1902): 357-61. The Pajarito Plateau area now includes Bandelier National Monument.

6. Ibid., 361.

7. Editorial notes, *Records of the Past* 2, pt. 5 (May 1903): 157. Ise, *Our National Park Policy*, 147, attributes this request to Hewett.

8. Lee, *Antiquities Act*, 57-60.

9. S. Doc. 314, 59th Cong., 2d sess., 1904, 4; NA, RG 79, Series 1, Records Relating to National Parks and Monuments 1872-1916, Letters Received by the Office of the Secretary of the Interior Relating to National Parks 1872-1907, Tray 166.

10. See H. R. 13349, S. 5603, H. R. 12247, and S. 4127, 59th Cong., 2d sess., 1904; NA RG 79, Series 1, Records Relating to National Parks and Monuments 1872-1916, Letters Received, Tray 166, contains copies of all these documents.

11. Henry Mason Baum, "Pending Legislation for the Protection of Antiquities of the Public Domain," *Records of the Past* 3, pt. 5 (May 1904): 149. See also S. Doc. 314, 1904, 5.

12. Baum, "Pending Legislation," 149.

13. Ibid., 147.

14. Ibid., 149-50.

15. William H. Goetzmann, *Exploration and Empire*, 512-13ff has biographical information on William H. Holmes.

16. Lee, *Antiquities Act*, 66-67; James Taylor Forrest, "Edgar Lee Hewett," in *Keepers of the Past*, ed. Clifford Lord (Chapel Hill: University of North Carolina Press, 1965), 145-46; Lansing B. Bloom, "Edgar Lee Hewett: His Biography and Writings to Date," in *So Live the Works of Men*, ed. Donald D. Brand and Fred E. Harvey (Albuquerque: University of New Mexico Press, 1939), 13-20.

17. See *Records of the Past* 4 (1905), frontispiece. Baum was also replaced as editor.

18. Edgar L. Hewett, "Report to the Commissioner of the General Land Office," 3 September 1904, NA, RG 79, Series 1, Records Relating to National Parks and Monuments 1872-1916, Letters Received, Tray 166.

19. Edgar L. Hewett to W. A. Richards, 14 September 1904, NA, RG 79, Series 1, Records Relating to National Parks and Monuments 1872-1916, Letters Received, Tray 166.

20. See H.R. 13349, 1904; Hewett, "Report to the Commissioner," 3 September 1904.

21. Ibid.

22. W. A. Richards to the secretary of the interior, 5 October 1904, NA, RG 79, Series 1, Records Relating to National Parks and Monuments, 1872-1916, Letters Received, Tray 166.

23. Lee, *Antiquities Act*, 70.

24. Edgar L. Hewett, "Preservation of American Antiquities; Progress During the Last Year; Needed Legislation," *American Anthropologist* 8 (1906): 113; see Lee, *Antiquities Act*, 72-77, for more detail.

25. *United States Statutes at Large*, L. 34 Stat. 225 (1906).

26. Dr. Harold C. Bryant, National Park Service memo for the files, June 1932. A copy of this can be found in NA, RG 79, Series 18, Records of Arno B. Cammerer. Cammerer's correspondence files are largely unsorted.

27. Darrell H. Smith, *The Forest Service* (Washington, DC: Brookings Institution, 1930), 20-35.

28. Francis W. Kelsey, "Recent Archeological Legislation," *Records of the Past* 5, pt. 11 (November 1906): 339-40.

4

The First Monuments

THE PASSAGE OF THE ANTIQUITIES ACT OF 1906 addressed regional
issues rather than national ones. The demands of an industrial-
izing society left little time to ponder the remnants of aboriginal Indian
culture. To a nation not far removed from the rigors of frontier
existence, the preservation of a non-European, non-English-speaking
heritage offered little symbolic sustenance. A civilized past in what
previously had been thought a cultural void had little meaning to the
average American. The Southwest remained of peripheral concern
to the United States as it modernized, and to many in the East, the
region seemed a backward yet romantic place. Archaeological ruins
evoked images of an intriguing past, but they were far from national
centers of policy and power. Few urban Americans saw any reflection
of the contemporary struggle to attain global power in the ruins of
prehistoric societies. Archaeological preservation seemed likely to remain the province of the upper classes and intellectuals.

Yet the Antiquities Act was a harbinger of change in the Southwest
and West. Its passage added a potent new method for the federal
government to impose order upon public lands, and it provided an
emotional and intellectual argument that merged with the scientific
rationale advocating wise use of dwindling resources. The Act gave
the aggressive administrations of the early twentieth century another
means to implement their agenda of controlled regulation of the assets
of the nation.

Although the framers of the Antiquities Act regarded the preservation of prehistoric ruins as an end in itself, others sensed an implicit affirmation of industrial America cloaked in the speeches that spurred its passage. The demise of prehistoric culture gave Americans confidence in their destiny. In the aftermath of the Spanish-American War, xenophobic Americans regarded their subjugation of the wilderness as evidence of the superiority of English-speaking people. The spread of industrial commerce in the Southwest offered a sharp contrast to the remnants of an aboriginal culture and reinforced that assumption. This quirky determinism suggested that the New World belonged to those who could master its often harsh environment. The ruins of previous attempts to bring order to a chaotic physical environment offered assurance that modern solutions were best.

Early in the twentieth century, the American public felt the beautiful and the scenic to be more accurate barometers of their superiority than were the ruins of lost civilizations. Americans found affirmation of their aspirations in the landscape of the national parks. The uproar over the articulation of the closing of the westward frontier and the back-to-nature cults it spawned revealed a general preoccupation with the relationship between humanity and its environment. Archaeological ruins were another way of confirming what the descendants of Europeans already knew: the North American continent was their rightful domain. From this perspective, the Antiquities Act was only the most recent law in a history descending from the Papal Intercaetara of 1493, which divided the unknown parts of the globe into halves ceded to Portugal and Spain.

The Antiquities Act also had some very practical functions given increased public interest in preservation. It allowed the Department of the Interior to protect the national parks, by creating an additional category for the permanent reservation of places of interest. One measure of the growing public acceptance for preservation was that congressmen began to covet national parks for their states or districts. Between 1900 and 1906, Congress created two national parks, Wind Cave in South Dakota and Platt in Oklahoma, as pork-barrel maneuvers. Sully's Hill, a tract of unspectacular scenery in North Dakota, also acquired informal designation as a national park. None of these areas compared in scenic beauty or size to previous parks like Yellowstone, Yosemite, and Mount Rainier, and the establishment of such parks called into question the motivation for the creation of national parks. The establishment of inferior parks prior to passage of the

Antiquities Act emphasized the need for some other category in which to place proposed areas. The passage of the Antiquities Act allowed the Department of the Interior to fend off the park proposals it did not want; after 1906, if a congressman wanted a national park in his district but the Department of the Interior thought such a designation was inappropriate, the area frequently became a national monument.

The Act also expressed the middle and upper-middle class values of decision makers during the Progressive era. The federal bureaucracy, operating as a managerial elite, acquired the right to make decisions in the interest of public good. As befitted the era, this power was unrestricted, yet narrowly conceived. The Act did not allow ad hoc funding for the new areas, and its punishment clauses were hardly sufficient to prevent vandalism. Progressive legislators believed that legal restrictions alone would inspire compliance and that a sign proclaiming federal property would deter a respectable citizen bent on excavating. They did not realize that the law might not have an impact upon someone not inculcated in middle-class traditions.

Despite the values of Progressive America and the ease with which national monuments could be established, the Act revealed a general lack of consensus over what should be preserved. The category it established—the national monuments—lacked the cultural trappings attached to national parks. These monuments were only proclaimed. Soldiers did not guard them, as they did the national parks. Railroads rarely promoted national monuments, and tourists did not go out of their way to find these often remote places. Established with little fanfare and sometimes with less thought, the monuments came to include an increasingly diverse spectrum of features.

Progressive sensibility alone did not account for the diversity of the monuments. In fact, the Antiquities Act lent legal sanction to an informal system already firmly entrenched in the GLO. Beginning in the early 1890s, the commissioners of the GLO actively pursued a policy of withdrawing places with archaeological, historical, or natural significance from settlement and other kinds of land claims. GLO special agents in the field brought these places to the attention of the bureau. To prevent development and exploitation, commissioners Binger Hermann and W. A. Richards removed a broad array of locations, including the homestead that Richard Wetherill staked out in Chaco Canyon, from the sections of the public domain available under the terms of the Homestead Act. A "temporary withdrawal" only required that the area had potential for something other than agriculture. The interesting features of many made them candidates for the then-amorphous national park category.[1]

The Antiquities Act allowed the conversion of the commissioner of the General Land Office's de facto system into a reality grounded in law. The GLO played an important role in questions of the disposal of land and worked to make its position understood throughout the legislative battles in Congress over the preservation issue. Its officials feared that measures like the Lodge-Rodenberg bill of 1904 might restrict their options. Edgar L. Hewett's close connections with the GLO made him aware that its officials needed considerable leeway. If the areas already withdrawn from entry could not be converted to permanent status, the work of early preservation advocates and their allies would be wasted. The Antiquities Act solved this problem. The transformation of land from temporary withdrawal to national monument status protected the work of prior commissioners of the GLO.

After the passage of the Antiquities Act, the commissioner of the GLO began to convert previously withdrawn places into national monuments. During the summer of 1906, the GLO staff reviewed withdrawn tracts and drew up preliminary proclamations for the secretary of the interior. On 24 September 1906 President Theodore Roosevelt signed the first of these proclamations, making Devils Tower the first national monument in the United States.

An 865-foot-high geological abnormality rising above the plains of eastern Wyoming, Devils Tower had first come to the attention of the Department of the Interior fourteen years earlier. In 1892 Sen. Francis E. Warren of Wyoming received a letter from GLO special agent L. S. Hanchett concerning this "great natural curiosity." Warren wrote to the commissioner of the GLO, Thomas Carter, to promote the region as a possible national park. He requested that the GLO "formulate a bill or suggest provisions for one which would cover the ground and receive the support of [the D]epartment [of the Interior]."[2]

But in 1892, the time was not ripe for the concept of preservation of its own sake. The regulation of natural resources, however, did already figure in federal policy; the Forest Reserve Act of 1891 allowed the president to select wooded areas of the public domain as forest reserves, primarily to protect watersheds. As a result, Carter developed a two-pronged justification concerning Devils Tower for the secretary of the interior. He argued that the feature had served as a landmark for early settlers in the West and that reserving it would help preserve the watershed of the nearby Belle Fourche River. Symbolic value and practical function, Carter insisted, made Devils Tower worthy of reservation.[3]

Six years later, in 1898, Carter's suggestion became reality. Although a temporary withdrawal required only a proclamation by the commissioner of the GLO, it was not a desired prize in the early 1890s. The GLO initially sought a more permanent solution. But the significance of the temporary withdrawal as an important tool increased throughout the 1890s, and in 1898, Commissioner Hermann completed what Carter had begun. He withdrew Devils Tower from the public domain.[4] As the scientific management of natural resources became an important social issue to Americans adjusting to the idea of a culture without a westward frontier, Hermann's move fit the changing political and cultural climate.

Yet until the passage of the Antiquities Act, Devils Tower remained in limbo, neither large enough nor important enough to become a national park. But there was no other category for it. It was ludicrous to add Devils Tower to a category that held Yellowstone as the standard to which other park areas were compared. In the federal system before 1906, Devils Tower was an anomaly. Its primary value was natural, which would have left it out of the preservation system had the Lodge-Rodenberg bill passed in 1904. Because the Antiquities Act of 1906 covered a greater range than did its predecessors, the main impetus for the first national monument did not come from the archaeologists, academics, or scientists who worked so fervently to pass the Antiquities Act. The proclamation reflected the dual function Thomas Carter suggested in 1892. An "extraordinary example of erosion in the higher mountains," Devils Tower was preserved for its historic and scientific value.[5] Inappropriate as a national park or forest, it became the first national monument.

The number and type of monuments grew rapidly. On 8 December 1906 Theodore Roosevelt proclaimed three more national monuments: El Morro, a rock abutment in western New Mexico that bore the inscriptions of Spanish and American soldiers and travelers as well as the petroglyphs of prehistoric people, and two areas in Arizona, the Petrified Forest, two extensive clusters of prehistoric petrified forests, and Montezuma Castle, a prehistoric cliff dwelling tucked into a hillside in the Verde River valley. Along with Devils Tower, the three December 1906 national monuments covered the gamut of potential monuments in the American West. All had previously been included in temporary withdrawals. These initial proclamations defined the boundaries of the monument category for the coming decades.

Rising above the surrounding desert, El Morro was a spectacular sight. Its small pool of potable water had attracted prehistoric people and later travelers. Beginning with don Juan de Oñate in 1605, Spaniards inscribed their names on the face of El Morro. During the nineteenth century, American military explorers, including Lt. James H. Simpson, who investigated Chaco Canyon in 1848-49, continued the tradition and left their mark. Late in the 1890s El Morro attracted the attention of the Smithsonian Institution. "A more beautiful and imposing bit of scenery is not to be found in the United States," the acting secretary of the Smithsonian wrote to the secretary of the interior on 22 December 1899. "I recommend immediate attention in this matter for many of the early inscriptions have been despoiled by vandal bands." The forestry report of the GLO in 1900 also noted the significance of the El Morro, a place "of such historical interest that ample protection should be thrown around it, especially in as much as added years attach new interest and value," and suggested that "if the lands upon which the rock stands were reserved from settlement, the property would be measurable [sic] protected for the present."[6] Because it was a unique and irreplaceable monument to the continuity of human existence in a harsh environment, El Morro was withdrawn by the GLO to await either national park status or the passage of a bill to preserve antiquities.

The Petrified Forest region in Arizona also attracted considerable attention in the period prior to the passage of the Antiquities Act. By the turn of the century, casual vandalism was threatening its features. Reports that thieves were using dynamite to break up the formations to haul them away reached the GLO. The crossing at the nearby Rio Puerco was littered with formations discarded when drivers found them heavy enough to prevent their autos from fording the creek. After numerous complaints by concerned people, the GLO withdrew the tract in 1903, pending consideration of a national park in the region. There was little progress toward a park bill in Congress that year, but in 1904 GLO special agent Stephen J. Holsinger received authorization to appoint an unpaid assistant with a specific purpose: to "prevent all persons from doing further damage to the natural curiosities within the proposed national park."[7] Park status for the Petrified Forest never progressed beyond the proposal stage, and like El Morro, it lingered in limbo.

In Arizona, Montezuma Castle was in a similar position. Nestled under a cliff overlooking agricultural fields, Hohokam and Hakataya aboriginals had built the "castle" as a defensive site. Nineteenth-century Americans, immersed in the romance of what they believed to be Aztec culture in the American Southwest, misnamed the secluded fortress. Cosmos Mindeleff of the Bureau of American Ethnology surveyed the site in 1892, and before 1900 it attracted the attention of the Department of the Interior. The GLO, nominally in charge of the area, did little until Gov. Alexander Brodie of Arizona wrote Secretary of the Interior Ethan A. Hitchcock inquiring about the ruins. In 1904 GLO special agent George Wilson inspected the ruin. He advocated the establishment of a national park, reporting that there were many visitors and that the ruin required better supervision.[8]

But a problem of semantics plagued such areas. Like the Petrified Forest, Devils Tower, and El Morro, Montezuma Castle differed from already established national parks. It did not have the scenery that characterized the national park class; it was a solitary, if massive, cliff dwelling. Wilson suggested that Montezuma Castle be proclaimed a national park because he recognized the need for its protection. But from the perspective of the Department of the Interior in Washington, D.C., Wilson's suggestion was implausible. In 1904 the interior department had already expressed concern about the inferior national parks, and if Montezuma Castle became a national park, the department would appear to contradict its emphasis. Although it clearly merited preservation, Montezuma Castle did not merit recognition as a national park.

Prior to the passage of the Antiquities Act, federal preservation efforts could not be comprehensive. Many areas worthy of preservation did not meet the amorphous standards for national parks. In addition, many were in the territories of Arizona and New Mexico, which had only a nonvoting territorial delegate in Congress and lacked the pork-barrel influence that often contributed to the establishment of national parks. Increasing private demand for land in the Southwest made the future of unclaimed areas uncertain. The GLO combated such problems with the power of temporary withdrawal. GLO commissioner Binger Hermann knew that Congress would never establish the Montezuma Castle as a national park, but late in 1904 he withdrew the ruin because he hoped for the early passage of the Lodge-Rodenberg bill or one of its counterparts. After the passage of the Antiquities Act two years later, GLO officials began to formalize such withdrawals.

As a result of GLO activism, the monuments became a much broader category than many of the supporters of the Antiquities Act had envisioned. Montezuma Castle was the first of many prehistoric ruins to attain national monument status. El Morro had historic and prehistoric significance; its walls held the answers to many questions about Spanish endeavors in the north of old New Spain, and its ruins were associated with some of the mystique of prehistoric life. Devils Tower and the Petrified Forest were natural areas, evocative of the culturally significant landscapes of the national parks.

The GLO used the Antiquities Act to codify in law what had been its standard procedure during the previous fifteen years. Although the Antiquities Act granted the president discretion in proclaiming sites, in practice the GLO made those decisions. Between 1906 and 1909, most monument proclamations formalized earlier temporary withdrawals, so that there was little argument about the suitability of reserving the places in question. Long in advance of the Antiquities Act, all had been withdrawn to protect them from the forces that the new law addressed.

The GLO carved the early national monuments out of the public domain and forest reserves, from land unclaimed by the public that lacked apparent economic value and that was predominantly located in remote, undeveloped sections of the country. Unproductive from an agricultural standpoint and generally too distant from the nearest railroad to support a profitable tourist industry, none of the early monuments had sufficient value to private citizens to make their reservation worth contesting.

The Antiquities Act had a severe limitation because it applied only to federal land. Railroads and other industries had acquired considerable land in the West and Southwest, and the GLO had little control over ruins upon railroad sections. The Homestead Act of 1862 had facilitated private ownership of land throughout the West, and by 1900 homesteaders claimed numerous objects of natural and cultural interest. In such cases, the Antiquities Act offered little protection for pictographs and petroglyphs, ruins, or other objects of value on private land.

The case of the pictographs and ruins of San Cristóbal pueblo in northern New Mexico typified the response of the GLO to suggestions involving privately owned sites. In January 1907 the *Los Angeles Times*, which circulated widely throughout smaller towns in the West, ran a Sunday article that featured these pictographs. In Beatrice, Nebraska, William Wolfe, president of the German National Bank, saw the article and asked Congressman John Lacey to bring San Cristóbal to the attention of Congress.[9] Wolfe had visited the pictographs and was willing to attest to their importance as relics of human history on the North American continent.

But the GLO found itself powerless at San Cristóbal. Lacey thought that the pictographs were an interesting possibility for a national monument and passed the request on to the Department of the Interior. It landed on Commissioner W. A. Richards's desk at the GLO. On 5 February 1907 Richards concluded that the Arroyo San Cristóbal lay within the confirmed E. W. Eaton land grant. Unless the owners, including New Mexico land baron Thomas B. Catron, wanted to make a gift of the tract, the GLO could not act.[10] Congress had not provided appropriations to purchase land for monuments, and a national monument was not sufficiently valuable to engineer an exchange of lands.

San Cristóbal was not the only worthwhile archaeological, natural, or historic area that remained outside of federal control. The GLO had limited resources for preservation and could not justify the time and effort that acquisition attempts required. Monuments were little more than a symbolic triumph, not worthy of extensive effort by the GLO. There were more than enough places of interest in the public domain to fill the time Commissioner Richards and his staff could devote to national monuments, and like most Americans, they lacked comparative standards to make qualitative assessment of such areas.

The GLO had few options in such cases and its officials chose the earliest national monuments from the best available areas that remained in federal hands. Barring donation by its owners, private land was out of the question. The public domain, the national forests, and military reservations formed a pool from which the GLO selected "objects of prehistoric, historic and scientific interest"; many places outside the category were of equal or greater importance than established national monuments.

Despite the limitations of the resources of the GLO, pressure to establish monuments mounted as Theodore Roosevelt's tenure continued. Private donations, threatened exploitation and development, and pressure from members of Congress, government employees, and individuals played a significant role in shaping the national monument category.

In a typical instance, the establishment of the Muir Woods National Monument resulted from conflict between the interests of utilitarian development and preservation in the San Francisco Bay area. Progressive-era administrators favored public control rather than private development of irreplacable resources, and Muir Woods became the first donation of private land for the establishment of a national monument.

California congressman William Kent, a long-time supporter of conservation and preservation causes, was the pivotal figure in the Muir Woods issue. On 29 August 1905 he purchased a large tract of redwood trees near Mill Valley, California, from the Tamalpais Land and Water Company. Aware of the increasing competition for land in booming northern California, Kent was determined to protect the few remaining stands of redwood trees in the San Francisco Bay area.[11] But when the massive San Francisco earthquake of 1906 decimated the city, local interests placed considerable pressure upon Kent to give up the land for development. Individuals and companies offered fair market value for the timber, but Kent regarded the redwoods as an irreplaceable resource and declined their offers.

The prospective purchasers saw the land only as a commodity and intensified their efforts. Rebuffed, James Newlands, the head of the North Coast Water Company and a nephew of the influential Nevada senator Francis Newlands, threatened to use his uncle's influence to wrest the land from Kent. Newlands filed a condemnation suit on a forty-seven-acre segment of Kent's redwood tract. The North Coast Water Company proposed to build a reservoir on the tract and to sell the water to the city of San Francisco.

In the name of the public good, commercial interests challenged rivate prerogative. Water was important to the city, and the North Coast Water Company sought to fill the need. Kent believed that

Newlands selected the redwood tract to force him to divide his estate. The wooded area would make an adequate reservoir, but it was not the only place that could serve the purpose. From Kent's perspective, the reservoir was a short-term solution that future generations would regret. But he held a minority view; public opinion was more interested in water than in the preservation of trees. If it came to a court battle, Newlands's lawyers intended to present Kent as a European-style "lord of the manor," whereas Newlands and the North Coast Water Company offered a public service, albeit at a profit. They could easily seem civic-minded in comparison with the caricature of Kent that might have emerged in court. Under the conditions that existed, Newlands had an excellent chance to win the condemnation suit in state court.

Kent had few options, but he made the most of them. As an ardent conservationist during his years in Congress, he was aware of the potential of the Antiquities Act. In response to the suit, Kent mailed the deed for 295 acres of his land, including the forty-seven disputed acres, to Secretary of the Interior James A. Garfield on 26 December 1907. Kent requested that Garfield accept it as a national monument under the terms of the Antiquities Act and that the monument be named Muir Woods, in honor of noted outdoorsman John Muir.[12]

Kent's situation required immediate action by the federal government. His attorney, William Thomas, explained the situation to United States forester and conservation advocate Gifford Pinchot. Thomas also urged Frederick E. Olmstead, chief inspector of the San Francisco branch of the USFS, to convince the government to accept the donation promptly. Kent had not been served with court documents and could still escape the lawsuit. "If I am forced to answer on behalf of Kent before the United States has any vested interest in the property," Thomas continued, "the result will be disastrous, as our statute provides that actions of this character will be given precedence on every court calendar." If the government acted quickly, federal ownership of the tract might preclude private or state-ordered condemnation. Secretary of the Interior Garfield believed that "these lands were deeded and accepted before the service of the process" and asked the Justice Department to protect the interest of the government.[13]

Kent's donation furthered his reputation for public service and gave the redwood grove the protection of the federal government. On 9 January 1908, twelve days after Kent sent his initial offer, Theodore Roosevelt signed the proclamation establishing the Muir Woods National Monument. The North Coast Water Company found itself suing the United States of America in federal court. Intimidated but undaunted, Newlands persisted. The court granted continuances in the case until Kent sold the North Coast Water Company another tract suitable for a reservoir, and Newlands finally withdrew the suit.

The controversy over Muir Woods juxtaposed two visions of public good. Newlands represented the utilitarian perspective, advocating the development of private land to create public services. Kent believed that the preservation of the redwoods provided a legacy for future generations. Both positions had merit, and in a way, the establishment of the national monument forced an accommodation. Neither side got exactly what it wanted, but both preserved their long-range objectives. The redwoods were saved, and Newlands built his reservoir elsewhere.

The divergent points of view that clashed over Muir Woods foreshadowed the fragmentation of the alliance of preservationists and conservationists in the dispute over the famous Hetch-Hetchy Valley reservoir. Although conservationists and preservationists had a natural affinity, in reality the two philosophies often produced contradictory programs for the same tracts of land. The terms of Progressive-era politics had dictated the resolution of the situation at Muir Woods. The North Coast Water Company was a private business that sought to condemn Kent's land for the public good, but lost. Public entities stood a better chance of success when it came to building reservoirs out of public or private land. In 1913 Woodrow Wilson signed into law a bill that allowed the inundation of the Hetch-Hetchy Valley in Yosemite National Park to create a reservoir for the city of San Francisco. In contrast to the Muir Woods case, the claim of the city was undeniable. There were no better options, and suspicions of private aggrandizement did not taint the arguments of the city of San Francisco. Ironically, Kent became a major proponent of the Hetch-Hetchy dam, and the controversy severed his friendship with preservationist John Muir.

Born out of competing values, Muir Woods also differed from its predecessors in other ways. It was the first national monument created close to a major population center, and the first that did not contain features that were somehow unique. Unlike earlier national monuments, its location as much as its stands of redwoods determined its significance. "There are, of course, many finer stands of Redwood in

California," Olmstead wrote in justifying the acceptance of Kent's gift, "but there are none owned by the United States nor are there any which might be acquired except at great expense. Moreover, (and here is the chief argument for acceptance of the land) there is no other Redwood grove in the world so remarkably accessible to so many people. Here is a typical redwood canyon in absolutely primeval condition, . . . it would be a living National Monument, than which nothing could be more typically American."[14]

In 1910 Muir Woods was an anomaly among national monuments. Proximity to San Francisco made Muir Woods worthy of preservation, and it became a popular picnic ground for day hikers from the nearby city. As a result of the traffic, Muir Woods became the first of the monuments to have a resident custodian, whose primary duty was picking up after picnickers. Muir Woods' problems resembled those of Central Park rather than those of the other monuments.

Had it been larger, Muir Woods might have been a candidate for national park status. It contained features similar to those in some of the national parks. But its small size was an obstacle to park status, and the urgency surrounding its proclamation and the ease with which it could be proclaimed a national monument pushed Muir Woods into the new category. With developmental pressure encroaching on one of the last tracts of wilderness in the San Francisco Bay area, the Antiquities Act provided the quickest way to guarantee the safety of the woodlands.

A similar impetus played a significant role in establishing the Grand Canyon as a national monument. Development in the area began in the early 1880s, and Sen. Benjamin Harrison of Indiana first proposed the region as a national park in 1882. Nothing came of the effort, and during the 1880s John Hance, who later became famous as a guide in the region, and P. D. Berry filed homestead claims on locations within the canyon. After he became president, Harrison proclaimed the Grand Canyon Forest Reserve in 1893, the first act to protect the region from private encroachment. Establishment of the forest reserve prevented further homesteading, although mineral claims were still permitted within its boundaries.[15]

By the late 1890s tourists began to visit the Grand Canyon, and amenities became necessary. In 1899 the only way for visitors to reach the canyon was by stage line or private transportation from Flagstaff and Ashfork. "Crude hotel camps" offered the only accommodations.[16] To alleviate the problem and to cash in on increased business, the Atchison, Topeka, and Santa Fe Railroad (AT&SF) began construction of a railroad spur from its terminal in Williams to the very rim of the Grand Canyon. The company planned a massive hotel, called El Tovar, to stand alongside their new station.

The Grand Canyon continued to attract public attention and its popularity grew. In May 1903 President Theodore Roosevelt deified the Grand Canyon during his only visit. He told an audience on the canyon rim that he preferred no "building of any kind, not a summer cottage, a hotel . . . to mar the wonderful grandeur, the sublimity, the great loneliness and beauty of the Canyon. You can not improve it. The ages have been at work on it and man can only mar it. What you can do is keep it for your children, your children's children, and for all those who come after you, as one of the great sights which every American, if he can travel at all, should see."[17] The power of the great gorge impressed Roosevelt. He saw before him the unscarred handiwork of nature and appreciated its awesomeness. Roosevelt sensed the importance of a place that could inspire such emotions. This was a place worthy of the American experience.

To Roosevelt, the Grand Canyon seemed part of the formation of the identity of the nation. From his perspective, the first sight of the continent itself could have been no less awe-inspiring than an initial view of the Grand Canyon. A reflection of the hardy spirit that Americans believed created the republic, the Grand Canyon was in a category by itself—too precious for commercial development. Its preservation in a pristine state would be a significant public good in its own right. It would be evidence of the power of the Progressive faith in regulated human achievement. When Roosevelt was told that the AT&SF decided to keep its hotel away from the rim of the canyon, he saw the decision as evidence of enlightened management and expressed pleasure at the restraint of the company.

But in the end, the AT&SF ignored Roosevelt's wishes. Business boomed at the Grand Canyon, and within a year of Roosevelt's visit, the El Tovar opened, "built upon the very edge of the canyon, its location afford[ing] the most intimate views of the great gorge."[18] Despite Roosevelt's use of the "bully pulpit," the AT&SF was bound only by statute. This private company was able to proceed because no law prevented its officials from building where they chose. The Grand Canyon became the first forest reserve to have a railroad terminus and a commercial lodge.

Yet the El Tovar offered something important at the Grand Canyon. According to the AT&SF and its staff of paid publicists, the construction of the railroad spur encouraged tourists, who began to visit the canyon in droves, and the El Tovar "came out of crying necessity." Managed by the Fred Harvey Company, the hotel was a tasteful, expensive place. Its colors were muted, to "harmonize perfectly with the gray green of its unique surroundings . . . its lines in harmony with the simplicity" around it."[19] El Tovar offered all the amenities of first-rate hotels elsewhere, mitigating the lack of facilities near the Grand Canyon. Yet the arrival of visitors and their accoutrements intruded upon the solitude of the Grand Canyon. The area boomed so rapidly that less than five years later Roosevelt felt compelled to limit its growth.

In 1907 pressure to develop the Grand Canyon area intensified. Under the terms of the forest reserve, Ralph Henry Cameron, a local politician who later became a United States senator from Arizona, staked out mining claims at some of the most advantageous tourist locations. His domain included the Bright Angel trail, the main route from the south rim to the bottom of the canyon. But Roosevelt's establishment of a game reserve in early 1906 prohibited the future filing of mining claims. Undaunted, Cameron continued to file illegal mining claims, and under the guise of a firm called the Grand Canyon Scenic Railway Company, he and his associates tried to secure a right-of-way to build an electric railway for sightseeing tours along the rim of the canyon.[20]

When conservationists discovered Cameron's plans, they mustered their influence. After being "bombarded by some man, who insisted that there was a trolley line about to be constructed around the Grand Canyon, which would not add to its natural attractiveness," longtime park advocate and civic leader Horace McFarland went to Gifford Pinchot and "made a loud noise in his ear." Pinchot informed Roosevelt, who was appalled by the prospect. He converted the game preserve into a national monument under the administration of the Forest Service. Monument status protected the Grand Canyon from random legal encroachment, and the Forest Service, placed in charge of the monument because it was created from national forest land, staunchly opposed exploitive private enterprise.[21]

Piecemeal efforts at preservation like that at the Grand Canyon were characteristic early in the twentieth century. The establishment of a national monument was not part of any grand plan to protect America's wonders. Instead, expediency in the face of pressure dictated the course of preservation. Initially, the government lacked mechanisms for permanent reservation, and it upgraded the status of the Grand Canyon in response to a variety of threats. The forest reserve prohibited all private entries except for mining claims. The game reserve prevented mining claims, but did not offer formal protection from exploitive development. The establishment of the monument under the Forest Service curtailed private development; Pinchot and the Forest Service took a dim view of capital development on public land. Although monument status did not exclude commercial development, acquiring permission to build within the boundaries of the reservation became much more difficult. The eventual reclassification of the Grand Canyon as a national park was inevitable as the need for comprehensive visitor-oriented management became obvious.

An unforeseen result of the formation of the Grand Canyon National Monument was that this action appeared to put the government in the position of favoring one organization offering tourist services over another. Without any public discussion or bidding process, federal authorities arbitrarily limited competition. This gesture was characteristic of the managerial elite applying its values to the society around it. The AT&SF was a successful business, and its board of directors came from the same social class as most high-level government officials. They shared perceptions of the world. Cameron and his friends did not belong to the same network. Cameron was a political boss who ruled Coconino County, Arizona. In part, the impulse for reform sprung from the desire to limit the activities of this breed of political animal and its equivalent in business. In the cultural climate of 1908, such preferences seemed justified. An established national entity took precedence over a local one perceived to be exploitive, and the good of the public outweighed the rights of any individual. Cameron retained his many mining claims, and he and his associates believed that they were unfairly prohibited from development. Later

Cameron created havoc with his lawsuits for a number of years, until a federal judge finally dismissed his contentions.

The Grand Canyon showed that Roosevelt and the GLO perceived the Antiquities Act from different perspectives. Prior to the establishment of the Grand Canyon, GLO proclamations established comparatively small monuments, beginning with a minimum size of 160 acres, one quarter of a section. GLO officials were conscious of the "smallest area compatible with the proper care and management" clause in the Antiquities Act, and concerned with a potential backlash, they limited their suggestions.[22] In comparison, the 806,400-acre Grand Canyon National Monument was the largest of the monuments. When an ominous situation threatened something that he valued, Roosevelt did what he thought was right even when his efforts smacked of flaunting executive authority. In 1907 he circumvented western efforts to limit his power to establish national forest lands by reserving more than seven million acres of forest before Congress passed legislation restricting his power.[23] By 1908 the only option for permanent reservation of public land that Roosevelt had left was the Antiquities Act. With one stroke of his pen at the Grand Canyon, he revived western fears of federal intervention.

Roosevelt's proclamation of the Mount Olympus National Monument further upset advocates of decentralization. In his last forty-eight hours in office, the president proclaimed 615,000 acres of the Olympic peninsula in Washington state as a national monument. Created at the behest of Congressman William E. Humphrey of Washington, the new national monument set aside much of the most rugged terrain on the western side of the Puget Sound and protected it from mining and timber interests.[24] Again, federal initiative and commercial development in the West seemed at odds.

The establishment of the Mount Olympus National Monument was a half-hearted conservation measure. It contained few of the restrictions that characterized the Grand Canyon and earlier monuments. During the 1880s, hunters and trappers broached the Olympic peninsula, and by the early twentieth century, excessive hunting had decimated its population of Olympic, also called Roosevelt, elk.[25] Intent on protecting the few animals that remained, Congressman Humphrey appealed to the hunter in the president, and Roosevelt made one final gesture for conservation. The proclamation also utilized the scientific justification for establishing a national monument, but it did not prohibit the development of resources within the boundaries of the monument. Nonetheless, mining and timber interests felt unduly restrained.

Commercial interests did not construe the reservation of a quarter section of archaeological ruins as a threat to development, but many thought that the Grand Canyon and Mount Olympus monuments were excessive gestures that restricted large tracts of valuable land for dubious reasons. Mining companies agitated for the immediate repeal of the proclamation at Mount Olympus, and in 1915 President Woodrow Wilson reduced its size by half. The Antiquities Act was a good way to initiate preservation, but it was not a guarantee of permanence.

Under any interpretation of the Antiquities Act other than Roosevelt's own, the Mount Olympus National Monument would have remained a part of the Olympic National Forest. With Congress out of session and little time left in his administration, the creation of a congressionally approved designation was out of the question. Mount Olympus National Monument was Roosevelt's going-away present to himself. He used the best available means to accomplish his ends, democratic or otherwise. That he stretched the Antiquities Act in a number of ways bothered him little. The law was a tool with which to achieve results.

Within three years of its passage, the Antiquities Act became much more than a way to preserve antiquities. The sentiments of the Progressive era and Theodore Roosevelt's activist vision of presidential responsibilities led to the creation of national monuments large and small that contained an array of features. Roosevelt set precedents that gave GLO and, later, National Park Service officials considerable freedom in the way that they applied the law.

The real catalyst for Roosevelt's interpretation of the Antiquities Act was his broad application of the "object of scientific interest" clause. This ambiguous definition gave him vast latitude, and without precedents to establish limits, Roosevelt created his own version of the boundaries of the monument category. Ostensibly preserved as examples of scientific principles in action, Devils Tower, the Petrified Forest, Muir Woods, the Grand Canyon, and others were proclaimed as "scientific" national monuments. Yet despite the obvious scientific *merit* of some of the monuments, scientific *use* did not figure in the reasons behind their establishment.

Nowhere were these ambiguities as obvious as at the Grand Canyon.

The president himself was awestruck by the sight of the gorge, and the AT&SF built a railroad and a monumental hotel on the rim of the canyon because nearly everyone who stood there felt the same way. Because he wanted to preserve the character of the Grand Canyon from the intrusion of the cable car, Roosevelt put limits on all growth there, not because it was "an object of unusual scientific interest, being the greatest eroded canyon within the United States."[26] The Grand Canyon certainly had scientific importance, but to Americans in 1908, its scenic and cultural attributes far surpassed its scientific value. Its establishment created a proper way to present this vast natural affirmation of American culture to visitors. Scientists bent on research were not battling over the canyon; hotelkeepers and tour guides were.

On the other hand, there was good reason to establish Devils Tower as a scientific national monument. It was a unique natural wonder, dwarfing its only competitor, an unnamed protrusion four miles away. As Thomas Carter pointed out in 1892, this geologic abnormality had conservation value as well as historical appeal. Yet after its establishment, the scientific significance of Devils Tower was overshadowed by its scenic appeal as the GLO groped to find a purpose for the existence of the monuments. At the first National Parks Conference, held at Yellowstone National Park in September 1911, Frank Bond, chief clerk of the GLO and the person responsible for the national monuments in the care of the Department of the Interior, proposed that "an iron stairway, winding if necessary, and securely anchored to the face of the vertical wall, should be constructed to the top of the rock."[27] The value of a stairway up the side of an 800-foot-high monolith was clearly not scientific. Bond tried to promote tourist interest in the spectacular view from atop Devils Tower.

Often the GLO or Forest Service took an interest in an area under consideration for national monument status because of its scenic merits, but the legal justification rested on its being established as a scientific monument. Commenting on the proposed Fremont (Wheeler) National Monument in 1908, Forest Supervisor F. C. Spencer wrote: "It is not probable that there is any immediate danger of devastation or vandalism to this bit of scenic beauty, but, with the settling up of the country, the place will be visited by many tourists, which will make its acquisition a source of profit for some individual or company." Spencer recommended a national monument "to prevent such acquisition and its attendant mercenary use." Despite Spencer's forward statement about the values of the area, the document that reached

Theodore Roosevelt's desk established a monument "of unusual scientific interest."[28]

Even a case like this aroused little controversy. The purported location where the Fremont expedition of 1848 met disaster, this series of limestone spires in southern Colorado was too remote and not economically valuable enough for anyone to contest its establishment. At Spencer's suggestion, the government reserved the tract to prevent future exploitation. The Wheeler National Monument was created in advance of widespread public interest to prevent undue profiteering after the public discovered it.

The term *scientific* in the Antiquities Act rapidly came to function as a code word under which scenic areas could acquire legal protection. This meaning was quite different from the intention of the anthropologists and archaeologists who had advocated passage of the Act. In practice, many of the areas proclaimed in the "scientific" monuments category served as little national parks before the establishment of the National Park Service. Government officials who believed in the ethics of Progressive America recognized the scenic value of many areas and incorporated them into an embryonic national park system. Regardless of the sentiments of Congress, executive action reserved such places for the future.

By the end of the Roosevelt administration in 1909, the national monuments were so diverse that they defied categorization. There were almost as many "scientific" reasons for the establishment of a monument as there were national monuments. The Antiquities Act placed few limits upon potential national monuments, and a variety of locations came to the attention of the Department of the Interior and the Forest Service. In different situations, the Antiquities Act could be, and was, interpreted loosely. The only link among members of the category was that after the GLO took care of its temporary withdrawals, many of the remaining areas that entered the system were threatened by what was perceived to be inappropriate development. By 1909 any clear sense of the intentions of the framers of the Act had disappeared.

Notes

1. Ise, *Our National Park Policy,* 147.

2. L. S. Hanchett to Francis E. Warren, 28 January 1892; and Francis E. Warren to GLO Commissioner Thomas Carter, 30 January 1892; NA, RG

79, Series 6, Devils Tower, file 12-5. The first letters to the Department of the Interior refer to the feature as "Devil's Tower"; the National Park Service dropped the apostrophe. Other parks have gone through similar transformations; for example, for many years, the apostrophe was left out of Sully's Hill. In *The National Parks: Shaping the System* (Washington, DC: National Park Service, 1984), bureau historian Barry Mackintosh includes the apostrophe.

3. Thomas Carter to the secretary of the interior, 16 February 1892, NA, RG 79, Series 6, Devils Tower, file 12-5.

4. GLO commissioner Binger Hermann to the secretary of the interior, 4 April 1898, NA, RG 79, Series 6, Devils Tower, file 12-5.

5. *United States Statutes at Large*, L. 34 Stat. 3236 (1906).

6. Acting secretary of the Smithsonian to the secretary of the interior, 22 December 1899, NA, RG 79, Series 6, El Morro, file 12-5; *Annual Report of the Commissioner of the General Land Office, 1900* (Washington, DC: Government Printing Office, 1900), 462-63.

7. Commissioner of the General Land Office to Special Agent Stephen J. Holsinger, April 1903, NA, RG 79, Series 6, Petrified Forest, file 12-5. An attached memorandum indicates that the letter permitting Holsinger to appoint a custodian was not sent until it was discovered in the files in March 1904. In April 1904 John Conner of Holbrook, Arizona, was appointed special assistant to special agent G. Henry Lesage.

8. Special Agent George Wilson to the commissioner of the GLO, 25 July 1904, NA, RG 79, Series 6, Montezuma Castle, file 12-5.

9. William Wolfe to Rep. John Lacey, 24 January 1907, NA, RG 79, Series 1, Records Relating to National Parks and Monuments 1872-1916, Letters Received, Tray 165.

10. W. A. Richards to the secretary of the interior, 5 February 1907, NA, RG 79, Series 1, Records Relating to National Parks and Monuments 1872-1916, Letters Received, Tray 165.

11. Horace M. Albright, *Oh Ranger!* (Palo Alto: Stanford University Press, 1928), 156.

12. William Kent to Secretary of the Interior James R. Garfield, 26 December 1907, NA, RG 79, Series 6, Muir Woods, file 12-5.

13. William Thomas to Gifford Pinchot, 26 December 1907; and Secretary of the interior to the attorney general of the United States, 9 January 1908; NA, RG 79, Series 6, Muir Woods, file 12-5.

14. Forest Supervisor F. E. Olmstead report, undated (circa New Year's 1908), NA, RG 79, Series 6, Muir Woods, file 12-5.

15. George W. James, *The Grand Canyon of Arizona* (Boston: Little, Brown and Company, 1910), 258; Robert Shankland, *Steve Mather of the National Parks*, 3d ed. (New York: Alfred A. Knopf, 1970), 226.

16. James, *Grand Canyon of Arizona*, v.

17. Quoted in Anna Sutton and Myron Sutton, *The Wilderness World of the Grand Canyon* (Philadelphia: J.P. Lippincott, 1971), 217-18.

18. Sutton and Sutton, *Wilderness World of the Grand Canyon* 217-18; James, *Grand Canyon of Arizona*, 16.

19. James, *Grand Canyon of Arizona*, 16.

20. Ise, *Our National Park Policy*, 232; Shankland, *Steve Mather*, 225-42, has the best chapter on the antics of Cameron and his cronies.

21. Horace McFarland, quoted in Lee, *Antiquities Act*, 91; U.S. Department of Agriculture, *Report of the United States Forester for 1909* (Washington, DC: Government Printing Office, 1909), 18.

22. See *United States Statutes at Large*, L. 34 Stat. 225 (1906).

23. Steen, *United States Forest Service*, 98-100.

24. Runte, *National Parks*, 73; see also Michael G. Schene, "Only the Squeal is Left: Conflict Over Establishing Olympic National Park," *The Pacific Historian* 27 (Fall 1983): 53-61; and Elmo R. Richardson, "Olympic National Park: Twenty Years of Controversy," *Forest History* 12 (April 1968): 6-15.

25. U.S. Department of the Interior, National Park Service, *Report of the Director of the National Park Service for the Fiscal Year ended June 30, 1918* (Washington, DC: Government Printing Office, 1919), 190.

26. *United States Statutes At Large*, L. 35 Stat. 2175 (1908).

27. U.S. Department of the Interior, *Proceedings of the National Parks Conference of 1911* (Washington, DC: Government Printing Office, 1911), 83.

28. Frank C. Spencer, "Report on the Proposed Fremont National Monument within the Cochetopah National Forest," February 1908, NA, RG 79, Series 6, Wheeler National Monument, file 12-5; Ferenc Szasz, "Colorado's Lost Monuments," *Journal of Forest History* 21 (July 1977): 33-45; Examiner of Surveys William B. Douglass to commissioner of the General Land Office, March 3, 1909, NA, RG 79, Series 6, Navajo, file 12-5.

5

"Warning Sign" Preservation

THE AMBIGUITY OF THE ANTIQUITIES ACT made it useful as a catchall preservationist law. The initial proliferation of national monuments showed the need had existed for a law that could permanently protect a wide range of places that government agencies and private citizens deemed worthy of preservation. The Antiquities Act became a weapon in the presidential arsenal, as well as a means that individual citizens could use to protect historic, scientific, and natural features. As a result, the Act became the authority for governance of the broadest range of areas ever established by any government. The twenty-eight offerings accepted between 24 September 1906 and 6 July 1911 included many types of areas that the framers of the Act had not considered.

In nearly every case, the proclamation of a national monument provided no supervision. Special agents of the GLO posted warning signs at each monument, but these signs offered the only form of protection for most early monuments. The establishment of an area as a national monument failed to deter vandals, who were oblivious to warning signs, although it did prevent law-abiding private citizens and companies from exploiting some unique features of the American landscape for commercial gain.

The cases of Chaco Canyon, Muir Woods, and the Grand Canyon showed that in some respects, the Antiquities Act was a success. But most monument proclamations failed to address pressing problems. Because Forest Service or GLO representatives visited most reserved areas only once or twice a year, the monuments were often targets of callous vandalism. Visitors in search of souvenirs destroyed sections of the Petrified Forest, and despite the efforts of government officials, archaeological vandalism persisted. After putting up a warning sign at the El Morro National Monument during his annual trip in 1911, GLO mining inspector Charles B. Barker noted: "The appearances indicate that unless more adequate protection and patrol can be given, the inscriptions on this rock will likely suffer."[1] El Morro and its peers were defenseless under the provisions of the Antiquities Act.

The problem was not just malicious vandalism. Without formal protection for monuments, people did not realize that their behavior was inappropriate. The lack of evidence of care, wrote GLO inspector Leslie Gillett in 1916, made it "doubtful whether visiting tourists, especially those who do not visit [El Morro] with the idea of its being a national monument in mind, are acquainted with the fact that the site has been withdrawn."[2] In the vast expanse of the West, the idea of a small reserved tract seemed incongruous. With only a sign to indicate the significance of each monument, people did not sense the special status of reserved areas.

Because of the lack of clarity of the monument designation and the remote location of most the reserved areas, the early monuments were victimized. The pothunting that had preceded the Antiquities Act remained endemic at archaeological sites, and the influx of people to the Southwest after 1900 increased the potential for scavenging, digging, and callous misuse. Unauthorized hunting and grazing affected the flora and fauna of many natural areas. Natural decay of historic and prehistoric features was another problem at many monuments.

Neither the GLO, the Forest Service, nor the War Department had the infrastructure to administer national monuments, and the lack of an organized system compounded problems. The three departments lacked budgets and specific personnel for these areas, nor did they have any clear sense of a reason for the existence of the national monuments. GLO special agents and Forest Service rangers visited monuments and made reports, but little action resulted from these efforts. The only link between the national monuments was the warnings signs posted by official representatives.

The lack of ascribed purpose for the national monuments as a whole posed an even deeper problem. The almost random creation of new monuments offered local and national special-interest groups such as the Sierra Club opportunity to implement their individual agendas. Because these groups saw the monuments from a range of perspectives, conflicts over the utilization of new monuments accelerated.

The archaeologists and anthropologists who had led the battle for the Antiquities Act were the most influential group to maintain interest in the monuments. They believed that they understood the purpose of the Antiquities Act and sought to use its provisions to encourage excavation. Scientists had advocated legislation for almost a decade prior to 1906, and they learned how to operate within the system that they had helped to establish. After passage of the Act, scientific and educational institutions both public and private began to exploit the crucible they had fought to protect. Many received permits, and they began excavations at many of the archaeological national monuments. The number of permits created dismay among GLO personnel, who worried about the motives of many privately sponsored excavators.

At that time, an unwieldly mix of people educated in Europe and the self-trained dominated American archaeology. Most trained specialists concentrated their research in southern Europe and the Middle East, and although they were sympathetic to the pursuit of archaeology in the American Southwest, they generally left the actual work to the self-trained. The GLO feared that unscrupulous excavators would use their permits to collect artifacts for private collections. From the perspective of GLO officials, this prospect meant the appropriation of public treasures for individual gain, an idea at odds with the social philosophy of the era.

While efforts were under way to establish an equitable and manageable set of rules governing excavations, federal officials and academic archaeologists tried to impose their own standards on fieldwork. GLO employees raced to find and reserve archaeological sites before scientists arrived and began to dig. In one case, William B. Douglass, the examiner of surveys for the GLO, visited extensive Anasazi ruins in northern Arizona. He found undisturbed remote ruins and advocated the establishment of the Navajo National Monument. On 3 March 1909 he informed the commissioner of the GLO that withdrawal of the land "embracing the Bubbling Springs group of ruins," about forty miles from the Arizona-Utah state line in northeastern Arizona, was imperative. Douglass's message revealed his motive; he had heard that a "pseudo-scientific expedition ... principally concerned in securing a priceless archaeological collection" planned to invade the area that summer. "It will probably be the last opportunity to explore important ruins that have not been marred and robbed by the pottery hunter," he concluded.[3] The solution he suggested typified his era; government regulation rather than professional consensus was the means to ensure proper excavation of the ruins.

Douglass objected to private individuals, even those with archaeological credentials, acting as if they owned the public domain. Undisturbed ruins held important information about the prehistoric past, and he insisted that the government regard more than the land and the structures upon it as valuable property. He wanted a record of "every article that comes from them, with accurate data as to its exact location in the building and the conditions under which it was found."[4] If archaeological science was to make new contributions, Douglass believed, it had to do more than uncover objects with which to fill museums.

To protect the new discovery, Douglass enlisted John and Louisa Wade Wetherill, who owned a trading post at Oljato, on the Utah side of the Arizona-Utah border, to be responsible for the ruin. Although John Wetherill was Richard Wetherill's brother, he had avoided the rancor that surrounded his brother's dealings with the Department of the Interior. He and his wife lived at Oljato the entire year and made their living by trading with the Navajos. Wetherill was a dependable man and very knowledgeable about the region. Louisa Wade Wetherill had earned the respect of Indians in the area and was an important conduit for information. A Navajo Indian told her of the ruins, and she alerted Douglass. Confident that he had done all he could for the moment, Douglass sent a description of the lands to be reserved to the commissioner of the GLO. On 20 March 1909 President Taft signed the proclamation establishing the Navajo National Monument.[5]

The Navajo National Monument situation seemed a repeat of the episode between the government and Richard Wetherill at Chaco Canyon, but in a reversal of roles, the scientists who had argued so vehemently in favor of the Antiquities Act became adversaries of the federal agencies responsible for the administration of the ruins. Archaeologists lobbied for federal sanctions against unbridled exploitation of the sites, but seemed astonished when men like Douglass tried to apply the same rules to them. They believed that they were acting credibly and resented the need to prove their reliability. Edgar

L. Hewett, who in 1907 became the director of the School of American Archaeology in Santa Fe, and Byron Cummings of the archaeology department at the University of Arizona, headed the group to which Douglass objected. In Douglass's view, southwestern scientists intended to become officially sanctioned pothunters, collecting relics to reap professional spoils.

The solution entailed determining which experts had the public interest in mind. Douglass accused the people who had maneuvered Richard Wetherill out of the picture of similar exploitive motives. He believed that the planned excavations were "detrimental to science" and recommended that the Department of the Interior deny all further requests for excavating permits in northern Arizona until scientists from the Smithsonian Institution had an opportunity to do preliminary work.[6] Smithsonian scientists were federal employees with established reputations, and Douglass believed that they behaved more responsibly than other archaeologists. Their discoveries also became government property.

In Douglass's far-sighted view, legalized pothunting was as detrimental as random digging for artifacts. If those with an academic affiliation were allowed to excavate wherever they chose, the archaeological sites they worked would be no more significant than those dug by amateurs. In eastern museum cases, treated as art objects only and lacking contextual information, the discovered relics would cease to be useful tools to reconstruct the past, and instead would merely be curiosities.

Alerted to Douglass's fears, the Department of the Interior closely watched Navajo National Monument. But in 1909 Hewett had immense influence, and the department routinely granted his requests for excavating permits. Earlier that year, he requested a permit to dig at the new Navajo National Monument. Departmental officials in Washington were not opposed to granting the request. Yet some officials at the GLO worried about the situation. S. V. Proudfit, the acting commissioner of the GLO, asked John Wetherill to keep him informed throughout the summer of 1909. On 24 August 1909 Wetherill wrote that "there is no one excavating on the Navajo National Monument except Prof. Cummings and party," which held Hewett's permit.[7] Douglass did not know that the permit had been granted, and he became furious when he discovered that the proclamation of the monument had not deterred Hewett and his friends.

John Wetherill's interpretation of the situation differed from Douglass's. Cummings and Hewett were colleagues of the experts who had harassed his brother. But although John Wetherill may have harbored resentment about the way the Department of the Interior had treated his brother, he clearly saw that the government had the legal power to control access to American prehistory. John Wetherill perceived the Cummings excavation as legitimate because it held the Hewett permit. But Douglass did not care about credentials. Motives interested him, and Douglass distrusted Hewett. In his opinion, the Hewett-Cummings party was out for personal aggrandizement, not for the advancement of knowledge; Douglass wanted to stop them.

Thanks to Douglass's diligence, the label "pothunter" came to include academic relic hunters who took advantage of their professional status to make collections for museums all over the country. With the help of William Henry Holmes, John Wesley Powell's successor as the director of the Bureau of Ethnology, Douglass was able to stop the Cummings excavation. Holmes ordered Cummings to cease except when Hewett was present. In the summer of 1909, Hewett was involved in projects other than Navajo and John Wetherill dogged Cummings's party. The excavators soon gave up.

In their place, the Smithsonian Institution sent its scientific representatives. Holmes selected two experienced and eminent Americanists, Dr. J. Walter Fewkes and Dr. Walter Hough, both of his bureau, to excavate at Navajo. Douglass went along on the expedition, and in 1910 Fewkes and Hough completed their survey, filing Bureau of Ethnology Bulletin No. 50, *A Preliminary Report on a Visit to the Navajo National Monument*. The report, complete with an extensive pictorial record, conformed to Douglass's expectations of proper conduct for archaeologists.[8] In Douglass's view, the Cummings party, concentrating upon artifacts and the training of students, would have paid less attention to the public interest.

The substitution of federal excavators for professional and academically affiliated ones strengthened the institutionalization of archaeology. This evolution began when Stephen J. Holsinger handed Richard Wetherill and Frederic Hyde the cessation order at the Chaco Canyon in 1902, and between 1902 and 1909 institutional affiliation became credential enough to authorize excavation. But a decade later, when it appeared that scientists were using excavation permits for personal aggrandizement, the GLO censured them.

Douglass presented Hewett in the same light that Hewett had once cast Richard Wetherill. In his view, former protectors of archaeological sites like Hewett had slipped into the patterns that had characterized the late nineteenth-century in the Southwest. Credentials and institutional affiliation were no longer sufficient for Douglass and his peers in the West. Because Hewett's and Cummings's allegiances to their furthering their reputations might outweigh their commitments to the principles of their discipline, they had to be watched. The government had an obligation to manage the sites, and the Smithsonian Institution and the Bureau of Ethnology sent government ethnologists to work in the monuments. The weight of government authority now supported the scientists' efforts.

Unlike Hewett, the careers of federal ethnologists were already established. J. Walter Fewkes had excavated in the Southwest during the 1890s, and Walter Hough had played an important role in the Columbian Exposition of 1893. In 1902 William Henry Holmes had succeeded John Wesley Powell as head of the Bureau of Ethnology. At the top of their profession, such men already had the respect of their peers.

Archaeological protection became a question of philosophy and guardianship. As long as making a collection offered an avenue to enhanced professional status, remote archaeological sites like the Navajo National Monument were vulnerable to pillage by professionals. In many cases, it took so long for an unauthorized dig to come to light that an astute entrepreneur could, depending upon his inclination, parlay his find into a financial or professional windfall. The situation encouraged archaeologists to behave irresponsibly, even overturning walls in search of pots and burial locations. In their haste, some did not even take field notes. Often a site excavated by these professional pothunters lost much of its potential value to archaeological science. Douglass believed that the advancement of the discipline, not solely the collection of artifacts for museums, was the greatest good, and that if random collection continued, the purpose of the Antiquities Act would be defeated, ironically, by the groups that had supported its passage. Whether Edgar L. Hewett or Richard Wetherill compiled them, irresponsibly made museum collections decreased the value of an archaeological site and threatened the credibility of the discipline.

The battle between archaeologists and federal administrators continued throughout the 1910s, but archaeological national monuments were not the only places in danger of depredation. Although Douglass focused upon a small group of the areas created under the auspices of the Antiquities Act and addressed problems relevant only to the administration of archaeological sites, the protection of natural and historic areas was also necessary. The diversity of the national monuments category made uniform administration impossible. Without budgets or personnel responsible for care on a full-time basis, the national monuments remained an unorganized collection of interesting places that grew in number every year.

In the Department of the Interior, efforts to administer the monuments gradually began. Frank Bond, the chief clerk of the GLO, assumed responsibility for the national monuments under its care and also evaluated monument proposals. Bond drafted proclamations for the establishment of various monuments and in general assumed responsibility for determining whether a proposed area would become a national monument.[9] Even the Forest Service solicited his opinion on its monument proposals. Although he rejected numerous requests that he thought were inappropriate, Bond wrote all of the twenty-eight proclamations establishing national monuments between 1906 and 1911.

But the conditions at many national monuments were so poor that after recommending the establishment of the Devils Postpile National Monument, a basaltic column formation, in July 1911, Bond passed favorably on only two more monument proposals in the following four years.[10] Battles over the philosophy of excavation, the haphazard process of monument establishment, and the pervasive absence of funds for monuments' maintenance all bothered Bond. Because he believed that the monuments were deteriorating, he completely reversed the policy of the GLO.

By 1911, five years after the passage of the Antiquities Act, protecting the monuments from wanton or inadvertent vandalism was a frustrating proposition. There were twenty-eight national monuments, and none of the three responsible departments had yet developed a formal administrative process to ensure their upkeep. The Forest Service regarded national monuments as a "makeshift," and at the Department of the Interior, only Bond and W. B. Acker, an attorney, took an interest in the monuments. The War Department had even less interest in its monuments. The three departments communicated little about common problems.

Conceived and executed in haste, the Antiquities Act left unanswered important questions on the issue of preservation. A system of paper entities existed; a proclamation affirmed the existence of places like the Shoshone Cavern National Monument in Wyoming, but it was possible to visit this monument, and many others monuments, without realizing that they were places under federal protection. For Frank Bond, proclaiming national monuments ceased to be an end in itself. The monuments needed more than protection on paper.

During the Roosevelt administration, the national parks had begun to attract more attention, and this interest carried over into Taft's presidency. Vocal advocates like Horace McFarland, the president of the American Civic Association, lobbied Congress and worked to enlighten the public. The Department of the Interior also responded, although slowly. In September 1911 Secretary of the Interior Walter L. Fisher convened the first National Parks Conference at Yellowstone National Park, at which government officials and concerned citizens argued for the creation of a federal bureau to administer parks and monuments. In the middle of the whirl of enthusiastic presentations, Frank Bond stepped to the podium to speak about the national monuments.

Bond's presentation revealed the problems he faced trying to manage areas on the periphery of the preservation movement. Tripartite jurisdiction created confusion in monument administration. To illustrate how management problems cut across departmental lines, Bond divided the monuments into two categories: the scientific and the historic. He noted that different departments managed monuments in both categories, and places as similar as the Gila Cliff Dwellings and Chaco Canyon, both prehistoric ruins, were under separate jurisdictions. In his view, duplicate administration limited the chances for comprehensive planning.

Bond correctly perceived that increased settlement in the Southwest and West was endangering the monuments, and the lackadaisical attitude of his department did not help. "It is only a question of time," he told the conference, "when [the national monuments] will be secretly attacked and pillaged piecemeal, until there is nothing left to preserve. . . . [They are] a responsibility which we now feel but can not make effective."[11] The realities of administration infuriated Bond; he could arrange for the proclamation of any number of national monuments, but he could not protect them in any way.

Bond tried a strategy that he hoped would arouse the audience of conservationists and government officials. Although many in his audience were leaders in shaping contemporary America, Bond realized that the government had not yet made a firm commitment to the monuments. As an alternative to the current chaos, he proposed privatization, turning monuments in danger of being spoiled to private owners, where "they would soon be made available at a price, which would be much better than not available at all." However "unpatriotic . . . the abandonment of any one of them would be," Bond suggested that private ownership and development offered the monuments a better future than benign neglect.[12] Privatization was Bond's ploy to attract attention to the plight of the monuments. As members of the reform generation, Progressive-era government officials eyed the motives of the business community with suspicion, and Bond played to these instincts. Private ownership of public treasures was the solution his audience dreaded.

Bond's oratory might have moved Theodore Roosevelt to initiate an immediate program of reform, but for his trouble, Bond received no substantive response from Secretary of the Interior Fisher, and it was on to the next speech in a seemingly endless succession. The lack of response, even to Bond's calculated attempt to rouse the passions of progressive-minded conservationists, confirmed his sense that, in 1911, the national monuments had little importance. The solution of his era was the creation of a watchful bureaucracy that would do no more than occasionally lament the continuous decay of the national monuments. Ironically, at a conference filled with pro–national park rhetoric and addressed by such luminaries as Sen. Reed Smoot of Utah, Rep. Scott Ferris of Oklahoma, chairman of the House Public Lands Committee, and William Kent, the donor of Muir Woods, the precarious position of the national monuments was not of interest. Although Bond declared the parks and monuments "as alike as two peas in a pod," it appeared that national park advocates felt otherwise.[13]

National monument status was a mixed blessing for the areas so proclaimed. Proclamation of a monument meant recognition of the value of a place, but little more. It reserved a place from private appropriation, but did not protect it from lawbreakers. In fact, monument status negated any chance of receiving direct administration. Established in law and ignored in practice, in 1911 the national monuments were in danger. Unless federal interest became stronger, the monuments would remain little more than places to post warning signs.

The national monuments began to acquire an identity of their own—albeit a somewhat confusing one—based more on what they were *not* than on what they were. They clearly were not like the national parks. The central features of most monuments were natural, archaeological, or historical, but many areas seemed barely to fit even this vague definition. The process by which the monuments were selected required the implementation of some type of standards. The category had become a repository for places of interest that were not considered eligible for national park status.

The long series of proclamations beginning with Devils Tower followed by the sudden dearth of proclamations after July 1911 reflected Bond's anxiety over the condition of the national monuments. He was no longer sure that establishing a new monument was any service to the place or to the nation. Increasingly frustrated, Bond referred fewer and fewer proclamations to his superiors. Only in rare cases did he believe that monument status was necessary for the proposals that crossed his desk. With this rationale in mind, Bond checked the growth of this amorphous system, preferring to wait and see whether Congress might establish a unit of the federal government to administer the parks and monuments.

Bond was not the only one responsible for developing new national monuments. Influential private citizens and elected officials could exert their will, and the two monuments proclaimed during the following four and one-half years resulted from such instigation. In 1913 the Order of Panama, which sought to commemorate Juan Rodriguez Cabrillo, the Spanish discoverer of California, pressed for the establishment of the Cabrillo National Monument on Point Loma, near San Diego. Upkeep and maintenance was not an obstacle; a lighthouse less than one acre in size and adjacent to Fort Rosecrans, a military installation, constituted the entire monument. There seemed to be little chance of vandalism because of the constant military presence. After Bond favorably reviewed the Cabrillo National Monument proposal, in October 1913 Woodrow Wilson established the new monument.

In the case of the second proclamation, Congressman Carl Hayden of Arizona desired a desert flora national park in the new state, and his efforts resulted in the establishment of Papago Saguaro National Monument in 1914. At Bond's request, GLO commissioner Fred Dennett tried to convince Hayden that "topographic conditions seem to offer nothing but scenery and . . . [the Antiquities Act] does not provide for the reservation of public land for the protection of scenery," but Hayden persisted.[14] He had watched as Theodore Roosevelt used the monument category to fulfill arbitrary conservation objectives and was not to be denied. Using his influence as a member of the House Public Lands Committee, Hayden's efforts resulted in the creation of another monument authorized for its scientific importance that had largely scenic and recreational value.

Throughout this period, the movement to establish a branch of the Department of the Interior to administer parks and monuments gradually gained momentum. In 1910 Secretary of the Interior Richard Ballinger advocated the idea, and two years later President Taft gave it presidential sanction.[15] Franklin K. Lane, Woodrow Wilson's secretary of the interior, and public-spirited organizations such as Horace McFarland's American Civic Association continued to press Congress for some kind of national parks bureau. In 1913 Lane appointed Adolph C. Miller as his special assistant in charge of national parks; he was the first, and at that time the only person in Washington, D.C., with full-time responsibility for national parks. When Woodrow Wilson drafted Miller for the Federal Reserve Board, Lane named Stephen T. Mather, a graduate of the University of California who had made a fortune in the borax industry, to replace him.

Mather came to Washington, D.C., to improve the parks, and to assist in this process, Lane assigned to him a graduate of the University of California, Horace M. Albright. Mather was an energetic dynamo with finely tuned promotional instincts and a network of influential contacts; the young Albright was persuasive, charming, astute, and underneath a polished veneer, hard as nails. Throughout 1915 the two men worked at laying the basis for a federal agency to manage the national parks and monuments, and by the end of the year, the prospects for a bureau of national parks and monuments looked very good.[16]

Once establishment of a parks bureau seemed imminent, Bond became less restrictive about establishing new monuments. On 4 October 1915 Woodrow Wilson established Dinosaur National Monu-

Table 1.   The National Monuments in 1916

Site Name	State	Date Proclaimed	Size (in acres)
1. Department of the Interior (NPS):			
Devils Tower	Wyoming	24 Sept. 1906	1,152
Montezuma Castle	Arizona	8 Dec. 1906	160
El Morro	New Mexico	8 Dec. 1906	240
Petrified Forest	Arizona	8 Dec. 1906	25,625
Chaco Canyon	New Mexico	11 Mar. 1907	21,509
Muir Woods	California	9 Jan. 1908	426
Pinnacles	California	16 Jan. 1908	2,980
Natural Bridges	Utah	16 Apr. 1908	2,740
Lewis and Clark Cavern	Montana	11 May 1908	160
Mukuntuweap	Utah	31 July 1909	15,200
Tumacacori	Arizona	15 Sept. 1908	10
Navajo	Arizona	20 Mar. 1909	360
Shoshone Cavern	Wyoming	21 Sept. 1909	210
Gran Quivira	New Mexico	1 Nov. 1909	560
Sitka	Alaska	23 Mar. 1910	57
Rainbow Bridge	Utah	30 May 1910	160
Colorado	Colorado	24 May 1911	13,883
Papago Saguaro	Arizona	31 Jan. 1914	1,940
Dinosaur	Utah	4 Oct. 1915	80
Sieur de Monts	Maine	8 July 1916	5,000
Capulin Mountain	New Mexico	9 Aug. 1916	681
2. Department of Agriculture (USFS):			
Cinder Cone	California	6 May 1907	5,120
Lassen Peak	California	6 May 1907	1,820
Gila Cliff Dwellings	New Mexico	16 Nov. 1907	160
Tonto	Arizona	19 Dec. 1907	640
Grand Canyon	Arizona	11 Jan. 1908	806,400
Jewel Cave	South Dakota	7 Feb. 1908	1,280
Wheeler	Colorado	7 Dec. 1908	300
Mount Olympus	Washington	2 Mar. 1909	633,300
Oregon Caves	Oregon	12 July 1909	480
Devils Postpile	California	6 July 1911	800
Walnut Canyon	Arizona	30 Nov. 1915	960
Bandelier	New Mexico	11 Feb. 1916	22,075
3. U.S. Department of War			
Big Hole Battlefield	Montana	23 June 1910	5
Cabrillo	California	14 Oct. 1913	0.5

ment, and preceding the passage of the National Park Service Act on 25 August 1916, national monuments were established at Walnut Canyon, Sieur de Monts, Bandelier, and Capulin Mountain. The new monuments represented the usual diverse array of archaeological, scenic-scientific, and historical entities (see table 1).

After the establishment of the new bureau, Bond saw that the role of the GLO in administering federal park areas would decrease. The rash of proclamations in late 1915 and early 1916 were evidence of the GLO's abdication of this responsibility. As long as Bond believed that he was responsible for maintaining monuments, for which he knew that he did not have the money or personnel, he kept a close check upon the creation of new monuments. Once he understood that a new agency would assume responsibility, he released the tight hold. The GLO system of preservation by warning signs had simply been a stopgap measure until a formal system of administration was established.

GLO officials looked expectantly toward a future in which they anticipated that a system of administration, and possibly even funding for monument upkeep, would be developed. Bond ended the self-imposed four-year ban on establishing new monuments hopeful that the chaos which had surrounded the first decade of the implementation of the Antiquities Act was over. Unfortunately, the kind of organization he envisioned for the administration of the monuments remained far in the future.

Notes

1. Mining Inspector Charles B. Barker to the General Land Office, 5 October 1911, NA, RG 79, Series 6, El Morro National Monument, file 12-5.

2. Mining Inspector Leslie Gillett to the General Land Office, 10 September 1915, NA, RG 79, Series 6, El Morro, file 12-5.

3. Examiner of Surveys William B. Douglass to the commissioner of the General Land Office, 3 March 1909, NA, RG 79, Series 6, Navajo National Monument, file 12-5.

4. Ibid.

5. Ibid.

6. William B. Douglass to the commissioner of the General Land Office, 22 March 1909, NA, RG 79, Series 6, Navajo National Monument, file 12-5.

7. John Wetherill to Assistant Attorney General S. V. Proudfit, 24 August

1909; and William B. Douglass to W. H. Holmes, 13 September 1909; NA, RG 79, Series 6, Navajo National Monument, file 12-5.

8. J. Walter Fewkes, *A Preliminary Report on a Visit to the Navajo National Monument*, Bureau of Ethnology Bulletin No. 50, (Washington, DC: Government Printing Office, 1910), chronicles the initial Bureau of Ethnology survey at Navajo National Monument.

9. "Report on the National Monuments" 1911, NA, RG 79, Series 4, Records Relating to National Parks and Monuments 1872-1916, Records of the Office of the Chief Clerk of the Department of the Interior 1887-1916. This document appears to have been made in preparation for Frank Bond's talk at the first National Parks Conference in 1911. It closely resembles the talk he later gave.

10. Devils Postpile was originally a part of the Yosemite National Park but was excluded when the boundaries were reduced in 1905. In 1910 a regional power company applied for permission to blast the formation and use it to dam the San Joaquin River. The officers of the Sierra Club petitioned the federal government, suggesting preservation of the area as a national monument. By March 1911 there was a crisis brewing as development and the need for water were pitted against scenic and scientific interest. In part because the Devils Postpile dam was proposed by a private company and because the need for water was not pressing, the Devils Postpile situation ended more positively for preservationists than did the crisis over Hetch-Hetchy. On 6 July 1911 Devils Postpile was proclaimed a national monument under the jurisdiction of the Forest Service (see NA, RG 79, Series 6, Devils Postpile, file 12-5).

11. Frank Bond, "The Administration of National Monuments," *Proceedings of the National Parks Conference held at the Yellowstone National Park September 11 and 12, 1911* (Washington, DC: Government Printing Office, 1911), 96.

12. Ibid., 80-81, 96-97, 99.

13. Shankland, *Steve Mather*, 52-53; Bond, "Administration of National Monuments, 95.

14. GLO Commissioner Fred Dennett to Congressman Carl Hayden, 28 April 1913, NA, RG 79, Series 6, Proposed National Parks, Papago Saguaro, file O-32.

15. Runte, *National Parks*, 99.

16. Ibid., 98-104. See also Shankland, *Steve Mather*, 51-53, 100-106; and Ise, *Our National Park Policy*, 185-93.

6

Second-Class Sites

THE CREATION OF THE NATIONAL PARK SERVICE (NPS) did little to alleviate the dismal conditions at most national monuments. The new agency had minimal resources and vast responsibility. The parks were its focus, and in the scheme of the fledgling agency, the monuments were mere complements to spectacular places like Yellowstone and Yosemite. During the late 1910s and early 1920s, political realities and the view of the leaders of the NPS made national monuments into second-class areas. Tourism became the raison d'être for the national parks, but the monuments were inaccessible and undeveloped, and most remained unsuitable for extensive visitation. Special-interest groups such as American scientists continued to propose various uses for areas set aside as national monuments, but no coherent sense of purpose emerged, and the suggestions failed to ameliorate the predicament of the monuments. Guarded almost exclusively by a loose-knit group of volunteers, the monument designation became a holding category. With support from the NPS, Congress regularly promoted the most important monuments to park status. The remainder were left outside of the vision that Stephen T. Mather and Horace M. Albright had developed for the agency.

As the first director of the Park Service, Mather embarked upon a broad and extensive program to ensure that the most awe-inspiring scenic places in the nation were reserved as national parks. His work reaped immediate dividends. As conditions in the national parks improved, Mather and his new agency developed a following among the public and a contingent of vocal supporters in Congress. By the time he retired because of his health in January 1929, the park system contained six new national parks, including five created from former national monuments: Sieur de Monts, Grand Canyon, Zion, Bryce Canyon, and Carlsbad Cave. The removal of the most visually spectacular of the monuments to the park category blunted the scenic dimension of the monument category. During Mather's tenure, Congress also authorized three additional parks—Shenandoah, Great Smoky Mountains, and Mammoth Cave—east of the Mississippi River, all the result of Mather's and Albright's vision of an agency with national scope.[1]

An important offshoot of Mather's development-oriented administration was the emergence of a system of concessions and accommodations. Before 1915 concessions in the national parks were a fiasco. Predatory hucksters competed for the attention of rail travelers, making grand and usually false promises. The food in the parks was dismal. During Albright's inspection of Yellowstone in 1915, twenty cases of ptomaine poisoning occurred. Mather advocated regulated monopolies in the parks and began to standardize accommodations. With quality as his objective, he initiated programs designed to offer visitors a range of economical services. As assistant to the secretary of the interior in 1915, he arranged for the railroads that served Yellowstone to allow visitors to combine their tickets, so that visitors could enter the park on one railroad through one gate and leave by another, on a different line, without paying an additional charge. Mather was determined to make the national parks into serious competitors for the attention of the American traveler. He wanted his visitors to be comfortable, often repeating his adage that "scenery is a hollow enjoyment to a tourist who sets out in the morning after an indigestible breakfast and a fitful sleep on an impossible bed."[2]

Mather also developed the "pragmatic alliance" between the railroads and the national parks. The link between American railroads and the national parks dated from the establishment of Yellowstone, which had been supported by Jay Cooke and the Northern Pacific Railroad. Early in the twentieth century, railroad entrepreneurs like Louis W. Hill, of the Great Northern Railway, began to see the parks as a boost to their business. Mather joined with such people, and facilities rapidly improved.[3] After the implementation of Mather's plans, record numbers of visitors flocked to the national parks. Western railroads such as the AT&SF, the Denver and Rio Grande (D&RG), and Hill's Great Northern carried visitors all over the West. Visitors found comfortable beds and food that did not incapacitate them.

But the parks still did not have competitive status as tourist attractions, and Mather continued to initiate plans to speed their development. After some cajoling, Robert Sterling Yard, Mather's friend from his days at the *New York Sun*, joined the Department of the Interior. Yard orchestrated a massive publicity campaign that culminated in the printing of the *National Parks Portfolio*, an oversize folio that contained large pictures of the best scenery in the national parks. Places like Yellowstone, Yosemite, the Grand Canyon, and Glacier National Park were the flagship areas, and the agency promoted them accordingly.

In contrast, the national monuments did not have a clearly defined place in Mather's and Albright's plans. Congress also ignored the monuments. The original NPS appropriation of $3,500 averaged out to $120 for each of the twenty-four monuments of the Department of the Interior. There was no money for salaries. Volunteers had to run each area. With the exception of places with national park potential, such as Grand Canyon and Zion national monuments, the promotional work of the agency also passed over the monuments. Most monuments with natural features were neither as spectacular nor as large as the leading national parks. They reflected comparatively little of the grandeur of the West. As a result, whatever identity the monument category had came from its archaeological component. But archaeology had only specialized appeal. Mather was primarily an advocate of inspirational scenery, and he did not believe that promoting prehistoric sites would help to develop the system.

The rising popularity of the parks also meant that there were more visitors at national monuments, which remained ill-prepared for tourist traffic. Railroads took people within striking distance of the national parks, and as the automobile began to encroach upon the American West, many of the national monuments in the Southwest experienced sizable increases in the number of visitors. By the early 1920s some monuments located along major thoroughfares, such as Papago Saguaro and the Petrified Forest, entertained more than 50,000 visitors a year. Their newly found popularity was a problem. Although publicity and technology brought more people to the national monuments, the Park Service lacked the means to protect the areas. Accessibility meant a significant human impact even upon places that were once sufficiently protected by GLO special agents visiting once a year. Areas that had not been well served by that system were in even greater danger.

The early programs of the Park Service inadvertently placed the majority of the national monuments in an inferior position. Lacking money and workpower, the agency did little to prepare these areas for the new influx of tourists. The parks and monuments were not "as alike as two peas in a pod," as Bond had suggested in 1911. Scenic monumentalism was what the parks epitomized; by rail and auto, Americans swarmed to see these spectacular sites in the late 1910s and 1920s.[4] The majority of the national monuments, however, contained features other than postcard scenery. When the agency established its priorities, the development of the monuments was largely left out.

The ambiguity of the definition of the national monuments affected the protection of the areas included in that category. It became impossible to speak of the national monuments as a cohesive category. Many monuments preserved for natural values lacked the features that characterized the important national parks. At the same time, these places had little in common with the archaeological reserves that formed the core of the category. Despite the preponderance of natural areas, the educational and scientific communities agreed with W. J. Lewis, a GLO special agent, who believed that the monuments were "reserved for scientific, historic and other educational purposes."[5] Historic, archaeological, and natural areas had few common values and fewer shared problems. Generalizations about the needs of the national monuments simply did not hold true.

The greatest obstacle to the development of the national monuments was that they had no clear purpose comparable to that of the national parks. Under Mather, the parks became the pinnacle of western tourism, and in May 1918 Secretary of the Interior Franklin K. Lane spelled out the criteria for administering the national parks.[6] There was no such clarity about the existence of the monuments. The ease with which they could be established ensured that the monuments defied categorization. Some had obvious potential as tourist sites. Others were so remote or obscure that visitation was beside the point. Nor were there evident standards for entry into the monument category. Many were consolation prizes, proclaimed as a favor to a member of Congress or to a special-interest group after the failure of a bill to establish a national park. Others were established as the result of public pressure on a representative, senator, the Department of the Interior, or the National Park Service. The monuments were simply a hodgepodge, the catchall category of federally held park areas. The NPS brought no more coherence to the national monuments than existed prior to its founding.

Scientists were the most important supporters of the national monuments. The diversity that hindered the administration of the category enhanced its appeal to a wide range of specialists. Archaeologists and anthropologists were the first to exert their influence, but after most of the important prehistoric ruins in the public domain became national monuments, the dialogue between archaeologists and the Department of the Interior stabilized. Natural scientists followed the lead of the archaeological community. They had a particular stake in the administration of the category and were eager to implement their programs among the monuments. But the goals of the scientific community differed from those of the Park Service. Tourism was never high on the scientific agenda, and the objectives of scientists were often at odds with what Mather envisioned for the park system.

The advent of extensive western and southwestern tourism created problems for preservationists, and archaeological sites became the first point of contention. The national parks were staffed, and the NPS could keep track of visitors there. But isolated monuments, particularly those with archaeological ruins, were susceptible to vandalism. Pothunting remained a cottage industry in the Southwest, and visitors who unthinkingly walked off with surface artifacts compounded the damage of vandals. The archaeological community sought monument status for archaeological ruins as a way to create legal sanctions against pothunting and destruction. Archaeologists wanted to discourage visitation at unsupervised archaeological ruins, but Park Service officials believed that the only way to build support was to encourage travelers. Mather's priorities won; as the volume of visitation grew, archaeologists rushed to excavate.

Ironically, the archaeologists who hurried to dig sites found themselves crowded out by the general public. During the first decade of the twentieth century, few besides archaeologists, sheepherders, and vandals had been interested in archaeological ruins in the Southwest. But by 1920 people were seeking out remote places. They carried away artifacts in their cars, and many carved their names into the walls of prehistoric ruins. Archaeologists often arrived at sites after the public had defaced them. The scientists who had fought against government restriction in 1909 pleaded for it in 1919.

The natural areas in the monument category were a coveted prize, and natural scientists in the government wanted to implement their programs in these areas. Staff members from the U.S. Biological Survey advocated using the monuments as wildlife sanctuaries. Ample precedent existed for this view. Theodore Roosevelt had referred to the Grand Canyon and Mount Olympus as important "wildlife preserves," and the Forest Service treated some of its remote monuments as game preserves. But if the monuments became wildlife refuges, there were obvious consequences for Mather's vision of the park system. This issue came to the fore in January 1917, at the fourth National Parks Conference, when Dr. T. S. "Tombstone" Palmer of the U.S. Biological Survey became an outspoken proponent of the idea that the national monuments were most useful as a refuge for wild animals.

Palmer sought to clarify the confused position of the national monuments by establishing a system of classification that ascribed a comprehensive purpose to the category. "The existence of some of the most interesting reservations is scarcely known to the public," the thin and bespectacled Palmer told the packed audience in the auditorium of the new National Museum in Washington, D.C. "Much less has the tourist or casual visitor a clear idea of what constitutes a national monument, of the diverse character of monuments, or of the distinction between a national monument and a national park." He offered more sophisticated classifications that focused on the value of some monuments as wildlife preserves.

What made national monuments valuable as wildlife sanctuaries was exactly what made them controversial in the first place: they encompassed areas of land large enough to allow animals to live and breed, unimpeded by humanity. Six of the eight monuments that Palmer thought had potential as wildlife reserves were in excess of 1,000 acres: the Grand Canyon, Mount Olympus, Pinnacles in California, Colorado National Monument, Papago Saguaro, and Sieur de Monts. Only two, Muir Woods and El Morro, were less than that size. In the view of this important government biologist, these eight monuments could serve as animal habitats in lieu of wild land.

Palmer's proposal inadvertently challenged the priorities Mather had established for the NPS. His ideas amounted to an unconscious attempt to resurrect the scientific designation of the Antiquities Act, something the emphasis on tourism had overwhelmed. Mather saw scenery as the primary value of natural areas, but seven of the eight areas with the potential to serve as wildlife refuges were included in natural monuments. They could not serve Mather's and Palmer's ends simultaneously.

Yet Palmer's perspective forced an analysis of the monument issue. He gave new significance to many previously ignored monuments. The Pinnacles National Monument, which Bond called unimportant in 1911, was critical in Palmer's view, because it had become one of the last breeding places of the California condor. Papago Saguaro, between Tempe and Phoenix, housed giant cacti; the saguaro, for which the monument was named, was the natural home of the elf owl, the gilded flicker, and the Arizona woodpecker as well as a many other desert birds. But before Palmer's presentation, the Park Service regarded Papago Saguaro, Pinnacles, and their counterparts as minimally important.

To dramatize his point, Palmer noted that even the Grand Canyon had potential as a wildlife reserve. The 806,400-acre monument went a long way towards protecting various kinds of wildlife from the increasing activity at the trailheads and along the rims of the canyon. People had access to only a few thousand acres at the Grand Canyon National Monument. There were hundreds of thousands of acres more suited to animals, providing the kind of inaccessibility that sheltered wild creatures from the focus of American travelers. The steep canyon walls "furnish[ed] a safe retreat for mountain sheep," a species that Palmer contended was numerous in the Grand Canyon. Smaller mammals and birds were also prevalent in the Grand Canyon, Palmer noted, "for the rugged walls naturally discourage and prevent pursuit."

On the cutting edge of modern biological science, Palmer revealed an environmental awareness that foreshadowed the development of modern ecological science. Yet he had to nod in the direction Mather and Albright led the Park Service if he was to have any impact upon agency policy. His view of Muir Woods as the "most accessible point at which to observe the [redwood] tree amid it [sic] natural surroundings" put him on a parallel track with Mather and the Park Service. But Palmer saw Muir Woods as a complete biota, the value of which lay not only in the preservation of redwoods, but in "all those species of plants, birds and other animals which find their native habitat in the peculiar conditions under which the redwood thrives." Scientists could study the interworkings of the natural world at Muir Woods. To that end, Palmer suggested that scientific and ornithological groups closely monitor the site, so that visitors could also "check up on the observations and perchance add to the records of the occurrence of rare species."[7]

In this respect, Palmer's foresight was limited. He did not envision the vast numbers of people that would come to places like Muir Woods, nor did he consider that unsupervised visitors, particularly those encouraged to watch rare species closely, might not share his reverence for wildlife. As visitation increased and the Park Service made its areas more accessible, the value of some of the monuments as wildlife refuges became dubious. Muir Woods could not have been much of a habitat the day after the *San Francisco Examiner* held its annual picnic with 9,000 guests there in 1920.[8] Despite Palmer's attempt to reconcile different functions, scientific use of the monuments in the way that Palmer envisioned remained incompatible with the vision of the NPS.

Palmer tried to give the monuments an identity of their own, but his proposal highlighted the weakness of this diverse category. He represented natural scientists, a special-interest group with its own agenda. Palmer's suggestions offered an unwieldy compromise that blurred the distinction between the wildlife monuments and the national parks. A place like Muir Woods or El Morro had value as a habitat only as long as few people visited it. In fact, the idea of promoting scientific study as a way to encourage tourism spelled disaster for the monuments. In their rush to see what the scientists and public relations people promoted, visitors inadvertently destroyed the very things they came to find.

In 1917 Palmer was the one person with a thorough understanding of the national monuments. His suggestions cut across the artificial boundaries established by the Antiquities Act and highlighted many of the same problems Frank Bond had seen earlier in the decade. Palmer stressed the issues that plagued the development of the national monuments for the coming decades. His entire presentation emanated from the fact that there was no clearly defined purpose for the monuments, which allowed him to make a new suggestion. His idea did not resolve the problem, but it did bring it to the attention of the Park Service.

Maintenance and protection of the national parks and monuments were critical issues in 1917. Mather began to take care of the parks, but a system of care for the monuments had still not been developed. Palmer pointed out that if the monuments received no protection, the qualities that inspired the reservation of the areas would deteriorate as more people visited. No matter what purpose finally emerged as primary, if the various monuments were destroyed in the interim, the reason for preserving them would disappear as well.

As usual, other issues closer to Mather's priorities overshadowed national monument questions. As the preeminent item in his program was to include the very best and most spectacular sites in the West among the national parks, Stephen T. Mather sought to convince Congress to make the Grand Canyon a national park. In 1917 the park conference focused on the status of the Grand Canyon. It was more important to the agency than all of the other national monuments combined. Mather, Secretary of Agriculture David F. Houston, and much of Congress agreed that the Grand Canyon deserved park status, and visitation figures bore this out. In 1915, 116,027 people visited the Grand Canyon, 6,415 more visitors than the combined totals of Yellowstone, Yosemite, and Glacier national parks for that year, and an astronomical increase from the 813 visitors recorded in 1900.

The Grand Canyon was not the first national monument that Mather coveted and subsequently acquired as a national park. The precedent for changing the status of a site dated from 1916, when Congress created the Lassen Volcanic National Park from two national monuments administered by the Forest Service. On the same day he signed the Grand Canyon National Park into law, President Woodrow Wilson signed a bill making Sieur de Monts, the first Park Service area east of the Mississippi River, into Lafayette (now called Acadia) National Park. During Mather's years at the head of the National Park Service, Zion and Bryce Canyon followed, and the agency laid the groundwork for the transformation of the Carlsbad Cave National Monument to national park status.

The monuments selected for park status contained the kind of scenery that characterized the national parks, but they often had to be altered to differentiate them from the remainder of the monuments. In order not to taint the park category with the second-class stigma of the monuments, areas that the agency wanted to transfer had to resemble existing parks more than the remaining monuments. Initially designated as scientific national monuments, these "way-station monuments" had been established because of their scenic value, but making them parallel to the national parks often required manipulation. Because the Antiquities Act limited national monuments to the smallest area that allowed effective management, most of the monuments were small areas. In contrast, western national parks were perceived as vast. At least in the West, the small size of most monuments doomed them to monument status. Enlarging a way-station monument became an important way to differentiate it from the areas left behind in the monument category.

By the late 1910s, Mather began to develop a strategy for the Southwest, with particular emphasis on the Four Corners area, where Arizona, New Mexico, Colorado, and Utah come together.[9] The Grand Canyon was the jewel of the nation, and Mather envisioned a network of park areas connected by roads to bring American motorists to the region in droves. The beautiful scenery of the Southwest appealed to Mather and Albright, at the same time that sparse settlement and the inhospitable climate meant that few people contested the development of park areas. The Grand Canyon was Mather's pinnacle, but as more Americans began to own automobiles, he also wanted to have national parks within driving distance along the dusty western roads.

Mather first looked for new southwestern national parks in the monument category, and the remote Mukuntuweap National Monument in southern Utah became one target of his vision. Mukuntuweap centered around Little Zion Canyon in the southwest corner of the state. There were few roads and fewer people in the region, and the railroads that traversed the area, including the Union Pacific and the D&RG, had difficulty finding passengers. When the monument was established in 1909, there had been little need to protect the site. As late as 1914, G. E. Hair, the division chief of the GLO in Salt Lake City, remarked that "were it not so far from railroads and the main travelled highways of the state, the number of tourists would have been greater than [the estimated three hundred]." Two years later Hair's subordinate T. E. Hunt commented: "It would be difficult for anyone to injure, deface or carry away anything pertaining to the principle features of this monument. . . . No supervision whatever is exercised over this reservation and little seems necessary at the present time."[10] The monument was established in advance of need.

During the 1910s, railroads began to promote travel in southern Utah, and activities in the Mukuntuweap area gained momentum. By 1917 W. W. Wylie, the originator of the "Wylie Way" system of camping in Yellowstone, opened tourist camps in Little Zion Canyon, the heart of the monument. Utah senator Reed Smoot engineered a $15,000 appropriation for road improvement at the Mukuntuweap monument, far outstripping the budget of the other twenty-three Department of the Interior national monuments that year. The NPS also became aware of the value of Zion Canyon. Director Mather mentioned the region as a possible "all year round resort."[11]

Compared to the size of most of the scenic national parks, Mukuntuweap was a small area. Road improvements made the monument accessible, but transforming its status required further work. On 18 March 1918 Woodrow Wilson enlarged the monument to 76,840 acres, five times its original size, and changed its name from Mukuntuweap to the more manageable Zion. The name change played to a prevalent bias of the time. Many believed that Spanish and Indian names would deter visitors who, if they could not pronounce the name of a place, might not bother to visit it.[12] The new name, Zion, had greater appeal to an ethnocentric audience. With its spectacular scenery and larger size, Zion resembled the other national parks more than the remaining monuments.

Woodrow Wilson's enlargement followed the precedent set by Theodore Roosevelt, but it represented a departure from most of Wilson's actions in land policy. His earlier efforts were directed toward appeasing special interests that wanted to make use of reserved portions of the public domain. In 1913 Wilson signed the Hetch-Hetchy bill. In 1915 he halved the Mount Olympus National Monument to accommodate mining interests, and two years later, he allowed sheep to graze temporarily in Yosemite.

Wilson's reversal revealed that Zion was clearly being groomed for higher status. The addition to Mukuntuweap/Zion made it larger by almost 120 square miles. Although still noticeably smaller than Yosemite, to which it was often compared, the combination of its spectacular scenery, increased size, and change of name made Zion worthy of consideration for national park status. In addition, the road appropriation was the first money Congress provided for any individual monument, a clear indication that Mather and Albright wanted Zion in the park category. Their objectives became more obvious when the agency banned firearms in the monument, resulting in a noticeable increase in the deer population. The Park Service also paid to fence the canyon mouth to prevent grazing, and "a marked improvement was manifest to all in the richness of the splendid canyon's appearance."[13]

The attention that Washington, D.C., lavished upon the Zion National Monument confirmed that the Park Service sought its conversion to national park status. Stephen Mather was certainly a strong proponent. During his first visit in 1918, he pronounced Zion Canyon "national park material of the first order."[14] Despite poor state roads, travel restrictions imposed by the government during the First World War, and the influenza pandemic of 1918, all of which cut deeply into the number of visitors during the 1918-19 travel season, Congress established Zion National Park on 19 November 1919.

Mather's enthusiasm for the southern Utah area also resulted in the rapid conversion of the Bryce Canyon National Monument to national park status. Albright visited the area in 1917 and told Mather of its beauty. Two years later Mather and a carload of friends, including a Salt Lake City banker named Lafayette Hanchett, drove for two and one-half days across dismal state roads to Panguitch, about eighteen miles from Bryce Canyon. Mather was astonished to find that more than half the people he talked to in Panguitch had never been to the canyon. When he and his friends drove the remaining miles the following day, Mather found out why. The "road" was little more than an animal trail. But the rigor of the trip did not detract from the spectacular view that the travelers found. As the car arrived, Hanchett, who had seen the canyon, had Mather close his eyes. When they reached the brink of the canyon, Mather opened his eyes and "let go with a fine burst of Mather enthusiasm." The eventual park status of the area was assured at that moment.[15]

Converting desire into reality was a tricky proposition, and Mather used the USFS and the Union Pacific Railroad to achieve his ends. In 1923 a national monument was established at Bryce Canyon. The Forest Service retained administrative control of the area because the monument was carved from national forest land. The proclamation declared the monument as the dominant use of the tract, but that meant little. The administrators of the Powell National Forest, which contained the monument, were allowed to use Bryce Canyon for the same purposes as the rest of the forest. The following year, Utah senator Reed Smoot, an important ally of the Park Service, convinced Congress to authorize the area as a national park, subject to the acquisition of private lands within its boundaries. Mather refused to assume responsibility for the new park until the Union Pacific Railroad exchanged its holdings in the area for other federal lands. Upon completion of the transaction in 1928, Bryce Canyon joined the national park category.

In the Southwest, it appeared that the quickest way to secure park status for a region was first to proclaim it as a national monument. The monument designation safeguarded the area from land claims, and the NPS simply awaited the best opportunity for conversion. Always a small area, Bryce Canyon did not threaten local interests. It had little commercial value to timber and livestock interests. Its exquisite scenery, often described as "Yosemite in Grand Canyon colors," ensured its eventual status. The establishment of Bryce Canyon as a national monument, even under the administration of the USFS, was only a prelude to its conversion to park status.

Mather saw the remaining national monuments in the Southwest quite differently. Most were inconsequential to his goals. Places like Natural Bridges and Rainbow Bridge in southern Utah were simply too far from existing roads and rails. Capulin Mountain, an extinct volcano in northeastern New Mexico, and others like it did not contain the kind of features that the Park Service generally promoted. As a result, while the areas made over into parks basked in considerable attention, the remaining monuments languished.

When highways began to connect the major national parks during the 1920s, Mather needed a new kind of national monument. Vast distances separated the western national parks, and motorists along the dusty roads sought places to stop for brief respite from the seemingly endless travel. Mather soon began to look at places that could serve as rest stops for motorists. The national monument category became the focal point for such areas. Usually of regional significance, they could rarely withstand the congressional scrutiny that national parks underwent, nor did they measure up to Mather's and Albright's standards. The ease of a monument proclamation made their creation simple, so to shape the system according to his vision, Mather relied upon the Antiquities Act.

Pipe Spring National Monument, a Mormon fort in northern Arizona, developed significance for Mather that far outweighed its historical importance. It became one of his pet projects because of its location on the highway between Zion and Grand Canyon national parks. Mather used persistence and charisma to acquire the seemingly unimportant site.

There were a number of conflicting claims upon the tract. Mormon settlers built the fort over the one spring in the area, and everyone in the vicinity needed its water. The Kaibab Indian Reservation included the old fort, but Jonathan Heaton, who once lived on the property, tried to reestablish his homestead claim on the buildings of the fort. Because of the complicated status of the land, both the GLO and the Bureau of Indian Affairs (BIA) challenged his claim.

After visiting the fort in the fall of 1920, Mather began to pursue its acquisition. On 21 June 1921 he wrote to the commissioner of Indian affairs, Charles H. Burke, suggesting that the area "should be preserved as a national monument from a historical point of view. . . . [I]t is a point at which tourists stop en route from Zion Park in Utah while visiting the North Rim of the Grand Canyon, or vice versa."[16] Mather wanted the BIA to appoint a caretaker to prevent vandalism. This was an important tactic for the Park Service. If the agency could convince another federal agency to place a guard at an historic or archaeological place, the Park Service could eventually present the need for *its* kind of management. Mather also sent a copy of the letter to GLO commissioner William Spry, attaching a memo insisting that "this splendid old landmark should be saved, either by direct purchase if J. Heaton's title is confirmed, or, if it reverts to the United States, it should be maintained as a national monument."[17] Mather intervened in an open public lands case in an attempt to secure the property as a stopping point for tourists visiting the crown jewels of his system, the national parks.

To win this victory for the NPS, Mather worked his network of influential friends. He contacted F. A. Wadleigh of the D&RG Railroad and President Heber J. Grant and Apostle George A. Smith of the Mormon church, and soon these disparate elements were working together for the public good. Although the GLO disallowed Heaton's contention in February 1923, Mather felt that paying Heaton's family for the claim was the best way to ensure local goodwill. Grant offered to be "one of twenty men to purchase [the] property," and Mather, Carl R. Gray, the president of the Union Pacific Railroad, and others contributed $500 each.[18] By May 1923 the acquisition of Pipe Spring was imminent.

But Mather's emphasis on this inconsequential place puzzled some of his supporters and friends. As the transaction concluded, the real reason for Mather's interest became clear. On 21 May 1923 Mather proposed to have Congressman Louis Cramton, the head of the House Appropriations Committee and a great friend of the fledgling NPS, take a "trip from Zion to the National Monuments and Mesa Verde made via the Pipe Springs, so that he will see the place for himself. . . . After he comes across the desert from Hurricane," Mather reasoned, "I am sure he will be convinced of its importance as a stopping place."[19]

Pipe Spring was an important link in Mather's vision of a complete park system. As highways came to the Southwest and began to assume the role that the railroads previously played in bringing visitors to the national parks, intermediary sites became important to the NPS. Located between the national parks that Mather was really trying to promote, Pipe Spring acquired a role in the growth of the park system that far outweighed its historical value.

Mather's priorities were increasingly clear; the most spectacular and extraordinary sites of any kind became national parks. The national monuments became intermediate stops between these stars of the system, building blocks from which to fashion grandiose national parks. They became complements to entertain the tourists who motored along the long and poorly developed western roads. The trend persisted throughout the 1920s, as places with special significance broadened the dimensions of the park category.

Parklands in the East were as important to the agency as those in the Southwest. Before Mather became assistant to the secretary of the interior in charge of national parks in 1915, a rumbling in favor of a national park in the East began. Even Henry Graves, the chief forester of the United States, felt that the development of remote national parks was "a waste." He contended that "the question of accessibility [to park areas] should be considered . . . from a national standpoint."[20] Despite the democratic rhetoric of those who advanced the park and monument cause, the western parks appeared to be playgrounds for those with the time, money, and inclination to travel into what was not always civilized territory. Questioning the value of remote national parks helped make some kind of parkland east of the Mississippi River an imperative.

Although the converted monuments gave the Park Service a stronghold in the West, serious rivals, particularly the Forest Service, threatened its position. The USFS also had an extensive western domain, but it valued its resources differently. The Forest Service worked to develop commercial uses of natural resources and to aid timber interests and local stockmen. The NPS became a threat to the Forest Service. When the Park Service proposed additions to its system, the land typically came from USFS holdings. Escalating conflict seemed inevitable, and by the early 1920s, the two agencies suffered from a growing rivalry that inspired mutual distrust.

The Forest Service also threatened the existence of the Park Service, and Mather and Albright needed a way to outdistance their most important rival. They realized that the best way to leave the USFS behind was to add park areas in the eastern half of the nation. The Forest Service had few holdings in the East, and there were few areas there with potential to become national forests. The American population centered on the eastern seaboard, and by creating parks and monuments close to its cities, the Park Service could build its constituency.

Mather and Albright had a mandate to build a system, but the raw material they inherited was strictly western. Transforming the NPS into a national entity was a complicated proposition. The support of eastern populations would help assure the growth of the park system. Most of the land east of the Mississippi River was not in the public domain, having been settled generations before; what was left was not particularly appealing for public reservations. The agency had to take what it could get from the sparse public holdings of the East. But because its standards for the national parks were designed by westerners for the expansive vistas of the West, finding eastern scenery that conformed to their criteria entailed considerable work. Eastern parks would never be as large as Yellowstone, nor could they contain the rugged peaks of the Rocky Mountains.

The problems of locating and acquiring suitable eastern park land seemed to stymie Mather's and Albright's dreams. The Park Service sought to acquire new land for eastern park areas, because there was little attractive public land in the East. But the agency budget did not contain funds earmarked for purchasing private land, and people willing to donate suitable private holdings were few and far between.

Thanks to the efforts of private citizens, the agency gained an eastern toehold at Sieur de Monts National Monument. A tract of rugged cliffs descending to the ocean near a favored vacation spot of American elites, the monument resulted from of the activities of a textile heir, George B. Dorr, and Dr. Charles W. Eliot, the former president of Harvard University. Both had summer homes in the area, and by 1903 the men and their circle of friends felt threatened by the development of the region. They formed an organization to acquire and hold lands in the area. The state of Maine granted their group, the Hancock County Trustees of Public Reservations, a tax exemption in 1908, and despite attempts to revoke the charter, Dorr solicited gifts of land near Bar Harbor. By the end of 1914, Dorr had amassed nearly 5,000 acres, and early in 1916, he went to Washington, D.C., to offer the land to Secretary Lane as a national monument.[21] On 9 July 1916 Sieur De Monts National Monument was proclaimed.

Sieur De Monts was another example of a way-station national monument, established to facilitate later attempts to create a national park. Dorr's letter offering the land suggested a region "rich in historic association [and] scientific interest," as required by the Antiquities Act, adding as if an afterthought, a reference to its "landscape beauty."[22] But its historic and scientific value were marginal; there were better examples elsewhere of "glacial action and the resistance of rocky structures."[23] Sieur de Monts was earmarked for eventual park status from the moment it was created. Its main features were scenic and recreational, and it was not likely to remain in the monument category for long. The Park Service worked to make the comparatively minuscule 5,000-acre tract into a national park. A national park was a more important prize than a monument, and the NPS needed to expand its base of power. In February 1919 Congress approved the new Lafayette National Park.

Sieur de Monts changed the national park criteria of the NPS. Its location made it a prime candidate for both monument and park status, and small size did not prohibit its entrance into the park category. It was close enough to Boston and New York to add a new dimension to the park sites already in existence. In 1919 more than

64,000 visitors came to the park, confirming that its transfer to the park category had not been a mistake. Sieur de Monts offered the agency what no western park could—a balanced geographic distribution of American national parks and monuments. It became the consummate way-station monument.

The establishment of Sieur de Monts was a strategically far-sighted move. It was much closer to American centers of population than any of the western parks and monuments. Its creation made a parklike area seem accessible to the majority of the American public, offsetting cries of elitism. No matter how far away from eastern cities the Bar Harbor area was geographically or culturally, it seemed closer than Yellowstone. The establishment of Lafayette National Park answered the clamor for a park in the East, as well as extending the reach of the NPS beyond the Forest Service. It was the first step toward making the national parks and monuments truly national.

Following the guidelines Lane put forward in 1918, Mather and his agency created a character for the American national parks. A handful of the most spectacular national monuments fit this model and, as a result of Park Service initiative, were elevated to the set of park areas that became the center of administrative attention. The unfortunate consequence of the loss of so many of the most spectacular monuments to the national park class was the relegation of the remaining monuments to a seemingly permanent second-class status, without sufficient funding and generally devoid of development. This tainted the remaining monuments, making them the stepchildren of the Park Service. The parks existed for visitors, and the best of the national monuments regularly became national parks. The remaining monuments lost any semblance of importance.

In spite of this lack of concern for the monuments during the late 1910s and 1920s, the rudiments of a cohesive system of administration began to emerge in the Southwest. Visitation increased, and as it did, crucial administrative issues emerged. Guardianship became paramount, and finding custodians to watch over the monuments on some regular basis became the first imperative. Unlike the GLO, the National Park Service did not have an already established system of personnel in the field, and its budget did not include the money to hire full-time staff to guard the national monuments. Instead, the NPS found local volunteers, most of whom were paid the token sum of one dollar a month, to watch over nearby monuments whenever they could. Two major problems perennially faced the custodians. There was often no available money for the upkeep of the areas, and the number of wanton acts multiplied. Careless visitors were responsible for frequent vandalism at nearly all of the national monuments.

In 1917 the NPS received its first appropriation, and the $3,500 allotted for the national monuments showed how inconsequential the areas were. If divided evenly, this amounted to a mere $120 a year per monument, not enough for any kind of substantial program. The reports of GLO special agents and the volunteer custodians offered the central administration of the NPS a picture of conditions in the monuments. Officials in Washington, D.C., decided which monuments needed the money most immediately, and these places received the bulk of the allotment. Uneven distribution meant that the places in the worst condition got some money while others, which often needed the money nearly as badly, got none. It was a race to see where conditions became intolerable first, before a monument received an inadequate appropriation that had little chance of delaying its disintegration.

The promotional efforts of the agency and the minimal funding combined to create a vicious circle that entrapped the national monuments for many years. Weather and the activities of careless, ignorant, or malicious visitors damaged unattended monuments. But without adequate funding, there was no remedy. Inevitably, the conditions at various national monuments worsened and visitors were unlikely to return and even less inclined to speak favorably of the places to their friends. As a consequence, justifying the appropriations the monuments received became more difficult, and increases in funding were inconceivable. The lack of funding also precluded finding full-time guardians, which virtually guaranteed continued deterioration. The best that concerned people could hope for under the circumstances was that deterioration could be slowed and vandalism kept to a minimum.

As the only national monument within walking distance of a major population center, Muir Woods was in a unique position. It required a live-in custodian, something that William Kent recognized and provided when he donated the tract in 1908. A hired man, Andrew Lind, lived on the grounds before the establishment of the monument, and Kent continued to pay his salary until 1910, when the GLO assumed financial responsibility. In 1916 Lind was the only full-time custodian at any of the national monuments of the Department of the Interior.[24] After the creation of the NPS, the funding for Lind's position ceased. The Park Service could not afford it. Other monuments received nominal care from nearby residents. At the Navajo National Monument, the GLO promised Richard Wetherill's brother John and his wife, Louisa Wade, one dollar a month to watch over the ruins from their trading post at nearby Oljato. In a typical situation, between 1909 and 1916, the Wetherills did not collect any of the money owed them for this work.[25] Elsewhere, volunteers or regional GLO personnel watched over the remaining monuments.

A parallel situation existed at the only congressionally established park site, the Casa Grande Ruin Reservation in Arizona. Like Muir Woods, it had a paid custodian. The development of Casa Grande was due to the boundless enthusiasm of Frank Pinkley, who assumed duties there in 1901 and remained closely associated with it and the other national monuments until his death in 1940. Wiry like a terrier, energetic, and inquisitive, Frank Pinkley was typical of the midwesterners who invaded the Southwest at the turn of the century. For better or worse, these migrants brought the values and perceptions of an industrial culture to a previously pastoral world and, in large degree, reshaped the Southwest. Pinkley typified the breed. The Missouri native moved to Arizona in 1900 after a medical examination revealed he was tubercular. Formerly an apprentice to a jeweler, Pinkley became a farmer near Phoenix until he was offered the position of caretaker and watchman at Casa Grande.

In 1892, President Benjamin Harrison had made Casa Grande a "national reservation." The presidential proclamation that established the national reservation also included a $2,000 appropriation. A custodian, the Reverend Isaac T. Whittemore, was appointed in 1892. His post was honorary because the funding for Casa Grande had been spent on repairing the ruins. Nevertheless, Whittemore took his responsibilities seriously. In 1895 he requested $8,000 for a roof for the ruin and for an excavation "of all the mounds in the vicinity for the purpose of learning the history of the wonderful people who once lived here." In late October 1895 W J McGee, the acting director of the Bureau of Ethnology, visited Casa Grande to report on the condition of the reservation. John Wesley Powell, the director of the bureau, recommended additional funds for Casa Grande, but Congress ignored the request.[26]

This was how things stood at Casa Grande in 1901, when Frank Pinkley pitched the tent that served as his residence there. Pinkley was full of ideas, and he had the determination to carry out his plans. A dedicated perfectionist, he developed a deep attachment to Casa Grande during his tenure. By the time Dr. J. Walter Fewkes of the Bureau of Ethnology began to excavate at the monument in 1906, Pinkley had already collected and displayed artifacts from the ruin, and he began maneuvering to get funds for a museum on the grounds. He also built a house in the compound and sunk a well on the premises. Pinkley and other local men assisted the Fewkes excavation, and sub-surface prehistoric artifacts further whetted Pinkley's appetite.[27] He continued his energetic management until 1915, when he resigned to serve a term in the Arizona legislature.

After the creation of the National Park Service, the Casa Grande was in an unusual position. Although it fit the criteria to be administered by the agency, on 13 November 1916 Frank Bond, the chief clerk of the GLO, discovered that the law authorizing the new agency did not cover Casa Grande. Bond thought that the NPS should assume its administration and initiated the process that resulted in the reclassification of Casa Grande as a national monument.[28] On 1 April 1918, following the close of his legislative term, Pinkley returned to Casa Grande after his replacement, James Bates, was discovered selling artifacts from the ruins. But Pinkley remained an employee of the GLO, not the Park Service. In 1918, when the transfer became imminent, Mather and Albright welcomed Pinkley as one of their own.

The NPS realized that in Pinkley they acquired someone with boundless energy. In his letter accepting reappointment at Casa Grande, Pinkley put forth his ideas about care for the national monuments. With fifteen years experience under similar conditions, he thought that he had a comprehensive understanding of the problems facing the monuments. Protection, development, and publicity were Pinkley's main concerns as custodian.[29]

Protecting the ruin came first. Pinkley's reappearance offered Casa Grande a degree of guardianship that had not existed during his absence. He was able to control vandalism by visitors. To prevent range stock from fouling and otherwise damaging the ruins, he proposed building a fence around the compound. Pinkley offered to supervise the erection of cement posts and helped to build the fence as part as part of his custodial duties. This showed Mather that he was not trying to use the improvements as a means of personal aggrandizement.

Pinkley also recommended a program of development for Casa Grande. Mapping was critical, he insisted, and as was his nature, Pinkley offered to make the map "at odd times during the next few months and locate on it the needed operations" if the U.S. Geological Survey would loan him the proper instruments. He also noted that during his absence, brush had grown up in some of the rooms of the compound. Water stood at the base of many of the walls, eroding the foundations of some of the buildings. Both clearing the ruins of brush and creating a drainage system were imperative before any other kind of development could begin.

Pinkley had even grander ideas for the promotion of his monument. By 1918 he had plans for a museum to display the artifacts he collected as well as to create "suitable buildings" for travelers who wished to remain overnight. His promotion campaign included convincing the "Phoenix and Tucson papers to play the Casa Grande up as an interesting automobile trip," taking up the matter of publicity with the railroad that served the region, the Southern Pacific, and cooperating with Byron L. Cummings's Department of Archaeology at the University of Arizona. He also wanted to mail a bulletin or newsletter to people whose names he had compiled from the register of guests he kept during his earlier tenure. Pinkley felt that such a mailing would rekindle the interest of former visitors to Casa Grande. Pinkley also proposed a referral service among the parks and monuments to encourage the people in charge of the various areas to exchange information concerning tourist accommodations and transportation.

Despite his grand scenario for the development of the Casa Grande, Pinkley was also a pragmatist. "I think of the protection of the Casa Grande against vandalism and disintegration as matters we must take care of;" he closed his letter, "the further devlopment [*sic*] and exploration as matters we wish to take up, as funds may be obtained; and the different methods of publicity as very desirable to experiment with until we determine the most effective methods to be used." His list of priorities was difficult to contest.

In Pinkley, Stephen Mather knew he had a man whose enthusiasm matched his own. Throughout April and May 1918, Pinkley wrote to the agency in Washington, D.C., regularly with many new ideas for the improvement of Casa Grande. A library relating to archaeology and ethnology was one of his proposals, an idea that the NPS took to Dr. Fewkes. Horace Albright wrote Pinkley that Fewkes "stands ready to assist us in every possible direction" and that he was "particularly pleased" that Pinkley reassumed management of the reservation. Albright concurred, noting that "the energy and enthusiasm that has marked your new administration is a source of keen delight to [the NPS]."[30]

Casa Grande, however, shared in the most serious problem facing the monuments. There was simply no money available for the upkeep and maintenance of the ruin. "I am going to be frank with you," Horace Albright wrote Pinkley on 7 June 1918, "the National Park Service and the General Land Office are both without a cent of money that can be expended on the Casa Grande Ruins during the current fiscal year." Casa Grande was in limbo, a problem exacerbated by its position as a national reservation. As Frank Bond pointed out in 1916, the ruins logically belonged to the Park Service. But there was no legal way that the Park Service could spend money on a reservation for which the GLO was responsible. The GLO already directed all the money it could for upkeep of the ruins. Because Albright was sure that "Congress [was] loath to make a special appropriation for the Casa Grande Ruins," he sought to reclassify the ruin as a national monument. "It would be in an eminently superior status from what it is at present," Albright remarked, "we must face the existing situation and do the best we can without the funds we desperately need."[31]

The problems at Casa Grande were part of the pattern affecting all the monuments. Although Casa Grande did become a national monument on 3 August 1918, the change in status did little to improve conditions. The newest addition was caught in the same cycle that encompassed the other national monuments. Pinkley still had no money with which to initiate his programs and he learned that the only way to counteract the situation was with his own hard work. Only his "indefatigable efforts" kept Casa Grande operating.

Pinkley believed that Casa Grande was an important part of the American past, and he worked to convey that idea to the public. His detailed annual reports on the monument did more than just recount its historical and cultural significance. Pinkley did his best to alert the bureaucrats in Washington, D.C., to the plight of the monuments. "It makes me sad," he wrote in 1920, "to see a prehistoric monument . . .

gradually disintegrating and to know that many other of our 24 monuments are in like condition, all for lack of a few thousand dollars a year."[32] He did all he could to bring it to the attention of anyone who would listen. Having a library and building a museum were ways to counteract the lack of funding and guardianship with the best alternative: widespread publicity that led to some sort of public hue and cry.

Pinkley's aggressive approach to promotion presented problems for Casa Grande, but his personal approach counteracted most of the danger. If visitation increased rapidly without any commensurate increase in appropriations, his efforts might have led to faster disintegration of the monument. But Pinkley was always on hand to counteract this eventuality. He took personal charge of his visitors, guiding them through the ruins, "explaining and describing things they would otherwise overlook, see[ing] that no vandalism occurs and in general, act[ing] as host on behalf of the United States Government."[33]

Despite herculean effort, Pinkley and the other custodians fought a losing battle against natural decay of and human impact on the monuments. In contrast to the top position at national parks, *superintendent*, the very title of the person in charge of a national monument, *custodian*, connoted rudimentary care and minimal responsibility. Pinkley had access to neither materials nor money for Casa Grande, and his cohorts fared no better.

The early custodians were a mixed batch, brought together by a few common threads. For most of them, performing as custodian was a secondary duty, far less important than maintaining their business. Many happened to own land close to the monument for which they became responsible. Proximity to the areas led to their selection. Evon Z. Vogt, who became the first custodian of the El Morro National Monument, lived on the road between the monument and nearby Ramah, New Mexico. In 1916 Vogt was already interested in the inscriptions at El Morro, and GLO special agent R. R. Duncan recommended him as a suitable custodian. He had, Duncan wrote the GLO, "the opportunity to notice [from his ranch] those passing on the main highway to the monument."[34] At Mukuntuweap National Monument in April 1917, locals recommended Freeborn Gifford of Springdale, Utah, as custodian, and the National Park Transportation and Camping Company, an offshoot of railroad interests, offered to pay him a salary. But Horace Albright contracted with a local man, Walter Ruesch, to build a fence across the canyon mouth. In November 1917, after he informed the Park Service that he had completed the fence, Albright asked Ruesch to add a self-catching latch to the gate. Ruesch obliged and, at Albright's request, sent photographs of the work. Albright was impressed with both his handiness and sense of responsibility, and after the enlargement of the monument, Walter Ruesch became custodian of the Zion National Monument.[35]

The men and women who filled the custodial positions in the early days of the Park Service were no more professional than Richard Wetherill, but they had the sanction of the proper authorities. Although the majority stayed as custodians for a number of years, a few were dismissed for selling relics that they took from the monuments, whereas others resigned when they discovered that "real" salaries for their work were far in the future. Most lived in the immediate locale and had some knowledge or interest in the monument before they were made custodians. They were selected because they could provide what their monument needed most. Guardianship of El Morro was essential; almost everyone headed there had to pass by Vogt's ranch. Ruesch proved himself reliable when he built the fence at Zion National Monument. He was also the only man in the region with whom Albright and the Park Service had direct dealings. But because there was no salary for these positions, most of the custodians had to earn a living. Consequently, they could only patrol the monuments in their care occasionally. Given an impossible job, the majority of the custodians served admirably. But the care they provided was at best sporadic, and the majority of the national monuments remained at the mercy of the elements and anyone who happened along.

Of all the monuments, El Morro was the most vulnerable to damage. Its historic significance centered in the centuries-old inscriptions upon the sides of its cliffs. Spaniards like don Juan de Oñate, who colonized New Mexico in the late 1590s, and American military men like Lt. James H. Simpson, who headed a cavalry expedition in the Southwest in 1849, left their marks on the cliffs. According to Frederick W. Hodge, a director of the Bureau of Ethnology, El Morro was "one of the most valuable historical places in this country." Were the monument in Massachusetts, Hodge said, "it would be protected by a gold fence with diamond tips and there would be thousands of people to see it every day."[36] It was also a magnet for those who felt compelled to add their names alongside those carved by explorers in previous centuries.

Few visitors saw El Morro before 1918, when the Fred Harvey Company opened the El Navajo Hotel in Gallup, New Mexico, about fifty miles from the monument. When the roads were passable, hired guides and cars from the Harvey hotel took visitors to the monument. Even with guides, the carloads increased the chances of vandalism at this fragile monument. Vogt could not leave his ranch every time a car passed, headed in the direction of the monument.

By the end of the 1910s, "name-scratching" had become a serious problem at El Morro. In 1919 "unthinking persons" inscribed their names so close to some of the most valued inscriptions that some kind of everyday protection became imperative. In 1920 Vogt reported that he had posted signs warning people not to deface the monument, and he began to send the names of vandals to Washington, D.C., for legal action. Anxious to do something to protect the inscriptions, Vogt also sent a sample of local sandstone to the Bureau of Standards. He sought a "transparent substance which will absolutely protect the writings from any weathering away and save these historical messages for all time."[37] No such substance was developed, and Vogt continued to chisel out any modern inscriptions that appeared at the monument.

Even federal employees were not immune to temptation, but the NPS had recourse against those on the government payroll who added new inscriptions. Two employees of the BIA "engraved their names so close to an old inscription that it is a desecration," assistant director of the NPS, Arno B. Cammerer, wrote to the commissioner of the BIA, Cato Sells, on 8 October 1920. "An example should be made of these men and of others whose names and addresses have been ascertained and [the Park Service] proposes to take legal action against them." Shortly afterward, Cammerer told a friend that he was "going to put the fear of God into them."[38] Cammerer did just that. As an assistant director of the Park Service, he wielded no small amount of power and he brought it down upon the two men. Both wrote Cammerer, pleading ignorance while apologizing profusely. "Your work has already had results," Vogt wrote Cammerer on 18 April 1921. "Last Sunday early in the morning a strange and unheralded car visited El Morro and erased the names."[39]

Although Cammerer's intensity ended this specific case, it did not prevent others from repeating the offense. Knowledge of rules about defacing national monuments was simply not widespread. "I was unaware that it was unlawful," wrote one culprit, E. A. Errickson of McGaffey, New Mexico, "as there were several names carved there in recent years and I did not notice any signs that a person was forbidden to do so." Dr. Albert Spears also pleaded ignorance, claiming that he "saw the names of many who were not historical characters—even the name of the custodian of the monument, I think. I cannot be sure of any particular name now as there were so many . . . [but] I have really felt ashamed of it ever since."[40]

Although the voluntary erasures by the occupants of the "strange and unheralded car" solved the question of legal culpability, the responses of the guilty parties revealed a deeper problem. As Leslie Gillett of the GLO pointed out in 1916, many did not regard El Morro as a monument. Ordinary law-abiding citizens, flushed with a sense of adventure after the difficult journey, saw the names of the explorers of yesteryear and felt compelled to join their company. Even though Vogt's ranch had become "a sort of public campground for tourists," he did not have the time to monitor the behavior of everyone who visited the monument.[41] The very character of El Morro invited what the Park Service regarded as vandalism. A full-time, on-location custodian would provide a solution, but without more than the token sum of ten dollars a month, Vogt could not give up his other responsibilities.

Yet, even without a salary, Vogt's enthusiasm for the monument rivaled Pinkley's. On 18 September 1921 he orchestrated a celebration of the seventy-second anniversary of the arrival of the Simpson Expedition at El Morro. There were almost ninety guests, including travelers from the East Coast, neighboring ranchers, and Gallup residents. Speaking eloquently, Vogt traced the history of humanity at El Morro, beginning with the prehistoric Indians who built the cliff dwellings on top of El Morro. He then directed his audience down the narrow stairway to the inscriptions below, where he described the conquistadores and interpreted their writings for the crowd. This was custodial care at its best, a model for the interpretive style the NPS later developed. Pleased with the results, Vogt asked that the anniversary of the first known Americans to come to El Morro continue to be celebrated every year.[42] It provided a unique opportunity to use the monuments as an educational tool, to teach Americans of the continuity of human culture and the viability of their own culture in a hostile environment.

Lacking adequáte funding and care, the position of the national monuments became more precarious under the first eight years of NPS administration. The custodians did the best they could, but there were many obstacles to consistent care of the monuments. Most custodial care was good, but no one but Pinkley at Casa Grande provided it on a full-time basis. Preserving the remnants of earlier civilizations, illustrating the continuity of human experience on the North American continent, was a secondary goal of the new agency. The primary goal of the NPS was to attract tourists to the awe-inspiring, breathtaking scenery in the national parks.

NOTES

1. Shankland, *Steve Mather*, 170-71; Ise, *Our National Park Policy*, 222-24.

2. Shankland, *Steve Mather*, 66, 134; Horace M. Albright as told to Robert Cahn, *The Birth of the National Park Service: The Founding Years 1916-1933* (Salt Lake City: Howe Brothers, 1985), 46-48, 77-80; Ise, *Our National Park Policy*, 196-99.

3. Runte, *National Parks*, 46-75; see also Alfred Runte, *Trains of Discovery: Western Railroads and the National Parks* (Flagstaff, AZ: Northland Press, 1984).

4. Bond, "Administration of National Monuments," 98.

5. W. J. Lewis, "Report on the Navajo National Monument," circa 1916, NA, RG 79, Series 6, Navajo National Monument, file 12-5.

6. Lane's directive, which many say was authored by Horace Albright, went a long way towards firming up policy regarding the national parks. It laid out both qualifications for park status and an implicit set of rules and regulations for the Park Service to follow. Mather closely adhered to these guidelines throughout his tenure and they became established as the most important statement of ideals concerning the national parks. The letter is printed in the *Report of the Director of the National Park Service Report for the Fiscal Year Ended June 30, 1920* (Washington, DC: Government Printing Office, 1920), 361-64.

7. T. S. Palmer, "National Monuments as Wild-Life Sanctuaries," *Proceedings of the Fourth National Parks Conference, 1917* (Washington, DC: Government Printing Office, 1917), 208, 210-223.

8. *Report of the Director of the National Park Service for the Fiscal Year Ended June 30, 1921* (Washington, DC: Government Printing Office, 1921), 6.

9. I would like to thank Charles S. Peterson of Utah State University for his idea that the NPS developed a comprehensive southwestern strategy.

10. G. E. Hair, report to the Department of Interior, 9 May 1914; T. E. Hunt, report to the General Land Office, 12 July 1916; NA, RG 79, Series 6, Zion National Monument, file 12-1.

11. *Report of the Director of the National Park Service for the Fiscal Year Ended June 30, 1918* (Washington, DC: Government Printing Office, 1918), 86.

12. Executive Proclamation 1435, 18 March 1918, L. 40 Stat. 1760. The issue of pronounceable names also arose at Bandelier National Monument in northern New Mexico. The proposed park often became impaled upon the choices—"Pajarito," Spanish for "little bird," and Cliff Cities—with commercial interests usually favoring "Cliff Cities," and anthropologists and archaeologists favoring the more traditional "Pajarito."

13. *Report of the Director of the National Park Service 1918*, 86-87.

14. Ibid., 117; see also Shankland, *Steve Mather*, 136-39.

15. Shankland, *Steve Mather*, 136-37; Albright, *Birth of the National Park Service*, 188-89. Excepting the fact it was never enlarged, the story of the creation and transformation of Bryce Canyon closely parallels that of Zion. For more information, see Nicolas Scrattish, "The Modern Discovery, Popularization and Early Development of Bryce Canyon, Utah," *Utah Historical Quarterly* 49 (Fall 1981): 348-62.

16. Stephen T. Mather to Commissioner of Indian Affairs Charles Burke, 21 June 1921, NA, RG 79, Series 6, Pipe Spring National Monument, file 12-5. See also Horace M. Albright, "The Origins of National Park Service Administration of Historic Sites" (Philadelphia: Eastern National, 1971), 13.

17. Stephen T. Mather to GLO commissioner William Spry, 21 June 1921, NA RG 79, Series 6, Pipe Spring National Monument, file 12-5.

18. Heber J. Grant to Stephen T. Mather 12 May 1923, NA, RG 79, Series 6, Pipe Spring National Monument, file 12-5.

19. Stephen T. Mather to Heber J. Grant, 21 May 1923, NA, RG 79, Series 6, Pipe Spring National Monument, file 12-5.

20. Chief Forester Henry Graves, quoted in *Proceedings of the National Parks Conference held at Berkeley, California March 11, 12, and 13, 1915* (Washington, DC: Government Printing Office, 1915), 144.

21. *Report of the Director of the National Park Service, 1918*, 91, 190; *Report of the Director of the National Park Service for Fiscal Year Ended June 30, 1919* (Washington, DC: Government Printing Office, 1919), 102.

22. *Report of the Director of the National Park Service, 1918*, 190.

23. *Report of the Director of the National Park Service, 1919*, 105.

24. Details of the financial relationship between Kent and Lind are found in the National Archives, RG 79, Series 6, Muir Woods, file 12-5.

25. The situation at Navajo National Monument is chronicled in the National Archives, RG 79, Series 1, Records of the Office of the Secretary of the Interior Relating to National Parks and Monuments 1872-1916, Letters Received, Tray 166.

26. The reports filed by Isaac Whittemore, Frank Pinkley, and other care-takers of Casa Grande prior to 1915 are contained in the National Archives, RG 79, Series 1, Records of the Office of the Secretary of the Interior Relating to National Parks and Monuments 1872-1916, Letters Received, Tray 166.

27. Ibid.

28. Frank Bond to Robert B. Marshall, 13 November 1916, NA, RG 79, Series 1, Records of the Office of the Secretary of the Interior Relating to National Parks and Monuments 1872-1916, Letters Received, Tray 166.

29. Frank Pinkley to Stephen T. Mather, 8 March 1918, NA, RG 79, Series 6, Casa Grande, file 12-5. Quotations in the next four paragraphs can be found in the same file.

30. Frank Pinkley to Stephen T. Mather, 8 April 1918; and Horace Albright to Frank Pinkley, April 13, 1918; NA, RG 79, Series 6, Casa Grande, file 12-5.

31. Horace Albright to Frank Pinkley, 7 June 1918, NA, RG 79, Series 6, Casa Grande, file, 12-5.

32. *Report of the Director of the National Park Service, 1920,* 249.

33. Ibid.

34. R. R. Duncan Report to the commissioner of the General Land Office, 8 September 1916, NA, RG 79, Series 6, El Morro, file 12-5. Duncan apparently did not yet know of the passage of the National Park Service Act on 25 August 1916.

35. Telegram from Doug White of the Salt Lake Railroad Route to Joseph J. Cotter, Acting Superintendent of National Parks, 25 April 1917, NA, RG 79, Series 6, Zion National Monument, file 12-5.

36. *Report of the Director of the National Park Service, 1920,* 252.

37. Ibid.

38. Associate Director Arno B. Cammerer to Commissioner of Indian Affairs Cato B. Sells, 8 October 1920; and Arno B. Cammerer to Howard Eaton, 11 October 1920; NA, RG 79, Series 6, El Morro National Monument, file 12-5.

39. E. Z. Vogt to Arno B. Cammerer, 18 April 1921, NA, RG 79, Series 6, El Morro National Monument, file 12-5.

40. E. A. Errickson to Stephen T. Mather, 20 March 1921; and Dr. Albert Spears to Stephen T. Mather, 23 May 1921; NA, RG 79, Series 6, El Morro National Monument, file 12-5.

41. E. Z. Vogt to Arno B. Cammerer, 4 September 1920, NA, RG 79, Series 6, El Morro National Monument, file 12-5.

42. E. Z. Vogt to Mather, 19 September 1921, NA, RG 79, Series 6, El Morro National Monument, file 12-5.

1. Frank Pinkley at the Casa Grande National Monument, circa 1925. Photo courtesy of the National Archives.

2. This skeleton was exhumed from Chaco Canyon by Richard Wetherill and the Hyde brothers during GLO Special Agent S. J. Holsinger's visit in 1901. Photo courtesy of the National Archives.

3. The Hotel El Tovar as it appeared on a postcard, Grand Canyon National Monument. Collection of the author.

4. Tourist "bus" owned by the Fred Harvey Company and Hunter Clarkson. Photo courtesy of the National Archives.

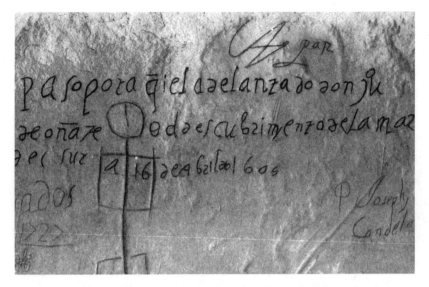

5. The oldest inscription (dated 1605) at El Morro National Monument. Photo courtesy of the National Park Service.

6. El Morro National Monument, established 8 December 1906. Photo courtesy of the National Park Service.

7. Kivas at Pueblo Bonito, Chaco Canyon National Monument, established 11 March 1907. Photo courtesy of the National Park Service.

8. Lassen Peak in Lassen Peak National Monument, established 6 May 1907. Photo courtesy of the National Park Service, photographer Fred Mang, Jr.

9. Muir Woods National Monument, established 9 January 1908. Photo courtesy of the National Park Service, photographer George Grant.

10. Pinnacles National Monument, established 16 January 1908. Photo courtesy of the National Park Service.

11. Tumacacori Mission, Tumacacori National Monument, established 15 September 1908. From a postcard in the collection of the author.

12. Blue Glacier on the northern slope of Mount Olympus, Mount Olympus National Monument, established 2 March 1909. Photo courtesy of the National Park Service.

13. Inscription House Ruin, Navajo National Monument, established 20 March 1909. Photo courtesy of the National Park Service, photographer Fred Mang, Jr.

14. Rainbow Bridge National Monument, established 30 May 1910. Photo courtesy of the National Park Service, photographer Fred Mang, Jr.

15. Big Hole Battlefield National Monument, established 23 June 1910. Photo courtesy of the National Park Service.

16. Independence Monument in Monument Canyon, Colorado National Monument, established 24 May 1911. Photo courtesy of the National Park Service, photographer George A. Grant.

DEVIL POSTPILE NATIONAL MONUMENT WAS
PROCLAIMED BY PRESIDENT TAFT JULY 6, 1911.
THE POSTPILE ITSELF IS A REMNANT OF A
BASALTIC LAVA FLOW THAT TOOK PLACE BETWEEN
100,000 AND 200,000 YEARS AGO. THIS EXTENDED
FROM MAMMOTH PASS TO JUST BELOW RAINBOW
FALL. UPON COOLING, THE BASALT CRACKED INTO
FOUR-, FIVE-, AND SIX-SIDED COLUMNS.
DURING THE ICE AGE, WHEN THE MIDDLE FORK
GLACIER ADVANCED FOR THE LAST TIME, IT
READILY QUARRIED THE BASALT AWAY, COLUMN
BY COLUMN, AND ONLY THE MOST RESISTANT
PARTS WERE LEFT STANDING. ONE SIDE OF THE
POSTPILE WAS THUS REMOVED, LEAVING THE
WALL OF COLUMNS 40 TO 60 FEET HIGH.
THE TOP OF THE FORMATION HAS BEEN WORN
SMOOTH BY THE GRINDING OF THE GLACIER,
LEAVING THE SURFACE WITH THE APPEARANCE
OF A MOSAIC OR TILE PAVEMENT.

17. Devils Postpile National Monument, established 6 July 1911. Photo courtesy of the National Archives.

7

Boss Pinkley's Domain

WITH AN AGENCY AUTHORIZED TO MANAGE the monument category, new areas proliferated. Between September 1916 and the beginning of 1924, thirteen new national monuments were established. Places as diverse as Scotts Bluff, a stop along the Oregon Trail located in western Nebraska; Aztec Ruins, an archaeological site on the Animas River in northwestern New Mexico; and Lehman Caves, limestone caverns in Nevada, were added. The new monuments were no easier to categorize than the old had been. Many lacked funds or even part-time custodial care, throwbacks to the days before the establishment of the Park Service.

By 1923 it was clear that there were too many national monuments, located too far from Washington, D.C., to be administered from the home office of the Park Service. Some sort of regional authority, geographically closer to the majority of the monuments, needed to be developed. Appropriations for monuments were determined by a haphazard process, primarily based on the reports of the custodians and occasionally on information supplied by GLO or USFS people near a specific monument. Because they had little first-hand knowledge of the monuments and were fully occupied with making the national parks the center of tourist attention, the Washington, D.C.-based officers of the NPS had neither the time nor the inclination to evaluate the monuments carefully. The monuments were peripheral oddities, anomalies in a system increasingly focused on scenic monumentalism.

Out of place in the park system during the early 1920s and difficult
to advertise as recreational playgrounds, the national monuments became a headache for the NPS. Tripartite administration with the
Forest Service and the War Department resulted in duplicated effort.
In addition, the NPS's emphasis on programs for the national parks
meant that monument questions were rarely scrutinized. As the condition of many of the national monuments made clear, scenery interested the Park Service more than archaeology. The agency needed
a better way to evaluate the monuments, and localized administration
offered the best answer. Looking for a way to be rid of the task of
caring for the monuments, Park Service officials decided that some
sort of field administration for the national monuments was a pressing
need. Someone responsible had to be found who knew the areas and
could be counted on to uphold Park Service standards.

The Southwest seemed a logical center for localized administration.
The majority of accessible monuments were there. Southwestern national parks ranked high on the agenda of the NPS, and the archaeological monuments of the region were particularly susceptible to
vandalism. There was comparatively little settlement in the Southwest,
and as western states built highways, the potential of the region for
tourism became increasingly clear. The leaders of the agency looked
for an administrator with commitment, intelligence, and an eye toward
development.

Since his return to Casa Grande, Frank Pinkley had been a favorite
with the Park Service. Following the reclassification of Casa Grande,
he had been the most active and inquisitive of the custodians. Pinkley
was an innovator who accepted challenges, and his vision was as broad
as Mather's. He saw the parks as a system rather than as individual
entities, and with more than twenty years experience at Casa Grande,
he certainly knew how to address the problems of national monuments. To Pinkley, the monuments were tools by which to teach Americans about a heritage of which they knew little. "Future generations
will censure us greatly," he mused despondently in 1920, "for our
lack of interest and for not properly caring for and preserving for
them these great relics of a long vanished race."[1]

When that most visible of national monuments, the Grand Canyon,
became a national park in 1919, the agency considered Pinkley for
the job of superintendent. Herbert W. Gleason, the Department of
the Interior inspector in charge of park conditions as well as the official

photographer for the Park Service, rated Pinkley a "no. 1 man,. . . exceedingly practical."[2] As the change in administration occurred, Mather asked Pinkley to report on conditions at the Grand Canyon, while simultaneously asking Irving Brant, a noted writer who was a friend of the agency, to assess Pinkley's qualifications for the superintendency. Despite favorable accounts, Horace Albright prevented Pinkley's appointment, pointing out his earlier battles with tuberculosis and the difficulties it might cause at the Grand Canyon. But more important, Albright insisted, Pinkley "is just the kind of man we need to look after our national monuments in the southwest—it would be impossible to get a man to fill his place."[3] Albright recommended keeping Pinkley with the national monuments.

Pinkley had found his niche, and promotions to other places held no appeal for him. When he discovered that he was not to become superintendent of the Grand Canyon National Park, Pinkley wrote Albright: "I would have gone to the canyon, had I been ordered there and would have considered it, in a sense, a promotion; but I am glad the rumor of my transfer was not well founded, and that you intend to let me work along lines which will be more congenial to me."[4] In 1919 Tumacacori Mission, decaying for generations, was placed under his care. In 1922 he convinced the Arizona legislature to appropriate $1,000 for repair work at the mission, the first state government gift to a specific National Park Service site. The governor of Arizona wrote that he "felt safe in signing the bill and signing over the money" in large part because he knew the monument was under Pinkley's care.[5]

An intense, assertive man who prided himself upon his candor, Pinkley became the leading proponent of the national monuments. On his shoestring budget, he initiated a variety of service programs at Casa Grande, mostly accomplished with his own money, time, and sweat. The attention and service visitors received at Casa Grande was as good as that at any national park, and for no other reason than that Frank Pinkley was in charge. There was no one who could match Pinkley's experience, zeal, or persistence in taking care of these often neglected areas. In October 1923 Frank Pinkley was appointed the superintendent of the fourteen southwestern national monuments over which the NPS had jurisdiction (see Table 2). The area for which he became responsible included all of New Mexico and Arizona, southwestern Colorado, and southern Utah.

Before he became superintendent of the southwestern national

Table 2. The Southwestern National Monuments Group, 1923–32

1. The Original Areas:

Park Name	Primary Value
Montezuma Castle	archaeological
El Morro	historic/archaeological
Petrified Forest	natural
Chaco Canyon	archaeological
Natural Bridges	natural
Tumacacori	historic
Navajo	aracheological
Gran Quivira	archaeological
Rainbow Bridge	natural
Papago Saguaro	natural
Capulin Mountain	natural
Casa Grande	archaeological
Yucca House	archaeological

2. Monuments added between 1923 and 1932:

Park Name	State	Size (in acres)	Primary Value	Year Added
Carlsbad Cave	New Mexico	719	natural	1923
Aztec Ruins	New Mexico	25.88	archaeological	1923
Pipe Spring	Arizona	40	historic	1923
Hovenweep	Utah	285	archaeological	1923
Wupatki	Arizona	2,234	archaeological	1924
Arches	Utah	4,520	natural	1929
Canyon de Chelly	Arizona	83,840	nat./arch.	1931
White Sands	New Mexico	143,086	natural	1932

monuments group, Pinkley had shown the ability to overcome whatever problems came his way. Looking beyond the two monuments in his charge, Casa Grande and the Tumacacori Mission, he offered advice and counsel to the custodians of other national monuments and frequently took up the general cause with the Washington, D.C., office of the NPS. Pinkley's appointment as superintendent was the logical outgrowth of his work in the agency. It gave official sanction to the unofficial role he had previously played.

The central administration of the Park Service was happy to unload the southwestern monuments on Pinkley. In the view of agency officials, more pressing concerns, such as acquiring private lands in the East and the development of roads in the national parks, relegated the national monuments to the background. Considering the difficulties and complexities associated with their upkeep, the monuments seemed to be more trouble than they were worth.

In fact, the central office of the Park Service was so pleased with Pinkley and so anxious to separate monument problems from mainstream issues in the parks that some talked of placing Pinkley in charge of all monuments. Some in the highest echelon of the agency favored this change. "Personally, I think it would be an excellent thing if all of the national monuments could be put under your immediate supervision, changing your title to 'Field Superintendent of the National Monuments,'" Assistant Director Arthur E. Demaray wrote to Pinkley on 3 June 1924. "Although I realize it would be adding largely to your duties, it would relieve a heavy pressure here."[6] Demaray thought his idea promising enough to send a memo to Director Mather encouraging another promotion for Pinkley.

The idea proved impractical. In 1923 national monuments were dispersed throughout the West. Automobiles were replacing trains as the primary means of travel, but western roads generally remained in poor condition. Getting from place to place was difficult, and Pinkley could not have kept a close watch on all parts of his domain without sacrificing the diligence that characterized his work in the Southwest. Spreading his authority all over the West might have diluted his considerable charisma and worn out his enthusiasm. The expanded responsibility would have been too much for anyone, and the net result might easily have been shoddy management at all the monuments, instead of the careful administration of those closest to Pinkley's heart.

The Washington, D.C., office also feared the implications of delegating authority for two-thirds of the areas that the agency administered. During the 1920s, Mather and Albright were the center of authority, and they believed that decentralization could lead to fragmentation within the system. The idea of a field superintendent went no farther than Demaray's memo. Too much autonomy for any individual in the NPS, even one connected with the national monuments, had divisive potential.

Pinkley's knowledge and experience were concentrated in the Southwest, and there was more than enough for him to do with the national monuments there. Almost as soon as he was appointed, Pinkley began to organize the loosely affiliated individuals who were watching over the national monuments into an orderly network of administrators. He instituted a system that prescribed an array of duties for the custodian of each national monument, culminating in a monthly report, due in his office on the twenty-fifth of each month.

As he tried to instill professionalism in his staff, Pinkley's demands led to problems. The volunteers who made up his staff had other responsibilities and could not keep up with him. Some did not share his enthusiasm. By June 1924 Pinkley was upset with the custodians at some of his monuments. Most were not meeting his deadline for sending their monthly reports. It was of the utmost importance to Pinkley that his unpaid volunteer staff conduct itself professionally, and he intended to quickly eliminate the lazy and the incompetent. "I am sure a report of some kind can be written about any monument any month," he asserted. "If your monument isn't worth reporting on there is something wrong either with you or your monument."[7] With such simple, straightforward logic, Pinkley set out to establish an orderly administration in which everyone abided by his rules. He began to change the meaning of the position of custodian, and some of his staff could not adjust. Indeed, several of the volunteers found Pinkley's constant demands a strain, and some resigned in search of less complicated work.

Although Pinkley always got right to the point, his communication with his staff was rarely abrupt. Typically, his letters ordered his staff to do something in a very specific way, and unfailingly, the superintendent took the time to explain his reasoning. He made certain that those who worked for him understood why he insisted that they abide by his standardized rules. The explanatory, teaching role became a significant part of the superintendent's job, and late in 1924, Pinkley issued a series of circulars designed to inform custodians of their obligations as he defined them. Pinkley envisioned a system of management based upon his experience at Casa Grande. He presented himself as a more experienced peer, telling his staff that he did not "want to seem dictatorial; it just occurs to me that if I place my twenty years experience at your disposal I may save you some of the mistakes I have made."[8]

The crux of his plan was to educate the public and protect the monuments from vandalism and depredation, and Pinkley offered ways to confront crises without resorting to threats or force. At archaeological areas, the ever-present "Name Scratcher and Souvenir Hunter," the tourists who wanted to mark their visit or take a piece of the site home with them, were his number one adversary. Be firm but even-handed, Pinkley counseled his volunteers, and "never give an order without an explanation and a reason . . . all but a few visitors are fair and want to do what is reasonable. They just don't think what their actions amount to if multiplied by a million."[9] When custodians remembered that they were public servants and when visitors acknowledged that they were citizens, Pinkley reasoned, most problems could be easily resolved.

Protecting a national monument meant more than stopping vandalism, because natural deterioration could be more of a threat than human depredation. Pinkley lacked the resources available to the superintendents of the national parks, and all he could do was try to bolster the morale of his staff. "I know it will be irritating," he wrote, "to have me tell you [that] you must study your monument with a view to getting the greatest amount of protection for the least money when we have practically no money for this purpose. . . . I used to think we needed a lot of money before we could do anything. I find that by plugging along with a little money we are gradually going to get our southwestern monuments in a fair state of protection."[10] Again, under difficult and frustrating conditions, Pinkley counseled diligence and patience.

Pinkley motivated a staff composed primarily of volunteers by appealing to their pride and sense of responsibility. The "Boss," a sobriquet he enjoyed, made the other custodians feel that they were a valuable part of the system even if they did not receive a salary or other perquisites of government service. At least once a year, Pinkley appeared at each southwestern national monument in the Model T Ford that the Park Service had provided for his official use. His personal style pleased his staff, and when he got down on his hands and knees with a trowel to assist in the stabilization of archaeological ruins or climbed rugged trails to view fire damage, his actions spoke much louder than mere words. His charisma and devotion considerably eased the frustration of his staff, but they also had to live up to his standards. Top-notch service was what Pinkley wanted, and with or without adequate funding from Congress, he was going to get it.

From the perspective of the Washington, D.C., officials, Pinkley did the NPS a great service. His enthusiasm and vigor were infectious, and by instilling them in the other southwestern custodians, he almost reversed the effects of institutionalized neglect. But even more amazing from the point of view of Mather, Albright, and Cammerer was that without their fulfilling Pinkley's constant requests for more money to spend on upkeep, conditions in his national monuments continued to improve.

Pinkley's ability was never in question. That he could develop first-class service from untrained, unpaid volunteers was nothing short of astonishing. NPS officials quite correctly concluded that Pinkley had an uncanny ability to motivate others, based on his way of communicating on an individual level with the custodians at the other monuments. This was an intangible asset, one that all the congressional support in the world could not buy. This approach made the custodians feel that Pinkley was "a helpful associate and co-laborer rather than a fault-finding critical boss," Assistant Director Arno B. Cammerer wrote him on 13 November 1924. "You will continue to spread helpfulness and the spirit of loyalty and pride as you have been doing."[11]

A man with astonishing personal charisma, Pinkley also slightly disturbed his superiors. He frequently seemed beyond their control, and he was the type around whom a personality cult could develop. The only man who could get action for the national monuments and a zealot by nature, Pinkley could have become the recipient of the fanatical loyalty of his subordinates. The kind of individual initiative that Pinkley exhibited could also have become a problem in an agency just defining its place in the federal bureaucracy and lacking a formal chain of command.

The agency had no evidence to indicate that Pinkley encouraged loyalty to himself instead of the system. It was just a possibility that nagged particularly at Arno B. Cammerer, whose genial nature often made him responsible for smoothing ruffled feathers. Pinkley always made multiple copies of every letter he wrote and spread them around the agency, yet Cammerer felt compelled to remind him to "keep on sending copies of your correspondence and good letters in to me. None of us can go a long way by ourselves," Cammerer gently told Pinkley. "We all like to know that we are being trusted and believed in."[12] Reading Pinkley's memos and letters gave Cammerer a way to monitor his feisty and invaluable monument man.

Cammerer rightly sensed that Pinkley knew that he and his monuments were not getting their due, and that as a result many involved with the monuments were becoming frustrated. As the official in the capital most aware of the problems of the field staff, Cammerer saw a way around potential conflict. If the Park Service acknowledged the significance of Pinkley's work, he could be pacified. Cammerer turned his attention to assuaging Pinkley's complaints. "We are all dependent on a little touch of sympathy and helpful appreciation here and there," Cammerer wrote Pinkley. "[T]hough I happen to be sitting in the Assistant Director's chair at the present time your letters and your loyal friendship . . . have meant a lot to me."[13] Cammerer tried to head off a showdown by providing Pinkley with the same kind of support that the superintendent offered to his subordinates.

But appreciation was all the agency could offer the person in charge of the southwestern national monuments, and Cammerer's attentiveness to Pinkley's problems only temporarily alleviated a troublesome situation. His actions created an illusion of concern, but Mather's and Albright's priorities precluded real attention to the issues of the national monuments. Pinkley's charisma was an asset to the fledgling Park Service because no one else thought the monuments were important enough to bother with; turned against the agency, his zeal could be a potent and destructive force.

Pinkley and the Washington, D.C., office valued the park system differently. The key points of contention centered on two interrelated issues: the lack of money for the monuments in the Park Service budget, and the constant attempts to turn the best of the national monuments into national parks. In both cases, Pinkley felt that the treatment he and his monuments received was shameful, whereas NPS officials maintained that political realities took matters out of their control.

Throughout the 1920s, the Park Service budget provided for the development of the national parks and largely ignored the national monuments. During the first half of the decade, money was scarce in the agency, and the agency used its funding to minimalize the impact of visitors. But the additional resources of the agency did not help the monuments, and the budget for the entire monument category compared unfavorably to that of even the lesser national parks. For the fourteen areas Pinkley administered during the travel season ending 30 September 1924, he received less than $15,000. That year, he calculated the cost per visitor in thirteen national parks and came up with an average of 68.4 cents. In contrast, the agency spent a nickel per visitor in a comparable group of thirty-one national monuments, and only 9.2 cents for each visitor to his southwestern national monument group.

The disparity persisted throughout the decade. By 1927 Pinkley took charge of four additional monuments, and the eighteen southwestern national monuments drew nearly 270,000 visitors. Yet the budget allocated less than $15,000 for the southwestern national monuments group. Pinkley did not even have the money to pick up the garbage visitors left. The other fourteen Park Service national monuments drew an additional 163,197 visitors, for which the agency allocated roughly $6,200. In comparison, Mesa Verde National Park received $72,300 for its 11,915 visitors that year, Yellowstone had a $398,000 appropriation for its 200,825 visitors, and Park Service officials at the Grand Canyon spent $132,000 on 162,356 visitors. Platt National Park, an unimportant pork-barrel park in Oklahoma, received $12,400, more than half the amount allotted to the entire monument category. Wind Cave, another inconsequential park, also received $10,275. That year, only Sully's Hill, a small wildlife park in North Dakota that Mather wanted to abolish since he entered the Park Service, was left out of the budget.[14] Even national parks that the agency regarded as insignificant received more money and attention than the national monument category.

In 1927 the budget of the entire monument category roughly equalled that of Mount McKinley National Park in Alaska. For the $18,700 spent there, the Park Service entertained 651 visitors. With less money, Pinkley was supposed to handle 270,000 visitors at eighteen southwestern parks. Without the network that Pinkley developed and minus his continuous encouragement, custodians of the fourteen national monuments not in the southwestern national monuments group served an additional 163,000 visitors on meager funding. In sum, the care and maintenance of a total of thirty-two diverse park areas had to be carried out on this minuscule budget. The superintendent of any national park would have complained at what the agency allotted Pinkley for all of the southwestern national monuments.

But throughout the 1920s, funding for the Park Service was always precarious. Although the prosperity of the 1920s dramatically increased the popularity of the park system and Mather built powerful alliances throughout Congress, when the Park Service drew up requests for money, Congress often overlooked the monuments. By 1927 Mather had spent more than a decade building a constituency to support the national parks, and he consistently asked a great deal more money for the parks than he did for the monuments. In his view, the monuments were complements, worthy of substantial expenditures only if they helped develop national parks. Because he constantly pressured Congress for national park programs, Mather had to be prepared to come up short in other areas, especially national monument funding.

The demands at some of the national parks were also different from those at the monuments. Some parks required extensive management of natural resources. Mount McKinley contained 2,645 square miles of wild land that miners and trappers often threatened. Part of its appropriation went for protection of the area. Hunters became a problem at Yosemite and Yellowstone, and the battle against poaching cost the Park Service money. Funding at these parks covered more than visitor services, whereas Pinkley's custodians generally had responsibility for areas small enough to protect with their presence. Managing natural resources became an agency priority because meadows, mountains, glaciers, and geysers were the attractions that brought visitors to the national parks. When protection for these resources required extra money or additional employees, the Park Service under Mather did all it could to convince Congress to allocate more funds.

Nevertheless, the discrepancy between the categories was too great. Pinkley wanted a budget that gave him a fighting chance, and in 1927 he settled upon an average of twenty-five cents per visitor as the bare minimum for adequate protection and care of the monuments. By the end of the 1920s, his staff clamored for salaries, an additional drain on his limited resources. Pinkley also had stabilization and preservation responsibilities for archaeological and historic sites, which could be as expensive as managing natural areas. His job included offsetting the impact of more than 100,000 pairs of hands and feet upon his monuments. But Pinkley's seemingly reasonable request amounted to nearly three times the annual sum allocated for the southwestern monuments and five times the total amount that the monuments had received the previous year. After making his pleas, he received little more than before.

In a way, Pinkley was penalized for his success. The work he did on his own time helped minimize the impact of visitation, and no one could match his personal dedication. As a consequence of Mather's drive to build public support for the agency, visitation became the basis for most Park Service funding. Pinkley understood those rules, and while he was in charge, he brought flocks of people to the monuments. The number of visitors at the southwestern monuments increased exponentially, and by agency standards, his record justified greater support. But Pinkley's monuments were not national parks, and increased visitation only guaranteed greater support in the national parks. The Park Service always had other holes to plug in the system, and even though Pinkley drew as many visitors as most national parks, he never received any more than a skeletal budget.

The need for money frustrated Pinkley, and throughout the 1920s, he challenged the priorities of the agency. In 1924 Pinkley exploded when Cammerer contended that the decision not to place full-time paid custodians at Montezuma Castle and Chaco Canyon was "a question of policy. . . . I never knew this was a matter of policy at all," Pinkley roared. "I always thought it was purely a lack of money which prevented us putting full-time men at all the national monuments which are open to vandalism or where a man in charge would be valuable for the distribution of information. No other policy could be backed by logic."[15] From Pinkley's perspective, such a contention revealed duplicitous conduct on Cammerer's part. It appeared to Pinkley that agency policy encouraged vandalism and neglect in the southwestern monuments.

If visitation was the standard that determined funding for park areas, Pinkley wanted to know why his monuments did not get more money. By his calculations, in 1924 the national parks averaged one dollar per visitor in allocations. Pinkley knew he would never get that much, but his monuments attracted more visitors each year. Significant visitation figures notwithstanding, funding for the monuments remained nonexistent. In 1924 more visitors went to Montezuma Castle, with its annual appropriation of less than $600, than to Zion, Sully's Hill, or Mesa Verde national parks, the last of which received $43,000 in appropriations. Pinkley wanted to know why visitation at Montezuma Castle did not merit at least $2,500, the annual cost of a full-time custodian.

To appease Pinkley, Cammerer explained that he had the "general situation of all the monuments in view" when he made his comments, and he tried to show that the agency did not completely neglect Pinkley and his monuments. When a caretaker "who will be willing to give his whole soul to the work" could be found, Cammerer told Pinkley, "there is no question but what an expenditure for a comfortable salary and comfortable living quarters is justified." Cammerer played to the biases of the superintendent. He suggested that E. Z. Vogt at El Morro deserved a salary, and that Tumacacori would also soon justify a paid custodian, but insinuated that places like Devils Tower, Capulin Mountain, and Verendrye needed little more than nominal care.[16]

Pinkley could tolerate such a compromise. A champion of the archaeological and historical monuments, he paid markedly less attention to natural areas. Cammerer was telling him that the places to which he had devoted half a lifetime were soon to receive adequate protection. Of the areas Cammerer named, only Capulin Mountain belonged to the southwestern monument group. Far from the main highways, it attracted few visitors, and Pinkley did not promote it heavily. The other natural monument in his care, the Petrified Forest, already had a full-time custodian. In order to pacify the superintendent, Cammerer agreed to Pinkley's vision of the monuments.

Despite his diligent service and effort, Pinkley felt like an outsider in the NPS. His concerns were at odds with many in the agency. He often reminded Cammerer that there were "phase[s] of monument administration which . . . park men ought to consider and there is no chance to bring up when we are in conference because park problems only have the right of way there."[17] While he struggled to administer the monuments, superintendents of national parks spent five times his annual allotment on road-building projects. Pinkley understood that the parks were and would remain the focus of the agency. His enthusiasm could help counteract the lack of funds, but he could do little about agency policy regarding the integrity of the national monuments.

Always a "strict constructionist," Pinkley fought to keep the areas that fit the terms of the Antiquities Act in the monument category. In his view, places of "pre-historic, historic or scientific . . . interest" belonged among the monuments.[18] This proved a difficult stance to maintain in a system that saw the monuments as bargaining chips and routinely reassigned the best of that class to national park status.

Pinkley's frustration with the status quo predated his appointment as superintendent of the southwestern national monuments and never lessened. There was always a proposal afoot to convert one or another of the important national monuments into a national park, and Congress and the Washington, D.C., office of the NPS irked him with their tendency to ignore the needs of the monuments when concerned with "park issues." When Dr. Willis T. Lee of the U.S. Geological Survey made his inspection of Carlsbad Cave and other southwestern national monuments in September 1924, E. Z. Vogt told Pinkley that Lee recommended that a state or local historical society take charge of El Morro. "What I think is better expressed with the shift key up among the exclamation points and asterisks," Pinkley exploded. "I have been stung by these monument robbers till I am sore. And every last time, if you make them come clean, it reduces itself to a matter of money. If we could get $50,000 to support El Morro as a Monument, would anyone be claiming it was not of monument status but ought to be turned over to some society or some individual for administration. . . . It is always a matter of turning a Monument into a Park or into something else, so as to increase its appropriation." There were distinct differences in law between what constituted a monument and a park, Pinkley bellowed, "and there *ought* to be a definite line between them, so that when a monument is once created its biased firends [*sic*] can not dress it up a little and bob its hair and run it over into the Park crowd simply because there is more feed in the Park trough."[19]

Pinkley thought that Mather's and Albright's tactics turned the monument designation into a liability. "Congress is never going to get enthusiastic over a lot of picked-over monuments," he stormed, "and unless we stop this talk of transferring the Carlsbad Cavern and the Petrified Forest and the Casa Grande Ruin and the Chaco Canyon, we are never going to get adequate appropriations for the National Monuments. When Congress realizes that the Monuments are a class quite to themselves and are not little Parks but are just as important as the Parks, we will begin getting enough money to handle them properly."[20]

Pinkley wanted a clear definition of national monuments and national parks to which both he and the agency would adhere. He told Albright that the agency needed to decide what constituted a national monument, and "when a newly proposed reservation falls under that definition, let us make a monument of it and ever after keep it in the monument class." He thought that the NPS caused some of the confusion "by making monuments of Zion and Grand Canyon when they didn't belong in that class and we never expected to keep them there."[21]

In his view, inappropriate proclamations gave ammunition to those who wanted to make national parks out of important national monuments.

Pinkley challenged agency attempts to broaden the definition of the national park category. Originally, Mather included only the most spectacular scenic areas among the flagship parks. NPS policy had to be revised for the agency to become an important federal entity. By the late 1920s, national park boundaries included most of what Mather and Albright desired in the West, but the survival of the agency dictated a policy of expansion, which in turn required a broader definition of the park category. There were very few places like Yellowstone, Yosemite, or Mount Rainier. Areas that were more than scenic mountaintops had to be included, and the monument category was the storehouse for the most appropriate places. The way-station precedents already existed, and the agency planned future conversions of monuments. But in Pinkley's hands, the move to preserve historic and prehistoric sites was on a collision course with the broadened definition of the national parks. As the agency began to regard one-of-a-kind natural wonders as national park material, Pinkley fought for his monuments. His position was grounded in statute, and he challenged the supremacy of the national parks in the park system.

Mather's and Albright's ideas and policies coincided more with Dr. Willis T. Lee's sentiments than they did with Pinkley's strict constructionism, and the possibility that Pinkley might damage the development of the park system became a threat that the agency had to address. Having created the priorities that initiated the conflict, Mather could not capitulate to Pinkley's vision of the system. Mather and Albright wanted the national parks to compete with the culture of Europe for the American tourist dollar. This required the inclusion of areas that were already designated as, and the might technically be, national monuments. No matter how the Antiquities Act was written, under Mather's and Albright's guiding hands, the best national monuments would be made into national parks and the remainder would continue to languish. The national monuments were simply not a priority in an agency with an orientation toward the national parks.

According to Mather's conception, the national parks inspired awe in those who came to visit. In contrast, most of the monuments lacked the commercial appeal and the postcard scenery of the majority of the national parks. But if the park category was to be superlative, if it was going to have a cultural significance equal to its scenery, places like the Carlsbad Cave National Monument in southeastern New Mexico were essential additions. Although its topography differed from the Grand Canyon or Yellowstone, its caves were awe-inspiring. Carlsbad drew more visitors than most of the national parks, and its popularity affirmed that Americans were interested in seeing places that highlighted the interaction between this extraordinary continent and the powerful individuals who had the will to tame it. Because it filled a need within the park system, agency officials broadened the ideology of the park category to make room for Carlsbad Caverns National Park.

The status of Carlsbad Cave as the most extraordinary feature of its kind set the stage for its transfer. It had the ability to inspire the kind of awe that Mather wanted. A commercial campaign by citizens of the nearby town of Carlsbad led to dramatic increases in travel. The limestone formations there also required protection, forcing the NPS to give it the kind of administration normally reserved for national parks.

The process of converting Carlsbad Cave moved slowly. Like many comparable national monuments, it lacked amenities. In 1923-24, the first year after its establishment, Carlsbad drew only 1,280 visitors, largely because the only way into the cave "was to be lowered 200 feet in a metal bucket attached to a pulley, through the natural opening at the mouth of the cave."[22] The roads in southeastern New Mexico were poor, and rail service only reached to El Paso, about one hundred miles distant. The NPS seemed content with the status of Carlsbad Cave National Monument, and the impetus for change came from other quarters.

The large limestone caverns appealed to the scientific community, which took responsibility for popularizing the site. Dr. Willis T. Lee explored the caves late in 1923. Lee compiled his findings in an article for the January 1924 issue of *National Geographic*. He persuaded the National Geographic Society to finance an expedition to explore the caves at Carlsbad further. In September 1925 *National Geographic* again carried an article about Carlsbad, and Lee began lobbying to convert it into a national park.

The Carlsbad chamber of commerce responded enthusiastically to the establishment and popularization of the monument. In 1924 and

1925 it paid $1,600 to finance the construction of a winding stairway through the natural opening, eliminating the necessity of the bucket and cable descent. Work on a road with an easier grade to replace the existing twenty-eight percent grade also began that year. People who read *National Geographic* put Carlsbad on their itineraries, and the improvements made it easier to reach the monument and to enter the cavern. In 1925-26, 10,904 people visited Carlsbad Cave, an almost one thousand percent increase from the previous year. By 1928-29, 76,822 visited the monument, 1,680 of whom came on 1 September 1929, the largest one-day attendance to that point at Carlsbad Cave.[23]

As the result of its popularity, the problems of Carlsbad Cave were very different from those of the rest of the national monuments. First and foremost, Carlsbad Cave became self-sustaining; at two dollars per adult for mandatory guided tours, 76,822 visitors—excluding children, who were admitted free—provided more revenue than any of the rest of the monuments generated in a decade. Despite the fact that the revenue went directly to the United States Treasury, the NPS had justification for spending money on this monument, and by 1928 it started spending $100,000 per year there. Carlsbad could bring in money, it had excellent support from the local community, and it was the focus of national interest. Carlsbad Cave resembled the national parks more than the mostly unimproved national monuments.

There were also concessions, which separated Carlsbad from the other monuments. By the 1928-29 season, the Cavern Supply Company, already established as a concessionaire in the monument, built a stone, pueblo-style building, from which it sold lunches and souvenirs. This was the first permanent concession structure at a national monument. In the same year, the company began to serve lunches inside the cave, 750 feet below the surface. These facilities increased the resemblance between Carlsbad Cave and the national parks, a fact Superintendent Thomas Boles emphasized in his report for 1928-29. Boles thought that the self-supporting status of the monument suggested that future appropriations "should be in keeping with the public demand for comfort and convenience."[24] Clearly, by the end of the 1920s, the status of Carlsbad Cave merited reexamination.

Carlsbad Cave increasingly seemed to fit the largely unwritten criteria that determined what constituted a national park. Visitation increased to 90,104 visitors in the 1929-30 season, and the situation at Carlsbad Cave resembled that at the original Grand Canyon National

Monument a decade before. Many Americans knew of it through *National Geographic*, and a promotional campaign further extolled its virtues.

Yet the initial monument proclamation made Carlsbad Cave a small area, confined to the land under which the magnificent caverns existed. The limestone formations at Carlsbad, its revenue, and advanced promotion and access gave it good qualifications for park status, but the Mather-Albright definition of a national park required more. Like the earlier monuments transferred to park status, Carlsbad Cave had to be differentiated from its peers. As a result, the proposals to convert Carlsbad Cave to a national park throughout the 1920s included extending the boundaries of the new park across the Texas border, into what is now the Guadalupe Mountains National Park. These attempts failed because the land between the caverns and the mountain was nondescript desert, not worthy of the national park designation.

By 1930 the situation was resolved. The bill that converted the monument to Carlsbad Caverns National Park authorized the president to add to its size by selecting suitable lands from the 193 square miles surrounding the known caverns. The size of the park was to be enlarged as new caverns were discovered, thus preventing private exploitation and allowing the new park to be distinguished from other national monuments by its increased size. In 1933 Herbert Hoover utilized this provision, and six years later Franklin D. Roosevelt added another 39,444 acres to the park, an area fifty-five times as large as the original monument. As in the case of the Zion National Monument, the new Carlsbad Caverns National Park grew to approximate the dimensions of the other national parks more closely than those of the majority of the national monuments.[25]

Pinkley did not protest the transfer of the Grand Canyon and Zion in 1919, but the reassignment of Carlsbad a decade later was another story. Pinkley had a great deal of time and effort invested in the monument system. Losing the one-of-a-kind park areas that dominated the national monument category reinforced the view that the monuments were inferior to the national parks and insinuated that the most important national monuments would become national parks as soon as congressional authorization occurred. The transfer of an area like Carlsbad Cave threatened Pinkley's world. He believed that the monuments were on the verge of being stripped of all vestiges of the identity he had been working to establish.

Agency policy trapped Pinkley and his monuments and forced him into controversy with the proponents of the mainstream views within the NPS. From its inception, the agency had directed its programs towards the improvement of the national parks. Between 1925 and 1930, the NPS spent $10,000,000 on road building within the national parks.[26] Most parks required this sort of physical improvement to make them suitable for tourism, and it was here that the Mather administration concentrated its efforts. As Pinkley correctly saw, the national monuments did not require highways—they required explanation for visitors to comprehend their significance. During the 1920s, "explanation" cost money that the agency was spending on the national parks. Pinkley could achieve significant results in the monuments with much less money than the agency spent on the parks, but he alone saw this as a primary goal for the NPS.

Despite these setbacks, Pinkley continued his energetic, innovative management, which began to attract attention as conditions in the southwestern national monument group improved. He continued to accommodate tourists, and in July 1927 the NPS promoted him a civil service grade. Later that summer, when Dr. Alfred V. Kidder put together the famous Pecos archaeological conference, Pinkley requested an unpaid leave of absence to attend at his own expense. In a gesture of appreciation of his work, the central office offered to pay both his salary and expenses. Pinkley also became a popular speaker on monument and archaeological topics. Despite protestations of unworthiness, he accepted numerous engagements, the highlight of which was a lecture series at the Southwest Museum in Los Angeles in November 1927.

Ever the perfectionist, Pinkley wanted to accomplish more. He began to establish a way to professionalize monument service, arranging for his former assistant at Casa Grande, George Boundey, to take over at the Aztec Ruins National Monument after the archaeologist Earl Morris and the American Museum of Natural History ceased their work at the monument. This move infuriated many of the locals in nearby Farmington and Shiprock, who saw the position as a local perquisite, but Pinkley stood his ground and began to develop other assistants for future openings.

By promoting through the monument system, Pinkley tried to make service in the monuments, with its all too infrequent rewards, comparable to service in the parks. Mather made the Park Service an organization that rewarded employees by moving them up a performance-based career ladder. This created a hierarchy among positions in the parks. By 1930 the superintendency of any of three national parks—Yellowstone, Yosemite, and Rocky Mountain—was a significant step on the way to a high-level administrative position in Washington, D.C. Pinkley emulated that system to build the self-esteem of his staff. He promoted custodians to the places he believed were most desirable. Through his scheme of career promotions, Pinkley sought an esprit de corps, stronger even than the camaraderie that he had already created. He inspired loyalty to the monuments as well as to himself.

An incontrovertible fact emerged from Pinkley's first decade as superintendent: no one could match his record when it came to the protection, care, and promotion of national monuments. Almost completely independent of the Washington, D.C., office of the NPS, he developed a system of management and care with which the casual efforts of the War Department and the Forest Service could not compete.

But despite Pinkley's efforts, the gap between services in the national parks and the national monuments widened during the 1920s. The parks were still the priority areas in the system and the second-class status of the monuments continued. Parks and park projects were generally well funded; Pinkley had to battle for every penny beyond a skeletal minimum unless the monument in question was targeted for eventual park status. Not surprisingly, his frustration showed on many occasions. "Congress," he wrote in 1929, "has never given us a fair chance with the monuments."[27] Pinkley's determination kept the condition of the monuments from deteriorating further, but even his effort could not prevent the public from regarding the monuments as places of secondary importance. Substantial numbers of visitors came to the monuments annually, but they often found deteriorating sites and inadequate facilities. This helped to confirm the generally held impression that the national monuments were of lesser caliber than the national parks.

NOTES

1. *Report of the Director of the National Park Service, 1920,* 250.

2. Herbert W. Gleason to Stephen T. Mather, 11 January 1919, NA, RG 79, Series 6, Grand Canyon, file 12-5.

3. Horace Albright to Stephen T. Mather, 6 March 1919, NA, RG 79, Series 6, Grand Canyon, file 12-5.

4. Frank Pinkley to Horace Albright, 16 July 1919, NA, RG 79, Series 6, Grand Canyon, file 12-5.

5. Frank Pinkley to Stephen T. Mather, 7 June 1923, NA, RG 79, Series 6, Casa Grande, file 12-5.

6. Arthur E. Demaray to Frank Pinkley, 3 June 1924, NA, RG 79, Series 6, Casa Grande, file 12-5.

7. Frank Pinkley memo to custodians, 14 June 1924, NA, RG 79, Series 6, Casa Grande, file 12-5.

8. Frank Pinkley, *What Does A Custodian?* circular, received by Department of the Interior, 1 October 1924, NA, RG 79, Series 6, Casa Grande, file 12-5.

9. Frank Pinkley, *Why Wear A Badge?* circular No. 2, October 1924, NA, RG 79, Series 6, Casa Grande, file 12-5.

10. Ibid.

11. Arno B. Cammerer to Frank Pinkley, 13 November 1924, NA, RG 79, Series 6, Casa Grande, file 12-5.

12. Ibid.

13. Ibid.

14. *Annual Report of the Secretary of the Interior 1927-28* (Washington, DC: Government Printing Office, 1928), 344-56.

15. Arno B. Cammerer to Frank Pinkley, 13 October 1924; and Arno B. Cammerer, quoted in Pinkley's Circular No. 5, attached to 27 December 1927 letter to Cammerer, NA, RG 79, Series 6, Casa Grande, file 12-5.

16. Cammerer to Pinkley, 13 October 1924.

17. Pinkley to Cammerer, 27 December 1927.

18. *United States Statutes at Large*, L. 34 Stat. 225 (1906).

19. Frank Pinkley to Evon Z. Vogt, 25 September 1924, NA, RG 79, Series 6, Casa Grande, file 12-5.

20. Ibid.

21. Frank Pinkley to Horace Albright, 25 September 1924, NA, RG 79, Series 17, Records of Horace M. Albright, Carlsbad Cave file.

22. *Report of the Director of the National Park Service for the Fiscal Year Ended June 30, 1924* (Washington, DC: Government Printing Office, 1924), 15.

23. Ibid., 48; *Report of the Director of the National Park Service for the Fiscal Year Ended June 30, 1928* (Washington, DC: Government Printing Office, 1928), 158.

24. *Report of the Director of the National Park Service, 1928*, 159-60.

25. Ise, *Our National Park Policy*, 330-32.

26. *Annual Report of the Secretary of the Interior for 1927-28*, 356.

27. Frank Pinkley to Stephen T. Mather, 1 October 1929, NA, RG 79, Series 6, Casa Grande, file 12-5.

8

Turf Wars

FRANK PINKLEY PLAYED A SIGNIFICANT ROLE in the development of
southwestern archaeological tourism. Before his arrival in Arizona, no semblance of organization existed. At the turn of the century,
railroads were responsible for promoting tourism, selling a southwestern mystique rather than any accurate representation of the past.
Pinkley changed the realities of tourism in the region. He created an
interrelated network of park areas, publicized them, and offered every
amenity that his limited budget could provide. Pinkley provided the
most up-to-date anthropological and archaeological information, albeit from the ethnocentric perspective that characterized his time
period. Like Mather, he recognized the importance of the automobile
early on and began to accommodate its users.

But he and the NPS did not administer all the archaeological sites
in the Southwest. Some belonged to private organizations, and Pinkley
could do little about them. The Forest Service also administered four
archaeological national monuments, Tonto and Walnut Canyon in
Arizona and the Gila Cliff Dwellings and Bandelier in New Mexico,
that he coveted. During the 1920s, Pinkley joined in the organized
assault against the USFS that Mather and Albright engineered.

The Forest Service and the Park Service had a complicated relationship, characterized by constant conflict and rivalry during the early
decades of interagency relations. The USFS initially opposed the establishment of the NPS, because its officials sensed that parks presented a threat to their preeminence. Both agencies administered

lands located primarily in the West, although they had different missions and constituencies. The Park Service became the federal agency responsible for preservation, and before 1920 the USFS advocated utilitarian conservation, the Progressive-era concept of wise use of natural resources. Both agencies often sought to implement their programs on the same tract of land, and between 1920 and the early 1930s, accusations and counteraccusations eroded friendly competition. Fierce territorialism rooted in incommensurable comparisons of the value of land replaced it.

During the 1920s, the Park Service acquired the upper hand in the conflicts between the two agencies. Although dynamic interaction characterized the rivalry, NPS administrators were closer to the pulse of the decade. Its leaders were effective lobbyists. Mather worked Congress like a carnival barker, taking congressmen, presidents, and other dignitaries on "catered" camping, fishing, and hiking tours of existing and proposed park areas. Horace Albright was a master of the politics of land acquisition, and his piranha-like instincts shaped the approach of the Park Service. It became the aggressor, identifying portions of the USFS domain that it coveted and giving specific reasons why the land should be added to the park system. Foresters then had to show that a tract the Park Service identified as unique, significant, and special was no different than other parts of the national forest.

The Forest Service attempted to broaden its obligations, but many in the agency resisted. As early as 1905, the USFS *Use Book*, the bible of Forest Service policy, listed recreation as one of the responsibilities of district rangers. Chief Forester Henry Graves ordered an inventory of recreational values in national forests in 1915, but out of the mistaken belief that the USFS would assume administration of the national parks. In 1924 Aldo Leopold, who later authored a crucial text in modern environmental writing, *A Sand County Almanac*, was instrumental in creating a wilderness area in the Gila National Forest in New Mexico, and the Forest Service established wilderness regulations in 1929. Yet despite this minor current, the USFS did not have recreational use in mind when it established primitive areas. Advocates of wilderness and recreation were a distinct minority with little influence. The utilitarian conservation of Gifford Pinchot remained the overwhelming emphasis of the USFS.[1]

A blurring of the roles of both agencies accelerated the rivalry during the early 1920s. Both shared the administration of the national monuments, and each agency tried to upstage the other. In partial response to the success of the Park Service, the USFS began to implement recreational programs for auto tourists. The Park Service tried to thwart such plans. By the middle of the decade, the two agencies reached an uncomfortable impasse. The Forest Service controlled large areas that Mather and Albright coveted, and it felt threatened by what it considered the wanton aggressiveness of the Park Service. Forestry officials regarded the transfer of their land to the NPS as outright defeat. The potential for interagency conflict was immense.

The joint administration of the national monument category provided Pinkley with a particular problem. There were two sets of standards when it came to monument administration, that of the Park Service and that of the Forest Service, and Pinkley approved of only one. He believed that the care and maintenance of national monuments by the Forest Service was "not up to [Park Service] standards of handling the public and giving information," and argued that "dollar for dollar, the Park Service delivered better service did than the Forest Service." The very best Pinkley could say of Forest Service personnel was that they would hold the monument "in status quo [and] give it a lukewarm police protection."[2] In the newspapers of the Southwest, he often charged the Forest Service with neglect.

Pinkley had plenty of ammunition for these charges. The Forest Service could not equal his efforts, and it often did not try. The USFS regarded national monuments as makeshift, and in many cases they did little to acknowledge the significance of areas under its care. Prior to 1929, USFS protection of the Tonto National Monument, a prehistoric cliff dwelling built by the Salado people of Arizona, consisted of "the irregular visits made by local Forest Officers, whose time was fully occupied with regular Forest work." In 1929 the Forest Service granted the Southern Pacific Railroad a "cooperative permit" to hire a watchman, but only after vandals managed to severely damage the more accessible of the two clusters of ruins. The railroad installed an Apache Indian at the ruins at a salary of $33.75 per month.[3] The man had neither archaeological training nor instruction. Visitor service at Tonto, Bandelier, Walnut Canyon, and the Gila Cliff Dwellings was noticeably inferior to that at Casa Grande, and when visitors arrived at the latter, they frequently asked Pinkley to explain the differences. These circumstances made uniform service impossible and largely negated the thrust of Pinkley's efforts.

But the Forest Service jealously guarded its monuments, and Pinkley's public expression of his feelings angered many in that agency. The USFS feared that Park Service acquisitions might establish precedents that in the long run would overwhelm the foresters. Although Forest Service people generally liked Pinkley, at times they thought him acquisitive and self-righteous. His contempt for Forest Service administration of archaeological national monuments was obvious, and he had a number of unfriendly exchanges with Forest Service personnel. Mather and Albright tried to keep Pinkley clear of confrontation, but because the superintendent enjoyed public tussling, it was only a matter of time until serious contention erupted.

The conflict exploded over the Bandelier National Monument in New Mexico. A 22,400-acre tract of archaeological ruins, high desert mesas, and steep canyons about twenty miles from Santa Fe, the area attracted the attention of late nineteenth-century archaeologists, anthropologists, writers, and later, artists. Adolph F. A. Bandelier, a self-trained anthropologist and a friend of Lewis Henry Morgan, wrote about Frijoles Canyon, the main attraction at the monument, in his novel *Die Koshare, The Delight Makers*. Noted author Charles Lummis, Edgar L. Hewett, and other anthropologists, archaeologists, and writers did much to imprint a picture of the monument and its wonders on the consciousness of the public.

The popularization of their work made the area a focus of American travelers. Their stories and books helped fashion a mystique that created another world of the Southwest, separated from modern America by layers of tradition and the constraints of a different culture. Here was the appeal to the urbanizing United States, rapidly losing its traditional cohesiveness in the wake of unprecedented immigration. Modern Americans saw an implicit validation of westward progress in the ruins of aboriginal cultures subjugated by a hostile environment. To an American public schooled in the Anglo-Saxon, Teutonic determinism of the first decade of the twentieth century, the ruins affirmed a belief in a sort of social Darwinism that acknowledged the strength of Christian society and its achievement in the New World.

Bandelier was the perfect site for Pinkley to administer. His programs revealed the nature of prehistoric Indian life on the North American continent and taught Americans about the cultures that shaped prehistoric life. Few places provided a better opportunity to convey this kind of information. Although he always regarded the ruins as less impressive than many, Pinkley recognized how useful the monument would be in the southwestern group. Located near Santa Fe, which had become a center of art as well as an increasingly popular destination for travelers, a well-managed Bandelier would serve as an entry point into his organized system of prehistoric and historic sites. It could be used to pique the interest of visitors who knew little of the other monuments.

Under the administration of the Forest Service, Bandelier was not developed to Pinkley's advantage, and he could only mutter about lost opportunity. The rangers of the Santa Fe National Forest administered the monument, and although they did not discourage visitors, neither did they offer educational programs. The ruins were anomalies on Forest Service land, managed by people more concerned with grazing leases, fire trails, and clearing dead timber than with the remains of a prehistoric civilization. Although he never doubted the competency of the Forest Service in matters of forestry, Pinkley believed that the wrong bureau managed the ruins. He was sure the Park Service could do a better job informing visitors to the monument of its cultural significance.

Although Forest Service management of Bandelier posed problems for Pinkley, the ever-present prospect of conversion of the monument to national park status was a more direct threat to his conception of a clearly defined group of national monuments. Mesa Verde, a collection of archaeological ruins in southwestern Colorado, received national park status shortly after the passage of the Antiquities Act in 1906, and if Bandelier followed the same route, Pinkley believed it would negate much of his work during the 1920s. The definition of parks and monuments would again be at issue, and the boundaries between the categories of public reservations would blur. Bandelier easily fit the definition of a national monument in the Antiquities Act. Its transferral would shatter the integrity of the category, as well as confirm once again the impression that all significant monuments were headed for park status as soon as Congress could be convinced to pass appropriate legislation.

There had been efforts to establish a national park in the Bandelier area throughout the first quarter of the twentieth century, and one attempt indirectly led to the establishment of the national monument. Between 1899 and 1915, more than fifteen separate bills to make the region a national park were introduced in Congress. All failed, and the establishment of the national monument in 1916 was the result of a maneuver by the Forest Service to circumvent a national park bill in Congress. Secretary of Agriculture David F. Houston sent Arthur Ringland, the district forester in northern New Mexico, and Will C. Barnes, chief of grazing for the agency, to the area. The men found impressive ruins that they termed "distinctive," but felt that monument status was sufficient protection for the region. Barnes suggested that the monument be named for Adolph Bandelier, who died in 1914. Under the terms of the Antiquities Act, the USFS retained jurisdiction of the monument.

But monument status was only a prelude to further efforts to establish a national park. Edgar L. Hewett, whose empire had grown considerably since 1906, considered the area his personal archaeological project. Hewett dug extensively in northern New Mexico and used his excavations to increase the importance of Santa Fe as a cultural center. In 1907 he arranged for the School of American Archaeology [now called the School of American Research], a division of the Archaeological Institute of America, to be located in Santa Fe, and he became its first director. In 1909, he founded the Museum of New Mexico, using it as a storehouse for many of the artifacts he collected on his frequent archaeological expeditions. When he thought the proposals to turn the monument into a national park served his interests, he advocated a national park. In the summer of 1923, Hewett visited Robert Sterling Yard, Mather's old friend who had become the executive secretary of the National Parks Association, and suggested that the time was right for a national park on the Pajarito Plateau.

With Yard's and Hewett's coaxing, the Park Service moved into high gear. Yard enlisted the National Geographic Society, and Hewett used his vast power base in the state to bring the issue to the attention of the public. Newspapers in New Mexico advocated the establishment of the park, and Hewett reprinted some of the best articles in his quasi-scholarly *El Palacio*, the journal of the Museum of New Mexico. As a result of the uproar, the Park Service jumped on the bandwagon. In 1924, Mather brought a proposal for a national park of more than

200,000 acres to the Coordinating Committee on National Parks and Forests (CCNPF). Stunned, the Forest Service began to devise a counterattack.

In response to Mather's development of the commercial potential of the park system, USFS officials sought to assume responsibility for strict preservation of the character of the region. The foresters believed that during the 1920s Mather and Albright had abandoned preservationist policies in order to garner support for the fledgling Park Service. The Park Service seemed more concerned with catering to its visitors with hotels and new roads than with protecting the resources that attracted people to a park area. In the view of Forest Service officials, this was poor policy, and it left a gap that they intended to fill. This gave the Forest Service the incentive to hold on to places like Bandelier.

Yet the Pajarito Plateau national park was a crucial addition for the Park Service. Within Mather's and Albright's plan to broaden the boundaries of the park category, the Pajarito Plateau gave them the opportunity to create a new concept—the "aggregate value" national park. Like Mesa Verde, the Bandelier vicinity included many prehistoric ruins. But the area also contained excellent scenery in the nearby Jemez Mountains, to the west of the existing monument. Mather and Albright did not want an exclusively archaeological park, and the mountains alone were not sufficiently important to make another mountaintop park. Combining the values gave the agency an area of national significance and the rationale for creation of many more national parks in the future.

With such a strong difference of opinion between the two agencies, resolution in Washington, D.C., seemed unlikely. Members of the CCNPF planned an inspection tour of the region for early in September 1925. Its members represented both NPS and USFS perspectives, but the Park Service was outnumbered. Congressmen Henry W. Temple of Pennsylvania, a staunch park advocate, headed the committee, and Charles Sheldon of the Boone and Crockett Club, Maj. William A. Welch, the general manager and chief engineer of the Palisades Interstate Park Commission of New York, Mather, and Forester William Greeley made up the commission. Welch and Sheldon frequently appointed substitutes for fact-finding trips, as did Mather and Greeley. Arthur Ringland, who was responsible for the creation of Bandelier and had also been the forester in charge of the Grand Canyon National Monument during the Forest Service tenure there, served as the secretary on the New Mexico trip and Assistant Forester Leon F. Kneipp represented the USFS. Mather could not be present and he appointed Dr. Jesse L. Nusbaum, the superintendent of Mesa Verde and a close associate of Hewett's, to go to central New Mexico as the Park Service representative on the tour.

The task of the commission was to gauge local sentiment about the park project. On 16 September 1925 Temple headed a public meeting in Albuquerque. Nusbaum found a sympathetic audience; he reported that all who came to a public meeting "desired a National Park or Monument area and were not hesitant about saying so." He decided that the people of Albuquerque recognized the economic value of the proposed park, and their support kept Forest Service representatives from offering substantive opposition to the proposal.[4]

The hearing the following night in Santa Fe began similarly, and the committee expected to hear additional expressions of sympathy for the park. Edgar L. Hewett chaired this public meeting. He traced the history of previous efforts to create a park in the region and pointed out the shortcomings of each attempt. Congressman Temple stood up to explain the purpose of his committee and to make it clear that he wanted a reading of local sentiment on the park question. As Temple sat, the Forest Service representatives took their cue, and efforts to stymie the establishment of a national park in north-central New Mexico began to unfold.

Forest Service resistance to the latest effort had begun long before the commission hearing. As Nusbaum reported to Mather the following day, in the months preceding the visit of the commission, a former Forest Service employee, A. J. Connell, who ran the Los Alamos Ranch School, a boarding school for boys located about ten miles from Bandelier, "started a campaign of defamation of the Park Service and the National Park idea." Nusbaum heard that Connell also threatened to close his school if a national park was created and "in the course of his talk [at a local gathering] and in subsequent talks, made public personal statements which any person knowing anything of the Park Service would know as absolute falsehoods." Connell convinced some area landholders that the Park Service would seize their land, that no one would be allowed to collect even dead timber for firewood, and that the Park Service would ban private cars from the park and force visitors to pay "to ride in the shrieking yellow busses of the transportation monopolies."[5]

Nusbaum felt that in an attempt to thwart the creation of the national park, Connell maliciously misstated both the objectives of the park project and the policies of the NPS. In fact, the agency followed a policy allowing any reasonable compromise that furthered the procurement of land in a region where a national park was proposed. For example, during the First World War, a unique agreement permitted grazing in Yosemite, and the Department of the Interior established the precedent that allowed the collection of dead timber for private use at Mukuntuweap (Zion) National Monument in 1914.[6] But Connell's insistence mustered strong and vocal resistance to the idea of a national park on the Pajarito Plateau.

Nusbaum found himself in a sticky situation. "The Forest Service had all the objectors to the plan lined up for the meeting," he told Mather, and they tried to make it seem that the region was inappropriate for a national park. Hewett, the most important advocate of a national park in north-central New Mexico, felt compelled to remain neutral because he chaired the meeting. Caught unprepared, the park advocates were leaderless and relatively unorganized. Two stand-ins on the committee, Barrington Moore, Sheldon's representative who had worked for the Forest Service employee and had become the editor of *Ecology Magazine*, and Assistant Forester Leon F. Kneipp, mercilessly pounded Nusbaum with "leading questions." Ringland, who originally worked to have the area set aside as a monument in 1915, was "apparently . . . bored to death [by talk of the region], and every remark he made belittled the area as a national park."[7]

The meeting proved uncomfortable for Nusbaum and the park constituency. Even with the support of New Mexico congressman John Morrow and Temple, Nusbaum felt that the evening was a failure. He had been ambushed because of his unpreparedness, and as a result, he felt that the question of the Cliff Cities National Park, the name given to Mather's proposal, was not fairly evaluated. Innuendo and propaganda formed the basis of public assessment of the issue, and its merit as an important artifact of the American archaeological past was ignored.

The Forest Service opposed creation of the national park because its policy dictated that economic development on the Pajarito Plateau was more important than the preservation of ruins. The foresters contested the Park Service premise that administration of the ruins was the primary issue on the plateau. In their view, there was little benefit for local homesteaders in promoting tourist travel, and economic development that focused upon ranching and timber cutting was far more important. As long as the Park Service insisted that effective preservation of archaeological ruins required restrictions upon the commercial use of large tracts of forest land, the Forest Service planned to oppose the project.

Homesteaders, stockmen, and timber interests comprised the Forest Service constituency, and the foresters' position dictated that the economic value of forest land was at least equal to the cultural value of archaeological sites. From the local perspective, Forest Service officials contended, the timber resources were far more important than the need for preservation of large areas of the plateau. If the archaeological ruins could be administered in conjunction with the use of forest land on the plateau, then perhaps a compromise could be worked out. But a large national park, restricting the use of the timber and grazing resources of the Santa Fe National Forest, was out of the question.

Although it was a despondent Nusbaum who continued with the committee to visit the ruins the following day, the damage to his cause, except for public embarrassment, was minimal. His performance in Santa Fe greatly disappointed him, and he was certain it hurt the chances of establishing a park. But Temple and Morrow remained strong proponents of the national park, even though the intensity of the resistance of the USFS surprised Morrow.[8] Despite the public battering Nusbaum took, it appeared that a national park in the northern half of New Mexico would become reality. The Forest Service representatives knew that Temple's support of the proposal put them at a disadvantage. He was the only elected official on the committee, the only member without a vested interest in the outcome, and his opinion outweighed all the others.

Kneipp, Moore, and Ringland sought opportunities to make their case to Temple without NPS interference, while Nusbaum complained about their tactics. During the visit to the Pajarito Plateau ruins the following day, Nusbaum did not have an opportunity to speak to Temple without a forester present. The Forest Service representatives took Temple to lunch at Connell's Los Alamos Ranch School and "wasted much valuable time" during the meal in a ploy Nusbaum interpreted as an attempt to steer the congressman away from the ruins in Frijoles Canyon. By the time the party arrived at the canyon rim, it was nearly dark. The travelers hiked down the trail and glanced around in the dusk, visiting the ruins in what Nusbaum called "a very superficial way."[9]

Finally, the group convened at the cottage where Congressman Temple lodged, and after another policy statement by both sides, everyone tried to settle the issue. Kneipp made a long, impassioned speech, during which he intimated that visitors were not interested in such unimportant ruins, and anyone who did stumble into them could be handled by the Forest Service custodian. He claimed that the Forest Service could do everything the Park Service could do and more for less money, and he questioned the need to sacrifice large areas of forest land to allow a national park big enough to fit the arbitrary standards that Mather and Albright had established. Then Nusbaum reiterated the Park Service position that the large area was necessary to protect the ruins and the unique physical features of the region. Finally, the time to deal with the question arrived. In the bureaucratic equivalent of the nineteenth-century gunfight, the men drew their maps, and the process of orchestrating an acceptable agreement began.

The two agencies had very different ideas of the acceptable size for the proposed national park. The Park Service envisioned a large area, including the existing monument, the Otowi ruins, the Puye ruins on the Santa Clara Indian reservation, the Baca Crater, and land connecting the various features. "The boundaries I laid," Nusbaum wrote Mather, "made the Forestry people gasp."[10] The USFS counteroffer reflected the thinking that had resulted in the establishment of the monument in 1916. After much consultation, the foresters offered to cede only the existing monument, the Otowi ruins, and a corridor connecting the two. Nusbaum immediately rejected the proposal. The initial counteroffer did not fit the image that NPS officials had of the size and stature of a national park. Kneipp then made another offer that included the area east of the Los Alamos Ranch School, inside of a line running north and south about one-quarter mile west of the Otowi, Tsankawi, and Puye ruins, and portions of the national forest between the Santa Clara Indian Reservation and the Ramon Vigil Grant, which bordered the existing Tsankawi section. This compromise offered the NPS archaeological control of the Pajarito Plateau, but Nusbaum turned it back in hopes of getting everything the NPS wanted at a later date.

Spurred by Temple's declaration that a national park was necessary to "preserve a tremendous outdoor Museum," the bargaining session continued until well after midnight, but the participants could not agree. In the hope that the NPS could use its advantage more effectively at a later date, Nusbaum, who was a lower-ranking official than Kneipp, his Forest Service counterpart, suggested that they table any permanent agreement until a meeting in Washington when Mather could attend. But the Forest Service representatives felt that their advantage lay in New Mexico, and they pressed for a settlement. Nusbaum refused, and Temple, tired after a long day and a longer evening, suggested that a delay might be a good idea, so that "others could be heard from."[11]

Unhappy at what it regarded as an acquisitive, one-dimensional land policy, the Forest Service refused to allow the Park Service to administer the ruins as a national park. Even under pressure from Temple and Morrow, foresters would not acquiesce. Rudimentary elements of a recreational policy had begun to surface within the Forest Service, and its officials were not willing to relinquish forest land to allow the NPS to develop programs for visitors. The foresters were willing to cede archaeological administration, but not at the expense of either the development of natural resources in the area or their own embryonic recreational programs.

The Park Service challenged Forest Service management, claiming that forestry personnel were not prepared to administer such an important part of the natural and cultural past of the continent. Park Service officials believed that the ruins fell too low among USFS priorities. Furthermore, USFS personnel lacked the background, training, and initiative to properly administer archaeological sites for visitors. By combining the archaeological importance of the region with the developing concept of national parks that Mather and Albright promoted, advocates made the Bandelier area appear to have a combination of natural and archaeological value worthy of national park status.

In the eyes of NPS officials, Forest Service recalcitrance in the face of what the NPS regarded as obvious merit made it appear that the foresters were trying to do the work of both agencies. In the words of New Mexico congressman John Morrow, the Forest Service "endeavor[ed] to set up little national parks of their [sic] own," a sense further affirmed by a USFS declaration in 1928 that included Bandelier as part of one of its wilderness preserves.[12] Park Service officials did not agree that the Forest Service ought to be in the recreation and tourist business; that was the province of the Park Service. It appeared that the conflict on the Pajarito could not be resolved to the satisfaction of both agencies.

The conflict between the two agencies reduced itself to a comparison of incommensurable values. There was a quantitative economic value to the disputed timber lands in the Santa Fe National Forest. A much less tangible value could be attributed to a national park filled with archaeological ruins. Each agency felt its use and its constituency should have priority, and each tried to manipulate the situation to its advantage.

But the pendulum slowly swung to favor the Park Service. Congressmen Morrow was already a long-time supporter of the various Pajarito Plateau proposals, and state government officials also showed renewed interest. Newspapers continued to trumpet the proposal, with Adela Holmquist, a reporter with the Albuquerque *Herald*, taking the lead. In order to assess the implications of the proposed park, the office of the governor of New Mexico asked Edgar L. Hewett to prepare a comprehensive report on the situation.

With Hewett's continued support, the project stood an excellent chance of success. On 8 December 1925 he presented a preliminary report to Temple's committee, indicating that he still supported Nusbaum's conception of a large park containing all the important features of the region.[13] His report to the governor reaffirmed this stance; it strongly emphasized the need to include more than archaeological ruins to make the area a national park of the first order. Hewett adopted the mainstream perspective of the agency, which seemed likely to prevail.

Under the auspices of the CCNPF, conciliation became the order of the day. But even with representatives of the NPS and USFS trying to devise an acceptable solution, little progress was made in 1926. Neither agency offered sufficient concessions to orchestrate compromise. The committee had an appropriation to fund inspection tours only until 1 July 1927, and early that year, Arthur Ringland became impatient with the lack of progress. He requested that the NPS send an official "to determine the feasibility of a National Park in the [Bandelier] region."[14]

There was only one person in the Southwest with the degree of knowledge and the level of responsibility that this job demanded. Frank Pinkley's Park Service credentials were also impeccable. His devotion and loyalty were unquestioned, for he had been an integral part of the most difficult decade of the agency. On 4 April 1927 he wired his acceptance of this job to Cammerer, and after receiving the files concerning the monument and the range of park proposals, he embarked on an inspection tour that included most of the leading southwestern national monuments as well as the Pajarito Plateau.

Although Pinkley's autonomy and outspokenness occasionally made the agency uneasy, the central administration of the NPS had great confidence in him. Albright expected that as a loyal Park Service employee, Pinkley would echo the departmental line on the proposed park; that he would visit the region and report that a large park, containing more than archaeological ruins, was essential. A national park on the Pajarito must be archaeologically significant, scenically spectacular, and able to compare to the existing members of the flagship category of Park Service areas.

These rigid requirements made it almost impossible for the NPS to compromise about land acquisition. National parks could only be established by Congress, and the NPS had succeeded in convincing Congress that it had stringent standards. If agency officials left out the scenic mountainous areas, opponents in Congress could accuse the NPS of violating its own criteria. Without the archaeological features, they had no basis for a national park. The scenery in the area alone did not justify park status. There was no room for compromise. At the highest levels of the NPS the Pajarito Plateau became an all-or-nothing proposition.

Despite Pinkley's frequent public outbursts on behalf of the national monuments, Horace Albright did not count on Pinkley's commitment to the concept of a distinct category of national monuments as defined by the Antiquities Act. "Boiled down," he wrote after his trip, "my report on the proposed Cliff Cities National Park is that the scenery is not of park status and ruins do not make a national park, not in any number, kind or quantity; they make a monument." He reiterated his long-standing contention that the ruins were inferior to those at Chaco Canyon and Mesa Verde and that scientists like Hewett were more interested in the area than the general public. "It would be," he continued, "a distinct anti-climax for the average visitor to come from the Mesa Verde to the proposed Cliff Cities National Park." There was little in the way of exceptional scenery in the proposed area. Most of it could "be duplicated several times over" throughout the Southwest. Because the Frijoles ruins were already protected as a national monument, Pinkley thought it best to transfer administration to the Park Service. But he asserted heretically, "I would rather see them left as a monument under [the Forest] Service than be transferred to ours as a Park."[15]

Few advocates of the park in Santa Fe agreed with Pinkley's rigid view of the categorization of sites. When he discussed the issue with its supporters, he found that they thought of the "proposed park in monument terms for when I suggested that we make a monument out of Puye and Frijoles [Canyon] and let them make a park out of the fine scenery which . . . was back on the Jemez Mountains to the west and south, they immediately said that such an idea would weaken the park proposition." When Pinkley suggested that the ruins were national monument material, the park supporters pointed to Mesa Verde as evidence to the contrary. "I could only reply that national monuments are clearly defined by the [Antiquities] Act . . . while parks are not clearly defined, so if Congress in its wisdom wanted to make a national park out of a duck pond that could be done but it would be no argument for making a national park out of every duck pond in the country."[16]

As far as Pinkley was concerned, national monuments and national parks were two separate concepts, and the conversion attempt represented an effort to minimize the legal and conceptual differences between them. He believed that in its attempt to acquire the Cliff Cities National Park, the NPS was violating the standards it had previously established. As superintendent of the national monuments, Pinkley felt as threatened by the acquisition attempt as did the Forest Service. In Pinkley's biased opinion, the area simply did not live up to established scenic standards.

Yet Pinkley was naive about the political realities that the Park Service faced during the 1920s. Although the statutes supported his policy, the Park Service could not use laws to establish itself as an agency. It had to prove its viability every year in front of congressional budget committees, and Mather's decision to promote the national parks shaped the policies of the Park Service throughout the period. The Forest Service was its primary adversary, and Mather and Albright were willing to use any tool at their disposal to put distance between the two agencies. Even altering the definition of the national park category was not out of the question.

Pinkley's report stunned Albright, the leading proponent of the project, as well as the strong pro-park element in the NPS. Albright thought that Pinkley took too narrow a view of the question, seeing it as an archaeologist instead of from the "broader standpoint of a national park executive."[17] In a blatantly partisan move, Albright tried to replace Pinkley with someone upon whose support he could depend. He suggested Nusbaum as a more qualified evaluator of the situation. Nusbaum, exhausted by the earlier fray, said he was too busy at Mesa Verde to take on added responsibilities.

The rift in the ranks posed a problem for the advocates of the park on the Pajarito Plateau. Pinkley's report undercut their position. They could not continue to promote the proposal as if they had the unanimous support of the Park Service. They could not even approach the CCNPF. If Pinkley's report became public, it would end any chance of convincing the still-intransigent Forest Service people that this was not just another acquisitive move by the Park Service.

As a result, the Park Service refrained from further action during the rest of 1927, keeping Pinkley's report out of the public eye. Even friends of the agency were kept in the dark. On 17 January 1928 Hewett wrote the Park Service to find out if the project was still under consideration. More than six months after Pinkley's report, the most important friend of the park proposal in the region did not even know of Pinkley's visit! Mather responded to Hewett's inquiry with the standard response concerning park proposals on the Pajarito. He complained that "the lack of a definite proposal hurt the project immeasurably," and if Hewett had clear ideas for the region, the Park Service "would be glad to present this for some definite action."[18]

The question hung in a Park Service-imposed limbo until late 1930, when Albright found his "national park executives." Upon Mather's retirement in 1929, Albright became director of the agency and began to implement his own agenda. Albright hated to lose to the USFS, and the Pajarito Plateau was high on his list of priorities. In October 1930 Roger Toll, the superintendent of Rocky Mountain National Park and the primary inspector of national park proposals in the West,

M. R. Tillotson, the superintendent of Grand Canyon, and Nusbaum went to inspect the region one more time. They spent eight days traversing northern New Mexico, visiting everything from the Otowi ruins to the Tent Rock Canyon, and reached important conclusions concerning the future of an archaeological park.

Surprisingly, their report supported Pinkley's position, and in light of the new opinion, even Albright went along. The report stated that the scenery was not "sufficiently unusual and outstanding" to merit national park status. "The choice," Toll wrote, "seems to be between having a large and important national monument and a rather small and unimportant national park." Although Cammerer thought that the agency should "aim high and then if necessary come down to what is possible to acquire," the report finally convinced Albright to put aside the park plans. On 2 January 1931 he wrote that he was "inclined to favor the national monument idea. . . . [T]he reports which we have now have before us have quite convinced me that we had better not try to get a national park in this section, at least not now."[19]

An influential Park Service supporter who did not participate in agency politics also offered an opinion that helped to kill the park proposal. On 10 February 1931 the noted anthropologist Dr. Clark Wissler of the American Museum of Natural History, a member of the Committee on the Study of Educational Problems in the National Parks, filed a report suggesting that the Park Service should "emphasize the archaeological function of the proposed park. . . . [It] relieves us of the necessity to combat the argument that the area lacks distinctive natural scenery. . . . The park can scarcely be defended on scenic grounds."[20] Wissler knew little about the politics of the situation. Albright took his perspective as an unbiased view, and it effectively put the idea of a national park on the Pajarito on hold. Despite Mesa Verde, the agency did not want purely archaeological national parks. Without an important scenic component, even Albright recognized that the agency was discussing national monument-caliber features.

Although Wissler's comments convinced Albright to give up on the park proposition, pro-park sentiment remained within the agency. Associate Director Cammerer expressed both disappointment and optimism in a memo he attached to Wissler's letter. "On the basis of this letter, if it stood alone," he wrote, "there would be no justification for more than national monument status for this area. From what I have heard, however, a good point could be made on scenic values.

. . . I should like to inspect the area some time with just that point in view."[21] Ambivalent about the acquisition of another national monument, the Park Service was not yet ready to concede.

Finally, late in 1931 Roger Toll took the lead in resolving the controversy when he proposed that the agency accept the USFS offer to transfer the monument. He concurred with Wissler's judgement, suggesting that the existing monument "would make a splendid addition to the archaeological national monuments, even if no other area were included." Forest Service officials agreed to turn over the administration of the prehistoric ruins, but "they did not wish to lose any more area from the Santa Fe National Forest than was necessary for the protection of the ruins."[22] Transfer of the monument offered an acceptable compromise, and Toll saw this as the best solution.

The compromise gave the Park Service what Frank Pinkley desired—administrative control of the archaeological ruins on the Pajarito Plateau. A rapid increase in visitors to the monument followed the completion of a new approach road to its boundaries, expediting transfer negotiations with the Forest Service. As Forest Service officials realized that the park idea had lost momentum, their position regarding the monument became conciliatory. Forester Maj. Robert Y. Stuart wrote Albright that he was prepared to transfer the existing monument and 4,700 additional acres on which "[all woodland] cutting of green timber has been completed" as long as the access roads through the additional acreage remained open for the use of local residents.[23] The additional tract no longer fit into Stuart's plans, but it united the previously segregated Otowi and Tsankawi sections. The Forest Service offered to cede the land to the Park Service in order to satiate its longtime adversaries and to alleviate the pressure to make large sections of the Santa Fe National Forest into a national park.

On 25 February 1932 the controversy was finally resolved to the satisfaction of Frank Pinkley. The Park Service assumed administrative responsibility for the new Bandelier National Monument, which included 3,626 of the 4,700 acres that Stuart offered.[24] Frank Pinkley finally had what he wanted, and Park Service development plans for north-central New Mexico could go forward.

The controversy at Bandelier was one example of how national monument issues divided the two agencies. Each agency had an agenda and a constituency, and often each wanted the same tract of land to advance its programs. Fueled by the already heated rivalry and compounded by Frank Pinkley's unorthodox position, the conflict at Bandelier illustrated the level to which relations between the agencies sunk during the 1920s. Yet it also contained the seeds of resolution and compromise, for when Pinkley forced the agency to assess the values of the area, a reasonable settlement emerged. The nearby Los Alamos Ranch School and the homesteaders in the Jemez Mountains barely noticed the change of administration in Frijoles Canyon, and the constituency of the USFS remained intact.

Pinkley also emerged a victor from the Bandelier transfer. He held out for the classification of areas according to statute, and in this case, the NPS followed his lead. In the aftermath of the Bandelier case, Pinkley's definition of what constituted a national monument took hold. Archaeological sites were and would remain national monuments. No longer would he have to worry that the best of his archaeological monuments would become national parks. Although his budget problems in the Southwest continued, Frank Pinkley's archaeological national monuments were safe from assaults from within the Park Service.

As the objectives of the two agencies became more defined, the potential for strife increased, especially in cases where both wanted to implement programs on the same tract of land. Ostensibly, the question of whether archaeological, recreational, scenic, or natural values should take precedence on the Pajarito Plateau forced the issue at Bandelier. But the real cause of conflict in New Mexico and elsewhere was that the contested area contained values that the programs of both agencies could develop. The resolution of the Pajarito Plateau situation addressed the specific issues of northern New Mexico, but set no precedents for other cases. Statute, not incommensurable values of land, dictated Pinkley's position. Pinkley's unlikely alliance with the Forest Service showed that commercial use of natural resources and archaeological preservation were not necessarily mutually exclusive, particularly when contrasted to the threat scenic preservation presented to both. A small national monument, centered on its archaeological component, posed no threat to the land management policies of the USFS because it required a comparatively small portion of Forest Service land.

But Pinkley's success at Bandelier created new difficulties in the Park Service. Horace Albright and others in the hierarchy were not happy with Pinkley's constant challenges to the status quo. From their perspective, the agency needed new and more professional standards. Pinkley had run the southwestern national monuments too long without proper supervision from above, and in their opinion, the monuments were being developed erratically and idiosyncratically, more in accord with Pinkley's standards than with those of the Park Service. With more than a quarter of a million visitors annually, the southwestern monument group had become too important to be left to the whims of a person who they saw as a cantankerous, aging iconoclast. Officials in Washington, D.C., began to feel that the monuments had to be run according to the same rules and regulations as other areas in the system.

This belief represented a major change in the policy of the NPS toward the national monuments, and it changed Pinkley's role in the agency. The Washington, D.C., office ceased to allow Pinkley the autonomy he had previously enjoyed. In the minds of many of the leaders of the Park Service, Pinkley represented an earlier, less sophisticated era of management, and although he maintained his position as the superintendent of southwestern national monuments, his influence waned during the 1930s.

During the 1930s, the Park Service became a self-consciously professional agency interested in creating its own traditions. Pinkley was a living reminder of an aspect of that legacy that the new hierarchy wanted to forget. With millions of dollars funneled into NPS areas through various federal New Deal works programs, the internal dynamics of the agency changed greatly. Pinkley's strict constructionism was antithetical to agency policy, and his personal style was no longer a factor in keeping up morale among monument employees. His achievements with the minuscule allotments of the 1920s seemed insignificant in an era of massive appropriation.

Notes

1. Harold K. Steen, *The United States Forest Service: A History* (Seattle: University of Washington Press, 1976), 153-59.

2. Frank Pinkley to Horace Albright, 27 July 1932, NA, RG 79, Series 6, Tonto National Monument, file 12-5.

3. T. T. Swift, Forest Supervisor, to Mr. Lee DeCalles, Miami, Arizona, 15 February 1930, NA, RG 79, Series 6, Tonto National Monument, file 12-5;

Frank Pinkley, Circular No. 5, attached to Park Service letter to Arno Cammerer, 27 December 1927, NA, RG 79, Series 6, Casa Grande, file 12-5.

4. Jesse L. Nusbaum confidential letter to Stephen T. Mather, 10 September 1925, NA, RG 79, Series 6, Proposed National Parks, file O-32, Cliff Cities.

5. Ibid.

6. During World War I, Franklin K. Lane's feelings of patriotism inspired him to grant grazing leases in Yosemite. The Sierra Club got wind of the project, and it was promptly terminated (see Shankland, *Steve Mather*, 203). Grazing was permitted in remote national parks like Lassen, and the precedent for grazing leases in national monuments was established at Mount Olympus National Monument in 1909 (see Shankland, *Steve Mather*, 170-71, for information about Lassen, and Ise, *Our National Park Policy*, 383-84, for Mount Olympus). Collecting dead timber first came up at Mukuntuweap in 1914. The GLO initially forbade collection of timber, but quickly reversed itself. It also allowed collecting at other remote monuments, particularly if there was a chance that the establishment of the monument inhibited the ability of locals to earn a living (see NA, RG 79, Series 6, Zion and Natural Bridges, files 12-5.

7. Nusbaum to Mather, 10 September 1925.

8. Jesse L. Nusbaum to John L. Morrow, 12 September 1925, NA, RG 79, Series 6, Proposed National Parks, file O-32, Cliff Cities.

9. Nusbaum to Mather, 10 September 1925.

10. Ibid.

11. Ibid.

12. Jesse L. Nusbaum to Horace Albright, 20 March 1928, NA, RG 79, Series 7, Bandelier National Monument, file 201. The announcement appeared in the 3 March 1928, Santa Fe *New Mexican*; Nusbaum attached a copy of the clipping to his bitter and despondent note.

13. A. B. Cammerer memo for the files, 3 December 1925; Minutes of the Eighth Meeting of the Coordinating Commission on National Parks and Forests, 8 December 1925; NA, RG 79, Series 6, Proposed National Parks, file 0-32, Cliff Cities.

14. Arthur Ringland to Edgar L. Hewett, 25 March 1927, NA, RG 79, Series 6, Proposed National Parks, file 0-32, Cliff Cities.

15. Frank Pinkley to Arthur E. Demaray, "Report on the Proposed Cliff Cities National Park," 23 May 1927, NA, RG 79, Series 6, Proposed National Parks, file 0-32, Cliff Cities.

16. Ibid.

17. Horace Albright to Stephen T. Mather, 8 June 1927, NA, RG 79, Series 6, Proposed National Parks, file 12-5, Cliff Cities.

18. Edgar L. Hewett to A. B. Cammerer, 17 January 1928; and Stephen

T. Mather to Edgar L. Hewett, 17 January 1928, NA, RG 79, Series 6, Proposed National Parks, file 0-32, Cliff Cities.

19. Jesse L. Nusbaum, Roger W. Toll, and M. R. Tillotson, "The Bandelier National Monument and the Proposed Cliff Cities National Park," 26 November 1930; Arno B. Cammerer to Horace Albright, 3 December 1930; and Horace Albright memo, 2 January 1931; NA, RG 79, Series 6, Proposed National Parks, file O-32, Cliff Cities.

20. Clark Wissler to Horace Albright, 12 February 1931, NA, RG 79, Series 7, Bandelier National Monument file 201.

21. Arno B. Cammerer memo for the files, 12 February 1931, NA, RG 79, Series 7, Bandelier National Monument, file 201.

22. Roger W. Toll to Horace Albright, 3 December 1930; Horace Albright memo, 2 January 1932; and Harold C. Bryant memo, 26 February 1931; NA, RG 79, Series 7, Bandelier National Monument, file 201.

23. U.S. Forester Maj. Robert Y. Stuart to Horace Albright, 10 November 1931, NA, RG 79, Series 7, Bandelier National Monument, file 201. Albright and Stuart corresponded about the Bandelier transfer for nearly two years.

24. Executive Proclamation 1991, *United States Statutes at Large*, L. 47 Stat. 2503 (1932).

9

The New Deal
and the National Monuments

THE IMPACT OF THE DEPRESSION OF THE 1930s changed the National Park Service and its national monuments in dramatic ways. The strong leadership of Franklin D. Roosevelt's secretary of the interior, Harold L. Ickes, the reorganization of the federal bureaucracy in 1933, and the federal emergency relief programs central to the New Deal made the NPS into one of the most formidable of federal agencies. By the end of the 1930s, the number of areas administered by the agency had more than doubled, permanent staff had increased substantially, and the scope of its responsibilities had greatly expanded. Conversely, the 1930s also ended the primacy of the national parks in the park system. As the park system encompassed a broader message, agency leaders recognized the importance of the national monuments and other new categories of park areas.

Changes during the decade accentuated trends toward central control and professional administration, and these shifts exacerbated existing conflicts between Frank Pinkley and his superiors in Washington, D.C.. Pinkley's position was incongruous in an agency that teemed with college-educated specialists. As the monuments became a valuable part of the system, the central administrators of the agency began to exert much more influence over the category than they previously had. Ironically, Pinkley's excellent work in the 1920s forced him into a battle for control of his domain. Pinkley refused to yield his autonomy, and a power struggle ensued between the aging superintendent and the developing Park Service bureaucracy, which was headed by

Albright, Cammerer, Demaray, and Dr. Harold C. Bryant, the head of the Division of Education, an Albright-inspired innovation to develop interpretive policy.

Although the trend toward professional administration first surfaced during the 1920s, policies established during Franklin D. Roosevelt's presidency became the catalyst for this reshaping of the Park Service. New Deal programs altered the role of the federal government in the economy. In 1933, after four years of unparalleled economic depression, federal agencies assumed many of the responsibilities of the private sector. The government provided credit for destitute farmers, unemployment compensation for workers, insurance on savings in banks, and an array of federally funded job training programs. In addition, federal programs funded the construction of roads, bridges, buildings, and dams across the nation. Large-scale government spending was the means to bring the United States back from the verge of economic ruin.

Nowhere was federal involvement more visible than in Ickes's Department of the Interior. A Bull Moose Republican in 1912, the irascible Ickes had always been an advocate of using government programs to further social goals. Despite differing political affiliations, Ickes and Roosevelt held similar views of the role of government in society, and when Roosevelt sought a Republican for his cabinet, Ickes was the logical choice for secretary of the interior. But his selection shocked many. Ickes lacked what most perceived to be the most elementary qualification for the post: as a resident of Illinois, he was not a westerner. But Roosevelt knew what he wanted when he recruited Ickes. The Department of the Interior managed large chunks of federally held land, and as the top man in Interior, Ickes became the leading advocate of many programs involving development of federal or state land by federal agencies.

Ickes was a staunch believer in the cause of conservation, but his point of view posed problems for the Park Service. To outsiders, the perspectives of the federal agencies responsible for the different facets of conservation, the Forest Service and the Park Service, seemed the same. Only insiders realized how distinct the two stances were. When Ickes arrived in Washington, D.C., early in 1933, the secretary seemed unaware of the subtle distinctions between the two agencies. Coming out of the Theodore Roosevelt-inspired Progressive tradition, Ickes announced that his sympathies lay with Gifford Pinchot, the former chief forester of the United States, and with the utilitarian conservationists, who advocated a policy of wise use of natural resources. Ickes acknowledged that he "learned the principles of conservation at [Pinchot's] feet." This squarely allied him with the primary adversary of the Park Service, and the spectre of Ickes worried the Park Service.[1]

One of Ickes's primary objectives was to rehabilitate the reputation of the Department of the Interior. Dating back to the nineteenth century, the department had an unequalled record of scandal, including the removal of the two commissioners of the GLO most instrumental in initiating federal efforts at preservation, Binger Hermann and W. A. Richards, early in the twentieth century. The Ballinger-Pinchot controversy of 1910 damaged the reputations of both Secretary of the Interior Richard A. Ballinger and Pinchot, and the notorious Teapot Dome scandal of the 1920s toppled Secretary of the Interior Albert B. Fall and further disgraced the department. Ickes thought that the Department of the Interior looked like a refuge of scoundrels and took it upon himself to restore public confidence in the department.

Ickes was prepared to be very tough, and the methods he used to upgrade his department terrorized the staff. He wanted the reputation of the Department of the Interior to rival that of any other federal agency. As a first step, Ickes selected Harry Slattery, a long-time associate of Pinchot's, as his personal assistant. Slattery had many endearing qualities to the reform-minded Ickes; the Teapot Dome scandal came to light largely through his efforts, and newspapers hailed the appointment as evidence of Ickes's sincerity. But in search of dishonesty and laziness in his department, Ickes condoned a variety of objectionable practices, including "intramural spying, telephone monitoring, eavesdropping, and the use of professional investigators." To uncover malingerers, Ickes himself patrolled the halls of the Department of the Interior. When they saw him coming, staffers from most agencies in the department quaked.

But the Park Service proved largely immune to Ickes's legendary wrath, and Horace Albright's personality provided most of the reason. Early in Ickes's reign, the competent and charming Albright made friends with his demanding superior. Ickes became convinced of Albright's reliability and respectability, and he probably admired the director's willingness to stand up to a man reputed to eat "half a dozen ten penny nails and few dozen buttered brick bats" for breakfast.[2]

Ickes came to trust Albright above anyone else in the department, and consequently, Albright played an important role in shaping policy at the Department of the Interior.

As a result of this relationship, Ickes became noticeably more sympathetic to the goals of the Park Service. The Forest Service was located in the Department of Agriculture and was beyond Ickes's control. He had vast influence over the Park Service, and as he learned to distinguish among the many perspectives that made up federal conservation, Ickes's allegiance to the Pinchot clique diminished, and he began to espouse a Park Service-like doctrine of preservation. He complained about road projects in the national parks, much to the delight of those within the NPS who opposed accommodating visitors under every circumstance. The secretary also thwarted conservationist projects that threatened the national parks, including a proposal by Idaho farmers and the Bureau of Reclamation to dam Lake Yellowstone for irrigation.

Ickes's approach to conservation and preservation emphasized federal initiative as a remedy for economic ills. He implemented programs in every agency under his control, and thanks to Albright, the Department of the Interior focused upon the Park Service. There was plenty to do in the park system; the 1920s had been a period of great growth unaccompanied by comparable expenditures for upkeep. Under the auspices of the Emergency Conservation Work (ECW) plan, the National Park Service became a vehicle for the employment of conservation workers. Five federal programs—the Civilian Conservation Corps (CCC), the Federal Emergency Relief Administration (FERA), the Public Works Administration (PWA), the Works Progress Administration (WPA), and the Civil Works Administration (CWA), also contributed heavily to the development of Park Service areas.

Policies that dictated massive federal expenditures upon federal and state property across the nation gave the Park Service a kind of leeway it had never enjoyed previously. The federal programs were so extensive that although the regular appropriation of the agency increased by approximately twenty-five percent between 1933 and 1940, the emergency appropriations nearly doubled the regular budget for each year from 1933 through 1940.[3] By 1940 the Park Service received more than $218 million in emergency funding, compared to a total of $132 million in regular appropriations.

The Park Service received so much money during the 1930s that it was able to spread its resources throughout the system. Frank Pinkley's complaints were muted by the extra money the agency received. The funding programs of the agency were no longer aimed almost exclusively at the national park category. The agency could initiate projects that had previously had low priority, could satisfy a much broader range of constituents, and could take on a more comprehensive vision of development. Many monuments, new and old, received their first attention from the Park Service during the 1930s, and the new programs filled a multitude of heretofore unmet needs.

The Civilian Conservation Corps was the most important of the programs that operated in Park Service areas. Modeled after a Forest Service program that put the unemployed to work in national forests in 1931, the CCC represented the kind of federal intervention that Roosevelt had promised the nation. It received the enthusiastic support of Park Service officials, who recognized it as a "potential bonanza." CCC camps in park areas proliferated rapidly, reaching a total of 118. National parks, monuments, and new designations like national historical parks all benefited from CCC programs. Camp workers did everything from refuse collection to technical conservation work such as planning and building fire roads. In twenty-three cases, the agency implemented programs focusing upon restoration, reconstruction, and new construction at places ranging from the Colonial National Monument to the Bandelier National Monument.[4]

Conceived out of social chaos, CCC camps attempted to embody order. In theory, successful enrollees were between the ages of eighteen and twenty-five, unemployed, unmarried, citizens of the United States, with no communicable disease or physical handicap, but often restrictions upon enrollment were waived or ignored. In practice, many who entered the camps were products of the depression who had grown up hungry, tough, and sometimes homeless. The discrepancy between ideal and actual enrollment contributed to the disciplinary atmosphere of many of the camps. Camp workers lived in a fashion styled after the military: officers commanded each camp and the men lived in barracks, dressed in government-issue military surplus clothing, and ate in the equivalent of mess halls. The bugling of reveille woke them each morning. They worked full forty-hour weeks, and were required to send home a substantial portion of their pay.[5]

Despite the rigor, CCC camps often integrated young men back into the mainstream of American life. Many of those unable to find work during the Depression of the 1930s felt alienated, and their experience with the CCC reintroduced values that they had long forgotten or never learned. The camp at Dinosaur National Monument had such an impact on some of its workers. In 1937 the project impressed A. H. Dahm, a visitor from Denver, "because the men in [the] camp have been taught to take an interest in life, and actually seemed very pleased, and had no desire to leave there." He complimented "the splendid way in which [the Park Service] taught these transient boys the finer things of life and how to make the most of their talents."[6] The Dinosaur camp seemed a fulfillment of everything Franklin D. Roosevelt dreamed of when he initiated the broadly based work relief recovery programs. Not only was the camp doing important work, but its leaders were teaching important values to people who might not otherwise be exposed to them.

Social accomplishments aside, the national monuments benefited from the development that CCC labor offered. The monuments were so diverse that the value of a CCC camp or side camp varied according to the three different kinds of areas in the category. Each of the three types of monuments—archaeological, natural, and historical—had a range of needs and newly found wealth allowed the agency to develop flexible programs that fit the peculiarities of individual areas. This presented a dramatic contrast from the 1920s, when the Park Service had little money and so few titular distinctions that Pinkley's archaeological assistants were labeled *park naturalists*. The increased significance astounded Pinkley and his associates. They resolved to take advantage of the new opportunities.

Prior to the New Deal, archaeological national monuments suffered most from lack of protection and inadequate funds for interpretation. As Pinkley watched the development of national parks throughout the nation, he became angry when he thought of the conditions at the monuments. Federal emergency relief programs offered a solution. Even the Southwest shared in the largesse of the decade. Pinkley had less to complain about as CCC workers implemented programs that he could have only dreamed about earlier.

Bandelier National Monument became one of the model CCC projects carried out at an archaeological national monument because of Pinkley's interest. CCC workers created a physical plant worthy of Pinkley's conception of the significance of the monument. Within a month of their arrival in 1933, CCC workers built the first automobile road to Frijoles Canyon. Initially the road was a twelve-foot-wide truck trail, but a CWA appropriation in 1934 widened it to twenty-two feet. Many tourists, to whom the previously existing foot trail was an actual barrier, now had a closer look at the mysteries of the canyon. Federal emergency relief programs also constructed a visitor center, an administrative building, and when Pinkley decided the existing lodge in the canyon interfered with his administration, a new hotel adjacent to the Park Service facilities. A trained archaeologist, Paul Reiter, supervised the stabilization by CCC camp workers of the Tyuonyi ruins, a primary feature at the monument. Later, when the road brought more travelers than the agency could handle, custodians at the monument trained CCC workers as summer tour guides. When the Park Service had acquired the area in 1932, there were two dilapidated forest ranger cabins in Frijoles Canyon, and the first park ranger drank his water from Frijoles Creek. By 1940 an extensive physical plant existed, complete with electricity, pumped water, five homes for Park Service people, and a paved road to the bottom of the canyon.[7]

The CCC also worked to conserve natural resources. Although it was primarily an archaeological national monument, Bandelier encompassed more than 26,000 acres, including steep canyons and open mesas. The CCC camp implemented wildlife conservation, forest maintenance, fire protection, and trail construction programs. Chaco Canyon also benefited from its CCC camp, where in addition to assisting archaeological investigation, the workers performed an array of development work to protect natural resources. Many other archaeological and natural monuments, ranging from Pinnacles in California to such new creations as the Capitol Reef National Monument in Utah, also benefited from CCC-sponsored development programs.[8]

The first candidates for CCC work were national monuments that contained natural features. They offered innumerable opportunities for conservation work. Many were large areas, consisting of tracts of rugged country and visual formations. Most had few roads, trails, or other facilities and lacked even rudimentary maintenance programs. Throughout the 1920s, the agency had never had the funds to manage places like the Glacier Bay National Monument in Alaska, which included more than 2 million acres. Remote and inaccessible, it received few visitors, and the little agency money for monuments was put to use in areas that attracted tourists. The Park Service also ignored places in the lower forty-eight states. The agency did not allocate funds for Lava Beds National Monument, a 45,000-acre tract of lava flows, natural bridges, and other volcanic phenomena in northern California where the Modoc Indians hid from federal troops in the 1860s, until the CCC camp there opened. Nearly all the natural-area national monuments that existed prior to 1933 received CCC assistance. CCC enrollees fought fires, battled insects and fungus, built roads and truck trails, and accomplished an array of other conservation work.[9]

Natural national monuments that the Park Service believed had tourist potential were prime candidates for federal emergency relief development programs. The Capitol Reef National Monument, established in August 1937, was this type of monument. For nearly a decade before proclamation of the monument, the NPS had pursued acquisition of the area. Located in southern Utah, the area which Steve Mather wanted so badly to develop for the park system, Capitol Reef encompassed 37,060 acres, approximately fifty- eight square miles. Because it had the potential for entering the southwestern network of agency areas and lacked facilities for visitors, it became a likely candidate for the ECW/CCC programs. A CCC side camp opened there in April 1938, staffed with twenty-five men and a foreman from the main camp at Bryce Canyon National Park. The workers embarked on a typical development program: construction of a camp for the workers, road improvement, and the construction of a ranger station, fences, a stock driveway, and horse trails. The attractions of the new monument were natural features; CCC labor and government money built an infrastructure to facilitate its administration.[10]

Cedar Breaks National Monument, created in 1933, also provided the Park Service with a way to use the CCC to its advantage. The Forest Service had administered the tract prior to 1933, but the Park Service sought it, and Cedar Breaks became the center of one more interagency dispute. As at Bandelier, Forest Service officials felt that NPS management would restrict other uses of land in the region. Unlike Bandelier, there were no archaeological ruins in the Cedar Breaks vicinity, and the Park Service had a more difficult time making its claim. Cedar Breaks was simply a series of vistas, which Forest Service officials did not believe required NPS interpretation. Albright insisted otherwise in a series of letters to Chief Forester Maj. Robert Y. Stuart, who suffered a nervous breakdown during the period. The weakened Stuart eventually acquiesced to his counterpart. The monument was established shortly after Albright left the agency in August 1933.

True to the Albright legacy, the NPS found a different way to present the monument. Park Service interpretation presented Cedar Breaks as the antecedent of the cliff formations at Bryce Canyon and Zion national parks and emphasized its place in the evolution of geology of southern Utah. Because the area was essentially visual, the CCC camp at Cedar Breaks built roadside stations that explained the scenic vistas in that context, and from an interpretive standpoint, Cedar Breaks became a valuable addition to the system.[11]

More important, development programs blurred the distinctions between the national monuments and the national parks. After 1933 monument custodians no longer had to maintain their monuments single-handedly. Development brought the cutting edge of agency planning to the formerly second-class monument category. The New Deal gave the Park Service the means and opportunity to fulfill its dual mandate to preserve and develop in a comprehensive fashion, and the agency responded to the challenge. No longer were the categories of nomenclature distinct. With federal emergency assistance from the CCC, WPA, PWA, CWA, and FERA, the monuments became as integral a part of the system as the national parks.

But not all national monuments required the kind of development that New Deal money provided, and CCC programs also created new distinctions within the monument category. Some monuments established during the 1930s, such as Organ Pipe Cactus, Channel Islands, and Joshua Tree, were not suited for the development programs of the New Deal. The Department of Commerce initially pushed the Channel Islands National Monument, five inaccessible islands off the coast of Santa Barbara, California, on the reluctant NPS. Because of lack of access and questions about its suitability as a park area, the agency chose not to implement development programs there. During the 1930s, scientific use became the primary value of the Channel Islands.[12]

As a result of the growing scientific orientation developing in national park planning, Organ Pipe Cactus and Joshua Tree were "representative-area" national monuments, established to preserve representative portions of land containing unique desert flora. In the view of the agency, Organ Pipe Cactus and Joshua Tree were also "primarily of scientific rather than popular value," and capital development seemed pointless.[13] Consequently, the 330,690 acres of Organ Pipe Cactus and the 838,253.30 acres of Joshua Tree remained outside mainstream planning during the 1930s.

These two areas were important evidence of the growing preoccupation with ecological communities in the Park Service. The national parks established during the first thirty years of the twentieth century were largely confined to mountaintops; Mount Rainier, established in 1898, and Grand Teton, in 1929, were the beginning and end of the period in which this kind of national park dominated. When college-educated biologists and their scientific peers began to shape Park Service policy, they came to believe that the system contained too many mountaintops and not enough ecosystems. The specialists sought a more comprehensive approach to the natural world than the preservation of scenery. This suited the objectives of Mather and Albright, who sought ways to broaden the national park category. The tenets of modern ecology formed a minority current within the agency, but this discipline offered a way to broaden the domain of the agency. As a result, during the 1920s the Park Service began to pursue the Everglades area of southern Florida.

Again the Antiquities Act offered the means to circumvent the congressional sanction that the establishment of a national park required. Scientific goals became important to the Park Service, and when hamstrung by Congress, agency officials resorted to the Antiquities Act as the most effective means to acquire areas that they believed the system needed. Saguaro National Monument, established by executive fiat in 1933, was the first "representative area" included in the park system. Prior to the creation of Joshua Tree and Organ Pipe Cactus, the Park Service finally succeeded in preserving the ecosystem of the Everglades. Yet the Everglades National Park was an anomaly among national parks. Congress remained more cognizant of the "visual experience" that Steve Mather promoted and did not yet recognize ecological communities as valid park units.[14]

The preservation of representative areas was important to more than specialists within the agency. Even during the greatest period of development of the Park Service the Antiquities Act provided officials with an avenue to shape alternative futures for the park system. Along with the Everglades, monuments like Saguaro, Organ Pipe Cactus,

Joshua Tree, and in the 1940s, Jackson Hole became precursors of
the later expansion by the agency into the preservation of biotas and
other less visually spectacular phenomena.

By the 1930s, most of the visually exciting natural areas in the nation
were already reserved. Scenic places in the West not included in the
park system generally belonged to the Forest Service. Two new national parks, Olympic and Kings Canyon, established in 1938 and
1940 respectively, offered exquisite scenic vistas, but each resulted in
extensive battles with the Forest Service, which grudgingly provided
much of the additional land. The price for scenic views became too
high for the Park Service, and its revived scientific interest offered a
different strategy. The continued expansion of its domain required
the agency to redefine the values for new areas.

The monuments became central to the future of the agency, and
Pinkley found himself further outside the mainstream than ever before. During the 1920s, the agency acknowledged his efforts but ignored his areas. During the 1930s, New Deal funding programs served
as a backdrop while the agency supported his areas but ignored his
efforts. In many ways, the New Deal gave Pinkley what he wanted
most: the money to implement programs at his national monuments.
But changes in the agency and the conditions that the central administration attached to funding minimized Pinkley's role. College-educated specialists and consultants dominated planning and policy-making
in the Park Service, Pinkley's autonomy in the Southwest diminished,
and he chafed at control from above.

The New Deal accelerated the trends that frustrated Pinkley. During
the 1920s, the agency began to move toward professionalization and
central oversight as Mather and Albright began to consolidate their
power. Albright particularly envisioned an institutional future for the
agency, and Pinkley's role at Bandelier did little to endear him to the
upper echelon of the agency. When Albright became director in 1929,
he implemented a rigid agenda, centered on rounding out the park
system, and he was less inclined than his predecessor to tolerate challenges from within the agency.

By 1930, the NPS hierarchy knew that it had to restrict Pinkley's
role in the Southwest. He ran his park areas so well that the southwestern national monument group attracted considerable attention.
Pinkley's position contradicted the realities of administering the Park
Service. From Albright's national park-oriented perspective, the su-

perintendent was an obstacle to the process of arranging the national park system to the advantage of the agency.

By the end of the 1920s, the Park Service had secured its position in the federal bureaucracy, and the process of professionalizing the agency began in earnest. The authorization of the three eastern national parks—Shenandoah, Great Smoky Mountains, and Mammoth Cave—during the 1920s ensured that the Park Service had a role that other federal agencies did not. From these roots, NPS officials sought to broaden their focus. Agency administrators wanted to provide visitors with more than an inspirational visual experience when they came to the national parks. Scenic national parks left an imprint on the visiting public, but the emotional response of the public often overlooked the agency that kept the parks. The Park Service needed to find a way to make the public appreciate its personnel and their efforts as well as its holdings.

As Mather's assistant, Albright considered the educational possibilities of the national parks. When he became director, Park Service interest in educating visitors, "interpretation" in the parlance of the agency, increased. Throughout the 1920s, individual rangers made casual efforts to explain the significance of specific areas to the public, and Pinkley and his staff explained prehistory, but Albright sought a more comprehensive approach. He engaged experts to develop a policy for serving visitors and created the Committee on the Study of Educational Problems in the National Parks in 1929. Albright enlisted Dr. Clark Wissler of the American Museum of Natural History, Dr. John C. Merriam of the Carnegie Institute, Dr. Harold C. Bryant of the California Fish and Game Commission, Dr. Hermon C. Bumpus of the American Association of Museums, and Dr. Frank Oastler, a medical doctor who had long been interested in the national parks, to design programs to convey the significance of the sites to the public.[15]

Like most of Albright's innovations, the educational programs focused upon the national parks. As Park Service visitation increased significantly throughout the 1920s, presenting national parks as vast playgrounds became too narrow a perspective for the agency. The Forest Service too easily copied this kind of presentation. In the climate of the late 1920s, when a reorganization of the federal bureaucracy seemed imminent, the Park Service needed to differentiate itself in order to assert its merit. Earlier in the decade, summer nature walks with rangers began at Yosemite, and Albright seized upon this concept as the way to make a visit to the national parks an educational experience.

But Albright had not reckoned with Pinkley. The idea of a comprehensive educational program was not new to him. By 1930, Pinkley had spent nearly thirty years explaining prehistoric people to the public. Even as the Park Service promoted the national parks as playgrounds, Pinkley used the national monuments as educational tools, but many of his most innovative programs were hampered by a lack of funding. From his perspective, educational programs that focused on the natural features of the parks were a waste of time and money. The archaeological national monuments offered a better medium. Pinkley had ideas galore. In his mind, all he lacked was money to implement them. As a result, he was instantly at odds with a commission of experts hired to tell him how to do his job.

The cantankerous Pinkley was on solid ground with these complaints. The places Steve Mather had made into national parks did not inspire the average visitor to ask questions about natural science. Instead, a view of the Grand Canyon, El Capitan in Yosemite, Mount Rainier, or Tower Falls in Yellowstone left people breathless. Pinkley believed that agency specialists were now trying to intellectualize a largely emotional experience to gain political advantage. He contended that the agency would spend a vast sum of money on interpreting the national parks, the effort would fail, and in a short while, the Park Service would find its interpretive policy in shambles.[16]

Pinkley's objections ran deeper than professional criticism. He saw the agency changing around him and felt threatened. Never a reticent man, Pinkley complained about the emergence of educational professionals and did his best to engage Harold C. Bryant, who became the head of the Division of Education, in controversy. Always ready to assert his position, the Boss loudly demanded better funding. Pinkley wanted a mandate to continue to develop the national monuments as he had throughout the 1920s.

Albright was less than sympathetic both to Pinkley and his national monuments, and by the end of 1931, he had had enough of Pinkley's carping. As director, Albright established an hierarchical central authority that was new to the agency and demanded compliance from his staff. Under Mather, park superintendents had run the day-to-day affairs of the agency, and after 1929 Albright had trouble centralizing authority. Albright soon decided that the field administrators of the agency, including Pinkley, were lax in implementing his orders. He saw a "growing carelessness" in carrying out his directives. Albright professed indignation, asserting that "omissions . . . in many cases have grown to alarming proportions."[17] Although not aimed specifically at Pinkley, Albright's comments summarized the widening gulf of discontent between the director and his most important employee in the national monuments.

The crux of the problem was that Pinkley was used to having his way, and he perceived executive oversight as interference. He had lost sight of the larger objectives of the agency, and in Pinkley's increasingly narrow view, Albright's creation of the educational division was a particular nuisance. Given the same resources, Pinkley was confident he could achieve more than the so-called experts could. No matter what Albright said, Pinkley was not prepared to relinquish his power to make decisions about the future of the places under his care.

Pinkley simply could not adjust to the new realities of the 1930s. He received the kind of attention he demanded, but could not compromise with those who gave it. Unfortunately, attention for the southwestern monuments came too late for the superintendent, who resented the intrusion into what he regarded as *his* sphere. Instead of compromising, Pinkley created adversarial relationships. He championed his achievements and compared them to those of other departments within the agency. By his own standards, Pinkley came out ahead, and this biased self-measurement became his justification for frequent assaults upon the policies of his rivals.

The national monuments were never in a secure position within the agency, and the new emphasis on education in the national parks made the superintendent wary. To retain his position, Pinkley attacked the Division of Education throughout the 1930s. In his view, the new entity duplicated his efforts and spent money that rightfully belonged to the national monuments. The *Nature Notes* publication series encroached upon Pinkley's area of expertise. He regarded Education as his chief competitor in the race for visitors, and Pinkley acted as if he thought he could regain his autonomy by outdrawing the places where the experts implemented their programs.

Although past the age of fifty, Pinkley felt like a fresh recruit, and his responses exacerbated conflict with the specialists. To consolidate his position, Pinkley pulled out old ideas and began to implement them. He also sought public support for his position, using pamphlets and printed material to reach a wider audience in the Southwest. One such endeavor was the *Epitaph*, Pinkley's answer to the *Nature Notes* series that Education published. Pinkley wrote for the publication in the colloquial style he had always used with his custodians, and he made it available to the general public. Bryant did not like the *Epitaph* and, on 12 May 1932, sent Pinkley a note that expressed displeasure at its style. Pinkley used familiar expressions like "you folks" and "the gang," and Bryant felt that the *Epitaph* was not professional. "If you desire a standing with scientists and educators," Bryant wrote in a classic bureaucratic tone, "care must be taken to avoid this kind of presentation. The general public can be interested fully as well by the use of simple words and thus the support of all can be maintained."[18] From Bryant's perspective, good grammar and proper English were essential components of any government document.

Perhaps intimidated by Bryant's fast rise in the agency, Pinkley took the criticism as a personal attack. Bryant embodied the trend toward professionalism; he had a Ph.D., whereas Pinkley lacked formal education. Pinkley announced that if requested, he would resign from the *Epitaph*, ostensibly to avoid embarrassing his rivals. Then Bryant could "drop the Epitaph in the same pod with the other Nature Notes, which are certainly alike as a row of peas," he cynically continued. "It will have a standing with scientists and educators and the chief end of man will be served."[19] Pinkley opposed Bryant's philosophy but the hierarchy obviously supported the trend towards professionalization. Against these odds, Pinkley knew he had little chance.

The battle over the tone of agency publications revealed a deeper rift over the constituency of the agency. Both Pinkley and Bryant sought to advance the standing of the agency, but they envisioned its audience differently. Pinkley sought to appeal to people on their own terms, and his experience showed that southwesterners responded to a colloquial style. He recognized that anthropologists, archaeologists, and scientists were an important part of his constituency, but he believed that in the Southwest, scientists were not as formal as their eastern counterparts. The *Epitaph*, he thought, did something unique. It crossed boundaries and appealed to both professionals and tourists. Bryant believed that credibility with the scientific community and popularity with tourists were compatible goals, and a well-constructed, professional publication could achieve both. Bryant thought that the agency had an obligation to elevate the standards of the traveling public. In his opinion, the *Epitaph* did not achieve either goal, and he insisted that Pinkley review his editorial policy. Pinkley refused and threatened to resign from the paper after writing one final and inflammatory column.[20]

Another individualist-professional split strained the agency. Bryant represented the modern professional agency, and Pinkley its traditional posture. The advent of specialists like Bryant affected the way the agency saw its mission, and conflict with proponents of earlier values was inevitable. The Division of Education believed that it served an increasingly educated constituency and wanted to impress it with formal agency publications. Pinkley thought that Bryant was posturing and that his ends were pretentious. "We have a lot of government publications on our office shelves which are as dignified as a plugged hat," Pinkley remarked to Albright, "and nobody ever read the first page of them."[21] In Pinkley's estimation, status interested Bryant more than attracting an audience.

The consequences of increasing professionalization denied Pinkley the latitude he had enjoyed during the 1920s, and the hierarchy came down hard upon its iconoclast. Associate Director Arthur E. Demaray took one look at the final column Pinkley proposed for his resignation from the *Epitaph* and curtly responded: "I don't think Pinkley should be allowed to use the Epitaph to put forward his own views." Albright landed even more heavily on the superintendent. "I am a little out of patience," he wrote, "with this attitude which is so different from any you have previously taken. I have always figured you as a good soldier. For you to sit back and pout [and say] you feel like quitting and not being associated with [the *Epitaph*], is taking an unusual position for you or any other of our representatives in the field." Albright would not tolerate this kind of insubordination and even went so far as to remind Pinkley that he held his position "solely because of [his] ability to interpret and apply Service, Departmental and Government rules and policies and to follow instructions from headquarters." While Albright guided the agency, Pinkley would have to obey the same regulations as everyone else.[22]

Ironically, as the monuments began to receive attention from the central administration of the agency, the man who made them important could not adjust to limitations upon his authority. Thanks to Pinkley's efforts, the monuments became too important to be left to the hard-bitten superintendent. Although Pinkley felt the task of structuring new policies should be his, Albright was not prepared to let him have that kind of control.

This fray shaped the evolution of interpretation throughout the southwestern national monument group. Pinkley continued to push for his understanding of the prehistoric Southwest, realizing that a new interpretive program that focused upon the national parks diminished his role considerably. He retrenched to his home territory, relying upon the public he had spent thirty years cultivating. Pinkley replaced the *Epitaph* with the *Southwestern National Monuments Monthly Report*, a mimeographed collection of reports of the custodians, which Pinkley liberally spiced with his own thoughts. Each month, the Boss authored a column called "Ruminations," in which he aired his point of view. Ostensibly aimed at custodians in the national monuments, the monthly report also circulated widely in the Southwest. Bryant and the other specialists chafed at Pinkley's colloquialisms and homespun aphorisms, but they could not wrest the Southwest from him. Direct confrontation failed. Pinkley would have to undermine himself before the hierarchy could limit his power.

The New Deal accelerated the conflict between Pinkley and the specialists by increasing the scope of executive oversight in the southwestern monuments. New Deal money was both the solution to Pinkley's problems and the cause of new, more severe antagonism with the central office. Despite successful programs such as the one at Bandelier National Monument, Pinkley found himself grappling with what seemed to him an amorphous bureaucratic monster. As his influence waned, Pinkley became even more rigid in upholding his version of agency standards. He held his ground, which put him continually at odds with the central administration of the agency. The eventuality that Arno B. Cammerer had envisioned a decade earlier came true. Pinkley became a destructive influence within the agency that he loved, and his superiors decided that they had to stop Pinkley before he hurt the public image of the Park Service.

In the end, Pinkley's personal intransigence took matters out of the hands of the Park Service. In February 1934, while Harold L. Ickes was settling into his job in Washington, D.C., Pinkley became involved in a controversy that called his judgement into question. He refused guide service at the Casa Grande to Arizona state senator James Minotto, Henry Horner, the governor of Illinois and an old friend of Ickes, and Ernest Palmer, commissioner of insurance for the state of

Illinois, because the men arrived almost an hour after the end of posted visiting hours. Minotto had come to Arizona as a millionaire and was well-known for his overbearing and arrogant behavior. Embarrassed and displeased at the treatment offered to himself and his friends, Minotto complained to Ickes.

Ickes seized upon the Horner-Minotto situation as concrete evidence of his suspicions and pursued Minotto's complaint vigorously. Albright's political sophistication made the Park Service largely immune to the terror Ickes inspired, but when Albright resigned as director in August 1933, the autonomy of the agency went with him. Ickes tried to replace Albright with someone from outside the agency. Albright then persuaded the secretary to appoint Associate Director Cammerer to the top post after Ickes's first choice, Newton B. Drury of the Save-The-Redwoods-League, declined. The genial Cammerer and the blustering Ickes were a less than optimal match. Ickes quickly took an obvious dislike to Cammerer that endured until Drury replaced him at the head of the Park Service in 1941. Ickes also distrusted what he thought was the bureaucratic mentality that promoted incompetence and covered for the mistakes of peers.[23]

Never as decisive as Albright, Cammerer faced a serious dilemma. Less than six months into his term as director, Cammerer was caught between two personalities more powerful than his own. Cammerer had known Pinkley for nearly two decades and was well aware of his devotion to the promotion of southwestern travel and Casa Grande, but Ickes was his superior. The morale of the agency and its position in the Department of the Interior were at stake. On 24 February 1934 Cammerer decided to uphold his field staff in the battle with Washington, D.C. He told Pinkley that he "would bet my last dollar that there is something wrong with these charges, since, if any discourtesies by any chance could happen in the National Park system, it would never be under your jurisdiction."[24] Cammerer hoped that the whole situation was a grotesque misunderstanding.

Pinkley did little to help his cause. Minotto sent him a copy of the letter to Ickes, and in response, Pinkley took the offensive. His letter revealed that he considered himself the supreme authority at Casa Grande. He believed that Minotto planned to "run in and look around for ten or fifteen minutes, and then drive on," Pinkley snidely remarked. "I gave you the regular treatment . . . I thought, as a snap judgement, that you would not steal anything, and were not the name writing vandal we have to guard against; so let down *my own rule* (not one from the Washington office!), and let you go without a guide." Indeed, Pinkley asserted that the men stayed only a short time, and in his mind, if a visitor could not stay more than a brief period, they certainly did not need his service as a guide. "A guide can no more tell you about the Casa Grande Ruins in twenty minutes," Pinkley rudely continued, "than you can tell a man all about the law, or Medicine."[25] Condescending and argumentative, Pinkley assailed Minotto. He accused Minotto of gracelessness equal to the discourtesy that the senator attributed to him.

Pinkley hoped to turn the situation to his advantage. He wanted Cammerer and Ickes to understand the nature of his major problems. In a more contrite response than he sent Minotto, Pinkley explained to Cammerer that the episode was typical of his problems with visitors. Ignoring the charges against him, he addressed what he perceived as the pivotal issue. Visitors frequently arrived after hours and demanded service, and their attitude bothered him. Few seemed to realize that although Pinkley lived in the compound, he was a government employee who worked regular hours. "We have them come in after dark many times," Pinkley complained, "and assume that we are some sort of watchmen who will light a lantern and lead them through dark and gloomy passages of the ruin where they can get a thrill."[26] Pinkley tried to educate his visitors, but not everyone appreciated his efforts. The unfortunate situation with Minotto helped him to outline a serious problem in his area.

Others in the Park Service were less supportive, but Cammerer still took Pinkley's side. Associate Director Demaray attached a memo to Minotto's complaint that read: "it looks as if Pinkley fell down this time." Cammerer, however, told Ickes that the incident was insignificant and submitted a draft of a reprimand for Pinkley. Although he suggested a five-day suspension without pay for Ranger Frank Fish, about whom Minotto also complained, Cammerer supported Pinkley completely and even wrote letters to Palmer and Horner exonerating Pinkley and implicating Fish.[27] Cammerer was Pinkley's friend, and his response seemed too conciliatory. Ickes also wanted his say.

The boisterous secretary of the interior was angry. Employees of his department had insulted two of his personal friends, confirming every bad feeling he had about perpetuated bureaucracy. Cammerer's lack of leadership in other situations perturbed Ickes, and his decisive support of Pinkley seemed out of character. This evidence of bureaucratic protectionism was too much. Ickes's assistant, Elbert K. Burlew, a veteran of the Hoover administration whose job Albright had saved when Ickes came to Washington, D.C., read Cammerer's reprimand and was also displeased. "If you send the 'reprimand' as prepared, Pinkley will not recognize it as such," Burlew told Ickes. "It is one of the best letters of recommendation I have seen in a long time." Ickes agreed, telling Cammerer that the letter went "out of the way to tell Pinkley what a fine person he is. It creates the impression that he could not possibly do anything that would subject him to criticism."[28]

Never one to ignore an opportunity to attack his favorite targets, Ickes followed through on the impulse to exert his authority. He told Burlew to write a letter that was an indictment of Pinkley, and irritated with Cammerer and Pinkley, Ickes chastised both. "The fact that charges of discourtesy against Mr. Pinkley have not in your judgement been proved," Ickes informed Cammerer, "does not call for a letter of such enthusiastic adulation as you have drafted." Ickes chose to believe Minotto, and when he castigated Pinkley, Ickes cited Governor Horner's response, which he believed corroborated Minotto's charges, as the important evidence in the case.[29]

In his indignation, Ickes let his personal dislike for Cammerer and bureaucracies in general interfere with his judgement. Horner's letter to Ickes supported Pinkley's version of the events much more than it did Minotto's. "Personally," the governor concluded, "I have no complaint to make. Please feel there is no apology due to myself or Mr. Palmer."[30] Humiliated in an effort to impress his friends, Minotto probably overreacted. But Ickes was determined to show everyone in the Park Service who was in charge of the Department of the Interior.

Instead of Cammerer's reprimand, Pinkley received harsh sanction. Ickes found Pinkley's response to the situation unprofessional. No matter how Pinkley justified it, his "established resentment against late visitors" was unacceptable to Ickes, who did not believe that "discourtesy to the unfortunate individual who may unintentionally transgress a code that you have fixed in your mind" was an appropriate solution. Furthermore, Ickes found Pinkley's response to Minotto "distinctly objectionable." The letter destroyed any qualms that Ickes had about judging Pinkley guilty, for it "clearly discloses an attitude that would motivate in the mistreatment of visitors." Ickes suspended Pinkley from duty for five days without pay and informed Cammerer that "a man who will write a letter like that should either correct his attitude instantly or be dismissed from the service."[31]

If Pinkley needed more evidence that the Southwest was no longer his autocracy, Ickes certainly provided it. Ickes was an advocate of strong centralized leadership, and he demanded that every employee of the Department of the Interior behave according to his standards. Horner and Palmer were his friends, and Casa Grande was his responsibility. The situation embarrassed Ickes, and he felt compelled to do something. Even after Horner's conciliatory letter, which Ickes seems to have purposely misinterpreted, his bias against bureaucratic behavior and personal dislike of Cammerer influenced his decision. In Ickes's Department of the Interior, underlings had to watch what they did.

But Pinkley also shouldered responsibility for the incident with Minotto. Long before Harold L. Ickes became secretary of the interior, Pinkley developed what Ickes called an "evident feeling of proprietorship" about Casa Grande.[32] Since the turn of the century, Pinkley had run the ruin and personally entertained more than 100,000 visitors. His work was indirectly responsible for the visit of Minotto and Horner. If Pinkley were not there, Casa Grande likely would have remained as obscure as the Gila Cliff Dwelling or the Fossil Cycad national monuments. Pinkley created visitor interest in Casa Grande and insisted upon the guided tours that figured in the incident with Minotto. Casa Grande was his home, and his life was closely tied to it. He was not prepared to relinquish that control, particularly to the people who ignored his predicament throughout the 1920s.

Although he felt wronged, Pinkley accepted Ickes's decision as gracefully as he could, and the episode changed the superintendent's view of his position within the agency. During the 1920s, Pinkley had decided that the spotlight could only help the national monuments. He gravitated toward it, attending meetings, making pronouncements, and generally calling attention to himself and the monuments. But later in 1934, he tried to avoid attending the annual conference of superintendents in Washington, D.C., his usual forum for airing grievances. Fearing humiliation at the hands of his growing number of rivals, Pinkley did not want to face his peers.

Relations between Pinkley and Washington, D.C. continued to deteriorate. Nothing the Division of Education did pleased Pinkley. If

Bryant did not offer assistance, Pinkley felt slighted. If specialists from Education proposed programs for the national monuments, Pinkley felt threatened. From Bryant's perspective, every effort was futile. The status quo did not please Pinkley either, and after 1934, his attacks upon Education escalated.

Pinkley's position became increasingly paradoxical. He wanted funding from Education, but disregarded its advice. No matter what Bryant offered, it fell short of what Pinkley thought he deserved, and to upset his rival, Pinkley often acted as if Bryant's offers were insulting. But Bryant had the ear of the leadership of the agency, and the interpretation programs in the national parks were successful. Educational money and advice were intrinsically linked, and Pinkley could not have one without the other.

Throughout the 1930s, the central administration and its authority on the periphery clashed. Pinkley publicly assailed the museum practices of the Division of Education, and Cammerer had to determine policy for the agency. Although he was the head of the Park Service, Cammerer had considerable sympathy for Pinkley's position. But in the end Cammerer was forced to accept that professionalization was the direction of the future for the NPS. On 5 October 1936 Cammerer flatly ordered Pinkley not to attack Education in public.[33] Cammerer wanted criticism brought up via the proper channels instead of in a public referendum. The agency had too much at stake to appear to be squabbling.

Pinkley responded as an outsider, loudly pronouncing his position. This set the stage for open conflict, and Cammerer had an intraservice war on his hands. Pinkley lacked another forum in which to vent his anger, and after Cammerer's rejoinder, he chose to continue his attacks. Cammerer did not want the situation to escalate, but he could not make Pinkley leave the educational division alone. Pinkley's wrath was no longer an occasional occurrence. He appeared to have a systematic plan of attack and did not think of letting up.

Pinkley had outlived his usefulness to the Park Service. Like Richard Wetherill before him, he could not see that his time had passed. Although the Park Service had developed in no small part because of what Pinkley had accomplished, there was little place for an uncompromising individualist like Pinkley in the new Park Service. He had to change or find himself bucking an increasingly powerful central administration on a regular basis. Although consistently able to achieve excellent results with very little money, Pinkley always went his own way. Adjusting to bureaucratic responsibility would not be easy.

By the 1930s, there was little other than his work in Pinkley's life, and the stress soon affected his health. His wife, Edna, died suddenly in 1929, and afterwards, he totally immersed himself in his work. Even failing health did not deter him. In 1937 he had a serious heart attack that forced him to temporarily reduce his work load. A kind of peace descended upon the Southwest. Pinkley became less aggressive, and the view of him in the agency softened. In 1938 Pinkley finally convinced Cammerer to approve a school to prepare future custodians for work in the national monuments in the manner that park rangers were trained for the parks. He had first suggested this idea during the 1920s, but it was not approved until the end of 1939. Throughout the winter of 1939-40, an ecstatic and again healthy Pinkley made plans for the opening of the school. On 14 February 1940, as he finished the introductory speech at the opening of the first session, Frank Pinkley collapsed on the podium and died of heart failure.[34]

It was a fitting way to die for a man so passionate about his work. The national monuments were his life, and he achieved the goal that perpetuated his system of care. Pinkley created the system that facilitated archaeological tourism and was instrumental in bringing the Southwest to the attention of the American public. Millions of people visited the monuments he had struggled to preserve, and because of his efforts, they left knowing a great deal more than when they arrived. Although Pinkley's enthusiasm and energy brought the southwestern national monuments to the attention of the Park Service and the nation, there was one thing he could not do. He could not make prehistoric culture more interesting to the American public than its Euro-American past.

Notes

1. Donald C. Swain, "Harold Ickes, Horace Albright, and the Hundred Days: A Study in Conservation Administration," *Pacific Historical Review* 34 (November 1965): 455-65; Donald C. Swain, "The National Park Service and the New Deal 1933-1940," *Pacific Historical Review* 41 (August 1972): 312-32; and Barry Mackintosh, "Harold Ickes and the National Park Service," *Journal of Forest History* 29 (April 1985): 78-84. *The Secret Diaries of Harold L. Ickes: The*

First Thousand Days, 1933-1936 (New York: Simon and Schuster, 1954) pre-
sents the activities of this time in the secretary's own words.

2. Swain, "Ickes, Albright, and the Hundred Days."

3. Harlan D. Unrau and G. Frank Williss, Administrative History: Expansion
of the National Park Service in the 1930s (Denver: National Park Service, 1983),
75.

4. Ibid., 84; Swain, "Ickes, Albright, and the Hundred Days," 313-14.

5. John C. Paige, The Civilian Conservation Corps and the National Park Service
1933-1942 (Denver: National Park Service, 1985), 70-75.

6. A. H. Dahm of Denver to Arno B. Cammerer, undated circa 1936, NA,
RG 79, Series 7, Dinosaur National Monument, file 201.

7. George Grant report to Director, 24 October 1932, NA, RG 79, Series
7, Bandelier National Monument, file 204-10.

8. Ise, Our National Park Policy, 360-64; Paige, The Civilian Conservation Corps,
7-19, 110-7. The original documentation for each camp is contained in the
National Archives, RG 79, Series 69, Records of the Civilian Conservation
Corps.

9. Ise, Our National Park Policy; Paige, The Civilian Conservation Corps.

10. NA, RG 79, Series 7, Capitol Reef National Monument, file 201, tells
the story of the creation of Capitol Reef.

11. Hal Rothman, "Shaping the Nature of a Controversy: The Park Service,
The Forest Service, and the Cedar Breaks National Monument," Utah Historical
Quarterly 55 (Summer 1987): 213-35.

12. The Channel Islands belonged to the Department of Commerce, which
was trying to get rid of the property. They repeatedly offered the islands to
the NPS, which was not really interested. Finally, the NPS agreed to accept
the area as a national monument (see NA, RG 79, Series 7, Channel Islands
National Monument, file 201).

13. "Summary of Data Pertaining to Proposed Organ Pipe National Monument, Arizona", undated, NA, RG 79, Series 7, Organ Pipe Cactus National
Monument, file 101.

14. Runte, National Parks, 131.

15. Ise, Our National Park Policy, 199-200.

16. Frank Pinkley to Frank R. Oastler, 7 November 1929, NA, RG 79,
Series 6, Casa Grande National Monument, file 12-5.

17. Horace Albright to Frank Pinkley, 22 October 1931, NA, RG 79, Series
7, Casa Grande National Monument, file 201-01.

18. Harold C. Bryant to Frank Pinkley, 12 May 1932, NA, RG 79, Series
7, Casa Grande National Monument, file 201-03.

19. Frank Pinkley to Horace Albright, 27 May 1932, NA, RG 79, Series 7,
Casa Grande National Monument, file 201.

20. Ibid.

21. Ibid.

22. Arthur E. Demaray memo attached to Pinkley 27 May 1932 letter; and Horace Albright to Frank Pinkley, 9 June 1932; NA, RG 79, Series 7, Casa Grande National Monument, files 201-02 and 201-01.

23. Barry Mackintosh, "Harold L. Ickes and the National Park Service," *Journal of Forest History* 29 (April 1985): 78-84.

24. Arno B. Cammerer to Frank Pinkley, 24 February 1934; Harold L. Ickes memo, 22 February 1934; NA, RG 79, Series 7, Casa Grande National Monument, file 201.

25. Frank Pinkley to Arizona State Senator James Minotto, 26 February 1934, NA, RG 79, Series 7, Casa Grande National Monument, file 201.

26. Frank Pinkley to Arno B. Cammerer, 8 March 1934, NA, RG 79, Series 7, Casa Grande National Monument, file 201.

27. Cammerer's letters to Horner, Palmer, and Minotto can be found in NA, RG 79, Series 7, Casa Grande, file 201; Arthur E. Demaray memo, 5 March 1934, NA, RG 79, Series 7, Casa Grande, file 201- 02.

28. E. K. Burlew memo to Harold L. Ickes, 30 March 1934, NA, RG 79, Series 7, Casa Grande, file 201. See also Albright, *Birth of the National Park Service*, 307.

29. Harold L. Ickes memo to Arno B. Cammerer, 30 March 1934, NA, RG 79, Series 7, Casa Grande, file 201.

30. Gov. Henry Horner to Harold L. Ickes, 26 March 1934, NA, RG 79, Series 7, Casa Grande, file 201.

31. Harold L. Ickes to Frank Pinkley, 3 April 1934; Harold L. Ickes memo to Arno B. Cammerer, 4 April 1934; NA, RG 79, Casa Grande, file 201.

32. Ibid.

33. Arno B. Cammerer to Frank Pinkley, 5 October 1936, NA, RG 79, Series 7, Casa Grande, file 201.

34. Pinkley's first illness was in 1936; he recovered and was well although weak until the fatal heart attack. The *Southwestern National Monuments Monthly Report*, in which Pinkley chronicled the progress of his organization, also kept track of his health.

10

History and the National
Monuments

THE REORGANIZATION OF THE FEDERAL BUREAUCRACY IN 1933, another important change that came to fruition under Franklin D.
Roosevelt, benefited the Park Service. Throughout the 1920s, Congress sought ways to streamline the federal system, but no workable
plan emerged. In the heady climate after his inauguration, Roosevelt
issued Executive Order 6166 to make the federal government more
manageable. Among its provisions was a clause that transferred the
responsibility for preservation within the federal government to the
Park Service. As of 9 August 1933, all the national monuments that
the Department of War and the United States Forest Service held,
along with an array of other areas, became the obligation of the Park
Service.

The reorganization of 1933 made the Park Service a national entity
with responsibility for much more than scenery. During the 1920s,
the administration of the agency had been relatively simple. Mather
and Albright had discussed the problems of each park with its superintendent. But the reorganization added nearly seventy areas to
the park system, and the agency had difficulty adapting to its new
condition. Many of the areas had titles that were new to the Park
Service. One result was that distinctions among areas other than national parks blurred, and the term *national monument* became more
ambiguous than ever before. Just as Frank Pinkley had warned, after
1933 the Park Service administered national battlefield parks, national

memorials, and a host of other areas that often differed more in "nomenclature than substance."[1]

The reorganization of 1933 did more than simply increase the number of areas in the park system. Included among the acquisitions were many places that were significant to the story of the American republic. Prior to the 1930s, American history had been a peripheral concern of the agency. Early in the decade, Horace Albright had propelled historic preservation within the agency forward, and the reorganization of 1933 catapulted the Park Service to the forefront of historic preservation in the United States. The need to interpret the historic past for the public changed the responsibilities of the agency. After 1933, the park system contained not only western mountain-top parks and archaeological monuments, but also a wide array of historical sites. After being keepers of the ceremonial landscapes during the 1920s, the Park Service had become guardians of a cultural heritage.

This changed not only the character of the national monuments, but the way in which agency administrators in Washington, D.C., regarded them. The peripheral areas of the decade before became central to fulfilling the articulated objective of the agency: building a constituency among the American middle class. As a result of the influx of New Deal money, the Park Service administered the monuments, historic parks, and their peers in a comprehensive fashion, integrating them into the system set up to manage the national parks. The significance of the monuments and the array of other Park Service areas increased as the agency began to inject the story of the history of the American republic into its interpretation policy.

By 1930 the National Park Service had clearly defined its role in the federal bureaucracy, and it could no longer accept Pinkley's narrow view of the monument category. Under Stephen T. Mather, the debates about the purpose of the park system had temporarily subsided. He made the park system a popular attraction for the American middle class. Mather's promotional campaigns also had patriotic undertones, and his emphasis on catering to visitors halted the debate over research use of the national monuments. The national parks were able to arouse interest in American achievement, broadening the constituency of the parks, and a previously elite system had gradually come to belong to the American public. The money and human resources of the New Deal enabled the Park Service to provide even more comprehensive service to its visitors.

But archaeology was not a primary interest of the American public before 1933 and it did not become one in the following decades. As long as the national monuments remained closely associated with archaeology and the public regarded the natural features of the category as inferior to those of the national parks, the monuments remained peripheral to the interests of all but a small group of aficionados. Pinkley was able to attract visitors to areas under his care, but his emphasis upon archaeology limited the appeal of these monuments. In the long run, visitors who were fascinated during their visits to archaeological sites did not maintain the kind of interest that the patriotic themes of places such as Gettysburg inspired.

At this time Americans were becoming more interested in making traditions of their traditions rather than looking to a European past. As the constituency of the agency grew, Americans wanted to see their heritage in publicly preserved places. Areas associated with the Civil War and the American Revolution served this purpose more fully than did places like Chaco Canyon. American mythology was less complicated and more inspiring for the average American than trying to make sense of a prehistoric presence on the continent. Commemorating the history of the American republic was one way for Americans to convey what they felt about their country, and the preservation of historic places offered a more accurate reflection of the mainstream values of the nation.

By democratizing the parks, Mather had laid the basis for this change in the emphasis of the agency. Early Park Service programs had focused upon the emotional impact of western scenery, but to expand its audience, the Park Service had begun to appeal to the intellect of an increasingly general audience. The three national parks authorized in the East during the 1920s—Shenandoah, Great Smoky Mountains, and Mammoth Cave—widened the audience of the agency, but offered no substantive change in the message that the Park Service presented. These three parks were eastern imitations of the ideal western national park, carved from a selection process that defined eastern park areas in the terms of the scenery of the West. Nor did the monuments that existed before 1933 offer a substantive message of cultural affirmation. Archaeological areas required prior knowledge on the part of visitors and often mystified uninitiated travelers. The emotional impact of the parks did not inspire sufficient intellectual curiosity in visitors. To change its role in presenting preservation, the Park Service needed places that the average American could understand.

Before 1933 the tripartite system of administration that the Antiquities Act had established kept the jurisdiction of areas associated with American history from the Park Service. Much of this early Anglo-American history had occurred on land that the military controlled, including battlefields and cemeteries from the Revolutionary War and Civil War and the series of forts throughout the West. The War Department focused its efforts at preservation upon battlefields and cemeteries. This commemoration was part of the obligation of the military, a component of its function as the upholder of patriotic feeling.[2] Except in unusual cases, the military did not comprehend the existence of public interest in its areas. Instead, its officials preserved the battlefields for veterans and for the descendants of those who had fought and died upon them.

Like the Park Service, the War Department had largely ignored its early national monuments. When compared to the military cemetery at Arlington, Virginia, or battlefields at places like Gettysburg or Antietam, Big Hole Battlefield in Montana and the Cabrillo National Monument outside San Diego appeared to be of little consequence. These two national monuments were small, remote places that did not remind Americans of the meaning of patriotism in the manner of Bull Run or Saratoga. With no sense that such places had cultural importance, the military left them unattended.[3]

As late as the end of the 1920s, the Cabrillo National Monument remained unmarked. Frank Tuthill, a Chicago industrialist who made a practice of looking for obscure national monuments, wrote to the Park Service in 1928 to complain that his efforts to find the Cabrillo National Monument were "fruitless. I went to the officer in charge of [the adjacent] Fort Rosecrans, who knew nothing about the monument. He referred me to the lighthouse keeper, who also knew nothing about it." Tuthill left, unsure if he had been in the right spot. Park Service officials informed him that they believed that the lighthouse was the correct location, but they were no more certain than he.[4] Despite the proclamation that established Cabrillo National Monument, its existence offered little to those intrigued by Juan Rodriguez Cabrillo and his legacy.

The War Department had regarded national monument status as an arbitrary inconsequential distinction, a perspective that the Park

Service challenged during the 1920s. In 1915 the secretary of war had interpreted the rules and regulations of the Antiquities Act as granting him the power to proclaim national monuments; as a consequence he issued War Department Bulletin No. 27, establishing fifty national monuments from military land. The collection included many old forts, as well as the archaeological mounds of Mound City, Ohio, and an array of other areas. Years later, when Park Service officials discovered military publications that referred to the secretarial monuments, they were puzzled. In 1923 Arno B. Cammerer cleared up the confusion when he asked the War Department about the authority behind the proclamations. Military officials realized that they had overstepped their bounds, and after reviewing the "monuments," they requested the authentication of five of the areas designated by the secretary of war. On 15 October 1924, the Statue of Liberty, Fort Marion, Fort Matanzas, Castle Pinckney in South Carolina, and Fort Pulaski in Georgia were all added to the monument category. In accordance with the system Edgar L. Hewett devised in 1906, the administration of the new historic national monuments fell to the War Department.[5]

There were obvious reasons for the error by the secretary of war. In 1915 the Park Service did not exist and the national monuments had no specific purpose. If the War Department wanted to add some of its property to the monument category, there was no one to object. Between 1915 and 1923, the Park Service was founded and asserted itself, and a clear definition of its categories and at least minimal standards of entry became critical to the future of the agency. Most of the fifty national monuments that the secretary of war had established did not fit the image that the Park Service had of its areas. Because the two agencies shared the administration of the monument category, areas that did not fit Park Service standards threatened the self-image of that agency. Such places denigrated the mission that Mather and Albright were trying to establish for the Park Service. By 1923 Frank Pinkley had begun to make the monuments identifiable, and despite later contention, the Park Service supported his efforts. When Cammerer queried the War Department about its monuments, he affirmed Pinkley's work in defining the category. The recategorization solidified Pinkley's definition of visitation as the purpose of the national monuments. Four of the five monuments proclaimed in 1924 had considerable appeal to the public.

Even after the reclassification of its monuments, the War Department had continued to emphasize the preservation of historic battlefields and cemeteries. The military paid little attention to the tourist potential of its new areas, instead finding local organizations to manage places for which it had no practical use. The War Department had leased Fort Marion [now called Castillo de San Marcos] in St. Augustine, Florida, to the St. Augustine Historical Society, which guided visitors through the fort. Castle Pinckney, a fortress in Charleston harbor, became a storage facility. The view of the War Department clearly differed from that of the NPS.

The premier military national monument was the Statue of Liberty. Since the 1880s, the garrison at the adjacent Fort Wood had administered the statue as part of the installation, and when Calvin Coolidge proclaimed the Statue of Liberty a national monument in 1924, military policy had not altered at all. Grime from industrial New Jersey coated the surface of the statue, and it looked like the rest of the fort. From the perspective of the military, the Signal Corps radio station, which handled all the radio messages for the Second Corps Area Headquarters on nearby Governor's Island, was more important than the Statue of Liberty.[6]

The Statue of Liberty was an exception among the areas that the War Department administered. It was an important cultural validator, part of the iconography of democracy. Considered a monument to the values of the nation long before it attained official national monument status, the Statue of Liberty was full of patriotic symbolism. It was truly a national monument, in a way that the public could appreciate. The message it conveyed was important to immigrant and native Americans alike. For many, it conjured up an image of the best ideas of the republic. Because of its symbolism and its location, near millions of potential visitors, the Statue of Liberty had resounding social significance.

But because of this importance, the military faced administrative problems at the Statue of Liberty. Many different organizations had tried to capitalize upon its symbolism, some of which were almost comic attempts to infuse causes with patriotic fervor. In 1926 the War Veterans Light Wines and Beer League attempted to use the statue as a backdrop to protest the fact that they had not been permitted to testify in front of a Senate subcommittee on prohibition. Three members of the organization had climbed to the crown and draped two sixty-foot black streamers from the windows to protest that their liberty had been unduly denied.[7]

A potent symbol of the American heritage, the Statue of Liberty National Monument required a type of care that the military was not prepared to offer, and the War Department soon realized that it had more than a military barracks on its hands. The Statue of Liberty was a responsibility that fell beyond the concerns of day-to-day military administration. In 1925 a military committee recommended the appointment of a civilian superintendent, and on 16 November 1925 William A. Simpson became the first superintendent of the national monument. Simpson's appointment mirrored the Park Service practice of placing supervisory personnel at important areas, and this was tacit acknowledgement that the Statue of Liberty was different from other military national monuments. Mostly, the War Department wanted Simpson to curtail the mayhem that had frequently involved the statue as a backdrop.

Simpson's problems at the Statue of Liberty paralleled those of Andrew Lind at Muir Woods and Frank Pinkley in the Southwest. All had more interested visitors than they could handle. Like Pinkley, Simpson received inadequate support from his department, and the War Department never defined a policy for the administration of the statue. Simpson saw himself as a caretaker, protecting the site from the antics of the public, similar to the way that Pinkley perceived Forest Service management of its national monuments. Unlike forest rangers, Simpson was in residence and could do something about upkeep and protection on a daily basis. But under the administration of the War Department, maintenance did not include explaining the significance of the Statue of Liberty.

Most of the War Department monuments paled in comparison to the statue, and like the Park Service, the War Department became befuddled as the number of monuments increased. In 1925 the military acquired three new monuments: the Meriwether Lewis National Monument near Hohenwald, Tennessee; Fort McHenry in Chesapeake Bay; and Father Millet Cross in upstate New York. The War Department understood the importance of Fort McHenry, where Francis Scott Key composed the Star-Spangled Banner, but places like Father Millet Cross and the Lewis grave site were not easily assimilated. Peripheral to the concerns of the War Department, these new areas did not inspire veterans or patriots.

The establishment of the Meriwether Lewis National Monument illustrated the problems that the tripartite administration of the national monuments posed. By 1925 the Park Service knew what kind of areas it wanted in the park system, and park areas east of the Mississippi River were high on its list. An acquisition in Tennessee like the Lewis grave site seemed to fit the strategy of the agency. But the proposal did not fit in with the image the agency had of its responsibilities. Fortunately for advocates of the proclamation of the area, the War Department was less concerned with the kinds of places that landed among its national monuments. All the classic conditions for the creation of a national monument existed at the Lewis grave site; it was a place of at least minor significance, on inexpensive land, and there were interested local citizens. Eager area residents and a reticent National Park Service thrust the area upon the War Department.

Local initiative began the process of establishing the monument. Early in 1924, Tennessee state archaeologist P. E. Cox began correspondence with the Park Service about the grave and the old inn where Lewis died in 1809. "The land surrounding this place is very cheap," Cox wrote Arno B. Cammerer, "being in an isolated location," and he wanted to assess the prospects of creating a national monument or park. But Arno B. Cammerer informed Cox that the Park Service was not interested in acquiring historic graves. "There is not, so far as I know, any grave of any noted American in the custody of the United States," Cammerer told the archaeologist. "I do not think the plan would be looked upon with favor because once the precedent was made, the United States would have thousands of graves offered to it for preservation." Nor did Cammerer think that Congress would fund the upkeep of the grave. The Park Service had little need for additional national monuments, and the Lewis grave seemed beyond the range of agency responsibilities.[8]

But Cox persisted. After much correspondence, the Park Service had not altered its stance, and Cox turned elsewhere. In October 1924 he and other interested state officials came to Washington, D.C., and on the eve of the general election, President Calvin Coolidge received them and listened approvingly as they told of their plans. With this considerable power behind him, Cox once again contacted the Park Service. "I was, after the interview with the President," he wrote Stephen T. Mather, "directed . . . to take the matter up with you as it had already been referred to your Department."[9]

Despite the mandate from the White House, the Park Service diverted Cox. Cammerer took him to see the acting secretary of war, Colonel B. Franklin Cheatham, who already had large numbers of graves in his care. The men explained the matter to the colonel, and he responded with interest. Cheatham suggested that Cox send him a deed to the property. Cox obliged, and on 6 February 1925 the grave site became a national monument under the jurisdiction of the Department of War.

The establishment of the Meriwether Lewis National Monument revealed the differences in the way the Park Service and the War Department saw the monuments. In keeping with Secretary of the Interior Hubert Work's policy to slow the establishment of new national monuments, the Park Service did its best to discourage the proclamation of the Meriwether Lewis grave site. The Park Service had assumed the administration of all previously donated sites, but Cammerer saw a qualitative distinction between these and the Lewis grave site. He foisted the Meriwether Lewis National Monument upon the War Department, which had no objection to acquiring another episodic piece of the American past.

The proposal for the Meriwether Lewis National Monument had forced the Park Service to compare its standards and its long-term objectives. Even inconsequential historic places would give the Park Service an avenue to approach the middle-class constituency that Mather sought to cultivate. Places that conveyed a small piece of the heritage of the American republic communicated much more to the average American than even the most intellectually accessible archaeological site. In addition, the Lewis grave was east of the Mississippi River, an area of vital importance to the Park Service. But in this case, the Lewis grave was deemed an insufficient prize, and the agency refused to amend its standards to further its long-term goals. In 1924 the NPS did not see historic grave sites as a part of its responsibility, nor would it today. As a result, the agency passed up an opportunity to increase its holdings in historic areas.

The War Department administered the Lewis grave in the same manner as its other unimportant areas. The educational fieldwork that was the hallmark of Pinkley's southwestern areas did not exist.

There were no facilities for visitors, and when people visited the Lewis grave site, they left knowing little more than when they came. Although officially protected, management of the Lewis grave site differed little from that of remote western monuments such as Big Hole Battlefield or Shoshone Cavern.

From the point of view of the Park Service in 1925, the Lewis grave was not a worthwhile acquisition. Despite its location in the East, it presented a different message than the main thrust of NPS efforts in the 1920s. Under Mather, eastern park areas were scaled-down versions of western ones. The military administration of historic places preceded the founding of NPS, but Horace Albright had aspirations in that direction. In the first annual report of the agency in 1917, Albright had indicated that the Park Service ought to someday acquire the historic areas of the War Department, but during the late 1920s and early 1930s, Mather's conception of a network of monumental national parks interspersed with conveniently located national monuments took precedence over such acquisitions.[10]

This stance was the result of events that took place at the time that the Park Service was established. In the 1910s and the early 1920s, the fledgling agency was busy developing supporters in Congress against rivals like the Forest Service. Mather struggled to develop the priorities of the agency, and like archaeological sites, historic places were largely peripheral to his concerns. As the agency looked to solidify its position in the federal bureaucracy and to expand its horizons, the packaging of the park system hastened the recognition of its historic responsibility. As Pinkley noted when he wrote to Frank Oastler of the committee for the study of education in the national parks in 1929, the day would come when the NPS would assume control of historical areas. Despite the implications of its rejection of Meriwether Lewis grave, by the beginning of 1930, that day was approaching.

Under the Mather regime, the impetus to acquire historic places grew, but its focus was primarily regional. Expedience or local initiative usually resulted in the creation of historic monuments, and some monuments, such as the Verendrye National Monument in North Dakota, which was a trivial monument that had been established to placate insistent locals, had little historic integrity. Even the best of the historic areas of the Park Service, places like Pipe Spring and Sitka national monuments, did not offer the American mainstream reinforcement of its ideals. Although the efforts of Mormon settlers at

Pipe Spring or Russian traders and soldiers at Sitka reflected the opportunity to forge an individual destiny in a new and foreboding continent, such places seemed like idiosyncratic incidents within on the patriotic canvas, the heritage of the unusual or the obscure. Regional in character, the early historical areas and their archaeological counterparts served only as auxiliary counterpoints to the development of the national parks.

Scotts Bluff National Monument was typical of the historic monuments of the Park Service before 1930.[11] A bluff overlooking the North Platte River in western Nebraska, the monument represented the journey of thousands of travelers along the trail to Oregon, California, Utah, Colorado, and other western states. It commemorated an important cultural impulse of the American mainstream, the idea of a manifest destiny that propelled the nineteenth century pioneers, but it did so in an oblique fashion. To the unimaginative, it revealed little of its historic moment. Cloaked in obscurity except to those who went looking for it, Scotts Bluff had a message, but its meaning was easy to overlook. Its ideological value was for people who had internalized American cultural norms thoroughly enough to imagine what they were supposed to see. Like the archaeological monuments, comprehending the significance of Scotts Bluff required indoctrination and prior knowledge.

Because the Park Service did not develop interpretation procedures until the end of the 1920s, the lack of explanatory mechanisms also made understanding Scotts Bluff difficult. Although Americans identified strongly with the westward migration, the monument gave visitors little tangible evidence of that movement. Scotts Bluff was a place of the imagination. It did not appear in grammar or high school textbooks, nor did it inspire bursts of patriotic fervor. Devoid of markers or buildings, it amounted to a view from a hilltop, and it left the responsibility for forging an understanding to the visitors who could look out over the plains and see in their minds the world of the pioneers, populated by buffalo, Indians, covered wagons, and mountain men.

Horace Albright dreamed of adding important historic sites to the responsibilities of the agency, and in the late 1920s, he reshaped the direction of historic preservation in the Park Service. By the time he inherited the directorship from Mather in 1929, the Park Service had major holdings in the West and the authorization for an embryonic park system east of the Mississippi River. Many of the best scenic areas on federal land were already included in the system. But like other federal agencies, the health of the Park Service depended on its continued growth and particularly on its ability to outdistance rivals like the Forest Service. Albright saw that the best avenue for growth was in the acquisition and development of places that told the story of the development of the American republic. As the United States became an increasingly urban, industrial nation, an articulation of its roots became more important, and Albright realized that selling the history of the United States to the public gave the Park Service a new obligation that no other federal agency had yet claimed.

As Albright took charge of the agency, historic preservation acquired new significance. But budget constraints and the position of the War Department limited his options, and Albright had to wait for the right opportunity. He watched "excitedly" as John D. Rockefeller, Jr., an important patron of the agency, financed the restoration of Williamsburg and donated much of the area to the agency.[12] Almost simultaneously, one of George Washington's direct descendants, Josephine W. Rust, began a campaign to reconstruct the house where Washington had been born. Although she raised almost $50,000 from private sources, Mrs. Rust met with little success in the federal government until the end of 1929, when she talked to Horace Albright. He immediately "warmed to the idea," and soon the George Washington Birthplace National Monument was established, followed closely by the Colonial National Monument. In the NPS report for that year, Albright announced the "entrance of [the Park Service] into the field of preservation in a more comprehensive way."[13]

The George Washington Birthplace and the Colonial national monuments represented a new mode of historic preservation within the federal system. The Park Service finally had jurisdiction over places that had significance for the development of the nation. The two monuments were the first restored historic sites in the park system, and as recreated evocations of a past, they revealed new possibilities to agency administrators. The George Washington Birthplace and the Colonial national monuments clearly differed from places like Scotts Bluff and Verendrye. Wakefield was the birthplace of the Father of Our Nation, a far cry in iconographical significance from a bluff overlooking the Platte River or cliff ruins in the Southwest. Americans recognized George Washington and his achievements, and most people revered places and events associated with his life. Despite an inaccurate reconstruction of the boyhood home at Wakefield, the monument there offered the public a usable past. Colonial National Monument also presented visible re-creations of textbook history with which Americans were familiar. The two restored monuments offered people tangible evidence of the heritage most Americans claimed as their own.

When Stephen T. Mather set the Park Service as the guardian of the ceremonial landscapes, he unwittingly impressed a one-dimensional role upon his agency. Mather had developed the system and left an indelible imprint upon it, but his personal experience limited his view of what was important. A Californian by birth and education, he had treasured the scenic magnificence of the western parks and when he laid the basis for national parks like Great Smokey Mountains in the East, he had created them in the western image. The parks included high elevations and the most spectacular scenery the agency could find, but they presented only one aspect of American tradition: their expansiveness showed the milieu that pitted humanity against its environment. Well-promoted, the parks doubled as recreational areas, but Americans eventually sought other facets of their heritage. By the 1920s, the American republic had a history of its own, revealed in places far more important than the Verendrye National Monument. It became more worthy of federal attention as the cultural distance between twentieth-century America and its westward frontier grew. As the United States emerged on the international scene, national sentiment supported federal preservation as a means to explore more than the interaction between humanity and the physical environment.

Prior to 1930, agency officials yearned for a significant historic presence under the jurisdiction of the Park Service. Colonial and Wakefield revolutionized the view the agency held of its responsibilities and gave agency officials a precedent not only for adding such places, but for sizable capital investment as well. The two areas became popular with travelers, and gratified by the response of the public, Albright and his staff sought more historic places.

The presence of the Park Service in historic preservation altered the role of the agency. According to Albright, the agency "doubled [its] efforts" to acquire important historical areas.[14] After the emergence of the educational division, which was staffed by museum and academic professionals, the agency began to see that the scenic beauty of the national parks had limited potential for interpretive programs. The addition of places like Williamsburg and the George Washington Birthplace National Monument allowed the agency to expand into interpreting the story of the American republic in a way that scenic parks never could.

In part, the growing emphasis upon history helped put the Park Service beyond the reach of the Forest Service. The majority of historic places were located on small tracts east of the Mississippi River, where the Forest Service had only a limited presence. Whereas the disposition of federal land in the West had forced the two agencies into competition, even the broadest vision of the responsibilities of the Forest Service did not include interest in historic areas. As the Park Service entered historic preservation, the Forest Service generally paid little attention. Finally, the Park Service found a way to circumvent whatever opposition to its plans the Forest Service may have had.

Even more telling, historic places were an avenue of interpretation that Frank Pinkley had not explored. As the highest echelons of the agency sought to curtail his role during the 1930s and as his work became less unique, Pinkley found others in the agency filling roles previously reserved for him. Because historic places offered meaningful opportunities for interpretation, the educational division seized upon American history in an effort to counter Pinkley's constant complaints. Harold C. Bryant and his staff used the gap in interpreting historic places to their own advantage to increase the importance of the Division of Education.

The educational division sought to establish a rationale for a systematic presentation of the historic past. The Park Service administered random episodes of American history, a perspective that Verne Chatelain, the man Albright hired as historian for the Division of Education, found inadequate. In 1931 he articulated the premise that historic areas had to be presented "not [as] a research program but [as] an educational program in the broader sense." Chatelain refined his thoughts over the following year and, with Roger Toll, the superintendent of Yellowstone who was headed for the highest level in the agency until his death in a automobile accident near Big Bend National Park in February 1936, reported that the agency needed to approach its areas from an integrative perspective. It was "unsound, uneconomical, and detrimental to a historical system and policy to study each individual area without reference to the entire scheme of things."[15]

Chatelain's proposals offered the agency a new perspective for interpretive programs. He suggested locating each episode within the larger picture of the American past. The idea, a comprehensive approach to interpreting the past, was new. Even Pinkley's efforts had been largely episodic. As a result, Chatelain's proposal had the added benefit of decreasing the significance of Pinkley's contributions to the interpretation policy of the agency.

Chatelain first tried to implement his concept at Colonial National Monument. After the creation of the monument, he guided the development of a historical program that the agency hoped would "serve as a link to bind the past to the present and be a guide and an inspiration for the future." The linkage between Jamestown, Williamsburg, and Yorktown neatly encapsulated what the agency and the public regarded as the important facets of the first two centuries of Anglo-American inhabitation of the eastern seaboard. As the Park Service developed its interpretation at Colonial under two young historians, B. Floyd Flickinger and Elbert Cox, the presentation of the monument became part of a move to link the foundations of the American republic.[16]

Chatelain continued to push the idea of synthesizing the message of historic areas within the system. "Unless there is a real philosophy of history," he told Arthur E. Demaray in April 1933, "it will be easy enough to spend our time in academic discussions . . . and never seriously tackle the bigger task." The larger "patterns of history" were what Chatelain sought, and rather than search for the story of each battlefield and house, Chatelain advocated exploring the larger questions and subsequently relating individual areas to broad themes.[17]

He also echoed earlier Park Service notions about adding areas of national significance to the system. As Cammerer noted in the Meriwether Lewis case, the federal government had to be careful what it chose to preserve lest every small town organization offer its local landmarks. Chatelain settled upon three types of areas that he felt belonged in the federal network. The places that offered an outline of the major themes of American history were important, as were the ones with strong connections to the lives of famous Americans and the locations of dramatic episodes in the American history.[18] To preclude inundation by insistent locals, he suggested that the agency ignore potential areas that did not meet his criteria. By 1933 Chatelain had established the roots of a system and solid reasoning for the continued growth of agency interest in historic areas.

But it was Executive Order 6166, which went into effect on 10 August 1933, that truly put the National Park Service into the business of historic preservation. Roosevelt's order to reorganize the federal government transferred the national monuments previously administered by the Forest Service and the War Department, as well as the battlefield parks and cemeteries and the public parks in Washington, D.C., to the Park Service. The centralization of the administration of the monuments was the result of three decades of lobbying by park advocates, and after 1916, by NPS personnel. This hard-won "inheritance" made the National Park Service an entity with a national constituency and multiple responsibilities. It also made the agency not only arbiters of the natural and prehistoric heritage of the nation, but the guardian of its federally preserved history as well.

In effect, Horace Albright's interests dovetailed with those of Franklin D. Roosevelt and Harold Ickes. Roosevelt wanted to reorganize government bureaucracies; from its inception in 1916, the Park Service had sought control of all the national monuments. The perspectives of Albright and Ickes interlocked closely in ideas about the value of historical experience. Their shared view also led to the development of educational programs for the newly acquired historic national monuments under the auspices of federal emergency relief programs such as the CCC and the WPA.

With this inheritance, the Park Service became the sole agency responsible for federal efforts at preservation. The reorganization presented the NPS with fifty-seven new historical areas to manage along with eleven additional natural areas, many of which required immediate administrative supervision and visitation programs. Fortunately, New Deal programs made funding available, but capital development was only one step toward a comprehensive system. With the added responsibility of historical parks of various kinds, something many old-line Park Service people felt was a burden, the Park Service needed a more flexible infrastructure.[19] Reorganizing the NPS was the first task that confronted Cammerer when he took over the directorship of the agency from Albright on 10 August 1933.

From its inception, the Park Service had relied heavily upon the personalities of its leadership. Mather and Albright ran every facet of the agency. But Cammerer was not as dynamic as his predecessors; although he spent many years carrying out the agenda that Mather and Albright designed, he played only a small role in shaping its priorities. With 137 park areas to administer, he needed to delegate responsibility, particularly for places of lesser importance. Pinkley had long ago taken care of the administration of the archaeological sites. Cammerer was left with responsibility for integrating the new areas into the established system.

As Frank Pinkley astutely predicted in 1929, the national monument category blurred as a result of the transfer. Although Pinkley succeeded in convincing many that the term *national monument* could be equated with archaeological preservation, Executive Order 6166 destroyed the clarity of his distinction. The Park Service now administered all kinds of historic places with an array of names; some were called national monuments, and of these, some were archaeological and others historical. The monuments were no longer alone in the system with the national parks. The agency also administered numerous other categories, such as national battlefields, national memorials, and national military parks. Park Service nomenclature had only begun to become confusing.

The obligations of the Park Service changed so dramatically as a result of the acquisition of these new parks that even the broad outline of the domain of the agency became murky. A generalization about natural or historic areas ceased to cover the range of areas under those headings, and the accentuation of the diversity of park areas presented new management problems. Mountaintop parks, representative-area national monuments, Civil War battlefields, Mormon forts, and archaeological sites did not offer a unified cultural message. The simple interaction between the director and the superintendents that characterized Mather's tenure became impossible with 137 areas, and Cammerer and his staff had to determine how to manage the broadened responsibilities of the newly expanded Park Service.

One response was the development of a more sophisticated system of administration. The Park Service moved toward integrated management, a process that began in 1937 as the agency divided itself into five geographic groupings of park areas.[20] The realignment created an intermediate level of administration between park superintendents and the office of the director. The *regions*, as the agency called these new entities, addressed the concerns of all the areas—historical, natural, archaeological, and recreational—within their jurisdiction.

Regionalization formalized the developing structure of the agency. After 1937 the informal hierarchy that had existed under Mather became a codified process. With the exception of Pinkley, who simply ignored the intermediaries at the Region III Office in Santa Fe, superintendents approached the Washington, D.C., office through their region. The new system sacrificed a degree of the personal contact between high-level officials and field personnel that characterized the Mather administration and, to a lesser extent, the Albright years. Despite protests to the contrary, the Park Service gave up some of its camaraderie in order to operate more efficiently.

Integrating its new historic areas into the system posed a major burden for the Park Service. Revolutionary War and Civil War battlefields in the East required intensive management if they were to fulfill their promise, but before the agency could implement its interpretation programs, it had to transform these historic places into Park Service areas. Agency personnel had to bring each area up to Park Service standards. Often the policies of the previous administrators—the Forest Service and the War Department—conflicted with the plans of the Park Service. Particularly objectionable to the NPS was the War Department policy of leasing historic places to private groups. Bryant and his staff regarded the activities of private organizations as inferior and unprofessional. From Bryant's perspective, the agency had to implement its programs so that the public would identify the new acquisitions with the Park Service.

The reorganization of Fort Marion became a crucible and a test case for the Park Service. The fort had a built-in constituency; the climate in St. Augustine made the fort a popular stop for people visiting Florida in the winter. This project offered Bryant the opportunity to show what the difference was between Park Service interpretation and the efforts of local groups. If the agency could wrest control of the area away from the locals, implement its history policy, and make the fort into an important place for tourists, Fort Marion would offer the educational division great advantages.

Fortunately for the Park Service, conflict among local people in St. Augustine predated the transfer of Fort Marion to the Park Service in 1933. As early as 1930, local residents contacted Albright to complain about the tactics of the St. Augustine Historical Society. When the Park Service assumed jurisdiction, serious tension between the historical society and two other local groups—the City of St. Augustine and the local Veterans of Foreign Wars—already existed. Both wanted to acquire the contract that the historical society held. In 1933 the society was firmly entrenched; its lease had more than a year to run. Herbert Kahler, whom Verne Chatelain recruited out of the University of Minnesota history department graduate program to serve as an historical foreman on the CCC project at Chickamauga-Chattanooga National Battlefield, became the Park Service representative in St. Augustine. It was his job to determine whether the lease should be renewed.[21]

What Kahler found was not impressive. Although only authorized to collect donations, the historical society guides were "hold[ing] the basket, so there is not much 'free will' about the offering." The guides told him that they had to be aggressive because visitors did not like to pay to inspect government property, but after watching the guides in action, Kahler was skeptical. The story the guides told consisted of "antiquarian details," Kahler reported, and they offered little in the way of interpretation. The usual tour took about fifteen to twenty minutes, and Kahler believed that its level was below the standards of the NPS. The public did not complain about the fees the NPS charged at its western parks, and Kahler suspected that people just did not want to pay for poor service. He thought that the existing guide service did little to maintain the interest of visitors and ought to be changed.[22]

There were other problems at Fort Marion, and Kahler believed the Park Service should not renew the existing lease. A museum containing "heterogeneous materials," including Spanish-American War relics and other items that had little to do with the history of the fort, particularly disturbed him. Following the procedures of the agency, he suggested its elimination. The City of St. Augustine, the historical society, and the local Veterans of Foreign Wars continued to quarrel over the monument, "primarily for its commercial value," Kahler observed. "I recommend that it be taken out of local hands."[23]

The Floridians feared that they would lose control of the fort and began to muster supporters, but the Park Service had no intention of changing its policy. The historical society enlisted Congressman W. J. Sears of Florida in its cause, and in January 1935 he approached the Park Service. The most direct person on the central office staff, Arthur E. Demaray, explained the position of the Park Service. He told Sears that it was a mistake to leave the historical society in control of the fort. Demaray believed that permanent administration by any local organization would create animosity among the factions, and that Park Service management of the fort was the only professional solution. "The practice of 'farming out' national historical parks and monuments," Demaray insisted, had to stop.[24]

As Cammerer considered the proposal, agency staffers made their opposition to the historical society clear. Kahler wrote to Cammerer that he believed the historical society to be "in the minority" and revealed that he had convinced Florida senator Park Trammel not to fight on behalf of the St. Augustinians. He urged the director to stick to his decision to terminate the agreement. Kahler's superior, Verne Chatelain, agreed. He thought that other elements in St. Augustine were jealous of the existing arrangement, "which is a *money maker* for the Society."[25]

The position of the Park Service at Fort Marion was typical of its stance in similar cases. Chatelain and Kahler argued that the agency represented the public good and that the historical society represented private profit. The Park Service disseminated information, whereas the guides of the historical society collected money from unsatisfied visitors. Within an agency that saw its role as serving the public, these officials found considerable sympathy. Cammerer decided that the Park Service should take over the areas as soon as the current lease expired.

In St. Augustine, Kahler began a publicity campaign to win friends for the Park Service, and his public proclamations enhanced the position of the agency. The Park Service had something to offer the community besides its administration, and Kahler made sure local citizens were informed. On 19 February 1935 the local newspaper, the *St. Augustine Evening Record*, revealed that the Park Service planned a budget allotment for the monument that would cover expenses and salaries. There would be no more "holding the basket." Kahler also said that the PWA intended to grant between $30,000 and $50,000 to restore decaying parts of the fort.[26] This meant jobs for local workers, the prospect of which made the community respond enthusiastically. By taking over a measure of economic responsibility for the people of the area, the Park Service outdistanced local organizations.

Kahler's work made the Park Service the more attractive alternative, and support for the local administration began to diminish. Despite the skepticism of David R. Dunham, the president of the historical society, who did not believe Kahler's press release, Mayor Walter B. Fraser announced that the city supported the Park Service. Local support for the historical society then evaporated. With the end of its lease approaching, members of the historical society became desperate and spread "fantastic tales" about the Park Service. To maintain the credibility of the NPS, Kahler countered with press releases. With the always persuasive Demaray handling the queries of the Florida congressional delegation in Washington, D.C., and with Kahler pursuing the interests of the agency in St. Augustine, by the spring of 1935, federal administration of Fort Marion was imminent.[27]

Kahler was an effective advocate for agency interests in Florida and the Southeast. He had arrived in the middle of this conflict and managed to turn it to the advantage of the agency. Although technically a CCC employee until June 1935, Kahler was already indispensable to the Park Service. On 1 June 1935 the agency added him to its permanent payroll as the junior park historian for Fort Marion, and he continued to inspect southeastern parks like Fort Pulaski, Fort Jefferson, Fort Frederica, and Ocmulgee National Monuments for the agency.[28]

Cammerer, Demaray, and Chatelain looked favorably on Kahler's work, and he shouldered increased responsibility for national monuments in the Southeast. With a visible need to develop decentralized authority as a result of the reorganization of 1933, and the central office promoted Kahler to acting superintendent of the southeastern monuments group on 16 December 1935. Kahler had "shown courage and initiative in his work and discretion in the execution of his plan. His unfailing tact [had] done wonders to remove many troublesome problems at St. Augustine."[29] He filled an important vacancy at the regional level. His new role paralleled that of Frank Pinkley's in the Southwest.

With only one organization to pattern themselves upon, the Park Service adapted Pinkley's southwestern structure to the Southeast. The southeastern monuments consisted of Fort Marion and Fort Matanzas near St. Augustine, Fort Pulaski, Fort Frederica, and Ocmulgee in Georgia, Castle Pinckney in Charleston, South Carolina, and Fort Jefferson in Florida. In structure, it was a geographic grouping similar to Pinkley's group. Organized similarly, with a superintendent at the top and custodians who reported to him, the southeastern national monuments group even put out its own monthly report magazine.

There were major differences between the two organizations and their leaders. The southeastern group was never as controversial as Pinkley's. Kahler joined the agency as its institutional structure was flourishing. He never had the autonomy that Pinkley enjoyed during the 1920s, nor did he ever become embroiled in the kinds of issues for which Pinkley was famous. Kahler's southeastern monuments generally covered historic themes and, from an interpretive perspective, were more coherent than Pinkley's areas. Only Ocmulgee, an archaeological mound near Macon, Georgia, did not relate to the European presence in the New World. Kahler also had a wider range of tourist figures to contend with. At one end of the spectrum, Castle Pinckney was closed to the public. At the other end, from June 1934 to June 1935, the last full year before the Park Service took it over, guides escorted 134,049 visitors through Fort Marion, a figure that equalled almost half of what all Frank Pinkley's monuments received in a year.[30] This level of visitation, particularly with the required guide service, created numerous headaches for Kahler.

The changes that the Park Service instituted at Fort Marion were typical of its development of historic places during the 1930s. The story of Fort Marion was closely related to textbook history, making Kahler's job easy. It revealed an early stage of European civilization in the New World, and the battles between the Spanish and English colonists added spice to its story. In a major tourist location, with extensive year-round visitation, Fort Marion was accessible, rich in history, and mild in climate. After wresting it from private concerns, the historical division of the Park Service, with help from CCC employees and a WPA allotment, administered the monument with complete educational programs, concessions, and other amenities more closely associated with the national parks. Areas like it were showplaces for the specialists that came to dominate the interpretive policy of the agency during the 1930s.

Fort Marion had broad appeal to a nation increasingly concerned with the development of its own traditions. It conveyed an image of a "usable" past, available to affirm American desires. Americans no longer had to look to Europe and the ancient world to see their cultural roots. The North American continent had a human past worthy of consideration. By the time the National Park Service moved to the forefront of historic preservation, Americans saw the European past on this continent as evidence of the advancement of civilization as they understood it.

The developments of the 1930s put the agency in the field of historic preservation in a manner that no federal agency had previously attempted. Fort Marion and the other areas acquired from the military, along with the Colonial and George Washington Birthplace national monuments, offered the best opportunities for the Park Service to make an impact with the interpretation of historical events. Interpreting the written record of the European past was easier than understanding the artifacts and structures of the pre-Columbian Southwest. The reorganization of 1933 gave the agency the chance to expand its horizons, and dynamic agency personnel did not allow the opportunity to slip away.

The reorganization of 1933 also transformed the NPS in other, more subtle ways. Besides giving the agency a national constituency and making it the primary agency concerned with preservation in the United States, the reorganization contributed to the move toward regionalization in the agency. The new historic areas forced the agency to reconsider the role of areas that did not belong to the national park category. Such places acquired a new significance as the NPS became the public arbiter of American values. As the Park Service interpreted historic places—these transformed by dynamic New Deal policies— agency officials took responsibility for conveying the continuity of European experience in the Americas.

Notes

1. Ronald Foresta, *America's National Parks and Their Keepers* (Washington, DC: Resources For The Future, 1984), 19-21, 30-32.

2. Ibid., 32.

3. Ibid., 32.

4. Frank Tuthill to Director, 29 October 1928; and Arthur E. Demaray to Frank Tuthill, 6 November 1928, NA, RG 79, Series 6, Cabrillo National Monument, file 12-5.

5. Walter Hugins, *Statue of Liberty National Monument: Its Origin, Development and Administration* (Washington, DC: Department of the Interior, 1958), 32-34.

6. Ibid., 38.

7. Ibid., 38.

8. P. E. Cox to Arno B. Cammerer, 23 March 1924; and Arno B. Cammerer to P. E. Cox, 23 March 1934, NA, RG 79, Series 6, Meriwether Lewis National Monument, file 12-5.

9. P. E. Cox to Stephen T. Mather, 24 October 1924, NA, RG 79, Series 6, Meriwether Lewis National Monument, file 12-5.

10. Horace Albright as told to Robert Cahn, *The Birth of the National Park Service: The Founding Years 1913-1933* (Salt Lake City: Howe Brothers Press, 1985), 234-47.

11. Executive Proclamation No. 1547, 12 December 1919, established the Scotts Bluff National Monument.

12. Horace Albright, The Origins of National Park Service Administration of Historic Sites (Philadelphia: Eastern National Park and Monument Association, 1971), 13.

13. *Report of the Director of the National Park Service for the Fiscal Year ended June 30, 1930* (Washington, DC: Government Printing Office, 1930), 6; see also Albright, *Birth of the National Park Service*, 246-47.

14. Albright, *Birth of the National Park Service*, 246-70.

15. Unrau and Williss, *Administrative History*, 163-65. An excellent leader blessed with clarity of insight, Toll's death deprived the agency of the one person who could have given it leadership during Cammerer's tenure.

16. Unrau and Williss, *Administrative History*, 167; Hosmer, *Preservation Comes of Age*, 2: 534-36.

17. Hosmer, *Preservation Comes of Age*, 2: 564-65.

18. Ibid.

19. Unrau and Williss, *Expansion of the Park Service*, 71.

20. Frank Pinkley to Frank R. Oastler, 7 November 1929, NA, RG 79, Series 6, Casa Grande, file 12-5.

21. Herbert Evison interview with Herbert Kahler, 1964. Manuscript on file, National Park Service Records Center, Harpers Ferry, West Virginia.

22. Herbert Kahler to Verne E. Chatelain, 30 December 1933, NA, RG 79, Series 7, Castillo de San Marcos, file 201.

23. Ibid.

24. Arthur E. Demaray to U.S. Rep. W. J. Sears, 25 January 1935, NA, RG 79, Series 7, Castillo de San Marcos, file 201.

25. Herbert Kahler to Verne E. Chatelain, 16 February 1935; and Verne E. Chatelain handwritten memo attached to Kahler's letter; NA, RG 79, Series 7, Castillo de San Marcos, file 201.

26. *St. Augustine Evening Record*, 19 February 1935; Herbert Kahler to Arthur E. Demaray, 21 February 1935, NA, RG 79, Series 7, Castillo de San Marcos, file 201.

27. David Dunham to A. E. Demaray, 20 February 1935; and Herbert

Kahler to Arthur E. Demaray, 21 February 1935; NA, RG 79, Series 7, Castillo De San Marcos, file 201. Demaray deflected the fears of Sen. Duncan U. Fletcher in a 27 March 1935 letter in which he showed the senator that the needs of his constituency would be better filled by the NPS than by the St. Augustine Historical Society.

28. Herbert Kahler memo to Verne E. Chatelain, 4 June 1935, NA, RG 79, Series 7, Castillo de San Marcos, file 201.

29. Arno B. Cammerer to Herbert Kahler, 6 December 1935; and Verne E. Chatelain memo to Hillary Tolson, 25 June 1936; NA, RG 79, Series 7, Castillo De San Marcos, file 201.

30. *Annual Report of the Secretary of the Interior 1934-35* (Washington, D.C.: Government Printing Office, 1935), 117.

11

The Antiquities Act and the
Modern Park System

IN MANY WAYS, the New Deal reinvented the federal system of preservation. Finally supported by adequate funding, the Park Service
could implement the kinds of programs that Stephen T. Mather and
Horace M. Albright had first conceived in the 1910s and 1920s. Areas
of previously low priority became prime candidates for development,
and many national monuments flourished. As a result, the focus of
the agency broadened, and after the end of the Second World War,
the way in which the Park Service perceived the Antiquities Act changed.
New expectations about the role of the agency and a different vision
of its future made the Antiquities Act less central to federal preservation than it had been prior to 1933.

The massive influx of money that the New Deal brought changed
both the way the NPS and the public perceived the obligations of the
agency. The New Deal brought many of the plans of the Park Service
to fruition, and by the 1940s, federal preservation had a physical plant
to support its constituency. After the New Deal, American travelers
expected amenities in their national park system. Despite the preservationist bent of Director Newton B. Drury, who headed the agency
between 1940 and 1952, the Park Service did its best to accommodate
an increasingly large and vocal public.

After the Second World War, the areas selected for inclusion in the
park system also changed. New parks and monuments were no longer
fresh discoveries, as were Navajo or Devils Postpile National Monu-

ment, hastened to establishment ahead of bulldozers and developers. Instead, additions were selected by a process not unlike that conceived by the agency during the 1920s when it sought parklands in the East. The rapid action that characterized the founding of many early national monuments disappeared among seemingly endless evaluation of similar areas in search of the right parks for the system.

As a result, the Park Service ceased to use the monument category as its place of experimentation. The agency tested its new concepts in a more sophisticated fashion that rarely included the kind of heady action that had been typical early in the century. Innovation was no longer at a premium. The raw expansion that the Antiquities Act facilitated disappeared into the structure of an increasingly specialized and hierarchical bureaucracy. The Park Service had become an established entity with a clearly defined role, and the testing of concepts for which the agency once used the monument category became a less important part of Park Service strategy.

These changes led to a diminished role for the Antiquities Act in federal preservation. The agency relied heavily upon the Act prior to 1933, but after the Second World War, its role nearly disappeared. The array of titles that became available for park areas contributed to the lack of distinction that surrounded the monuments, but the primary obstacle was that, despite its vast powers, the Antiquities Act did not grant the power to fund the development of an area. With the emphasis placed upon development throughout the 1950s and 1960s, the Antiquities Act became a smaller part of the process of creating a new park area. Establishment was only the beginning of the battle, and the Antiquities Act ceased to fill the needs of the Park Service. A decline in the number of uses of the Act and informal restrictions upon its use led to a limiting of the roles that the Antiquities Act played. After 1945, its primary use was the same as one of its initial ones: as a last resort in extreme cases.

Since its passage in 1906, presidential use of the Antiquities Act had inspired serious opposition. Western congressmen regarded direct federal intervention in regional affairs as a violation of state sovereignty. Protests arose intermittently throughout the first forty years of the twentieth century, but from the administrations of Theodore Roosevelt to Franklin D. Roosevelt, the Department of the Interior continued to take advantage of the discretionary powers granted by the Act. It was only a matter of time until some president and Congress clashed over what could easily be perceived as uncontrolled executive power.

The controversy over the establishment of the Jackson Hole National Monument in the Yellowstone-Grand Teton National Park region in 1943 brought matters to a head. Typical of portions of the West in its scenic beauty and economic potential, the region acted as a magnet for the desires both of preservationists and the ranching industry. Park Service requests for an extension of Grand Teton National Park began almost as soon as the original park was established in 1929. John D. Rockefeller, Jr., was instrumental in the establishment of the original park, and his holding company, the Snake River Land Company, purchased and managed more than 33,000 additional acres in the area until the NPS could find a way to include the land in the park. Under Cammerer, the NPS had little success; in 1938, opponents calling themselves the Jackson Hole Committee outflanked the agency during a Senate public lands committee hearing in Jackson Hole. The Wyoming congressional delegation dropped the bill from the congressional agenda and no one reintroduced it. The NPS could not convince Congress to make laws concerning Wyoming lands if representatives of the state did not favor them.[1]

After the debacle in 1938, Rockefeller questioned whether he should continue his support of the project. Rockefeller had become uncomfortable with Cammerer, and his right-hand man Kenneth Chorley echoed Rockefeller's feelings when he remarked that he could not "recall seeing any organization decline as much as the Park Service since Mr. Albright left it." Indeed, the philanthropist had a legitimate complaint. He had been involved in the Grand Teton project since his initial visit to the region in 1927, and all he had to show for his benevolent efforts was an annual tax bill of $13,000. By the early 1940s, Rockefeller felt that the time for action had arrived. On 27 November 1942 he told Ickes that if the project did not progress, he had every intention of divesting himself of the property he owned. This was Rockefeller's way of initiating action; his son, Laurance later referred to the letter as "undoubtedly more of a bit of maneuver and pressure kind of thing than [an] indication of a change of purpose or policy."[2]

Rockefeller's veiled threat got the response he sought. Ickes and the Park Service suggested the creation of the Jackson Hole National

Monument as an attempt to circumvent the kind of congressional disapproval they encountered in 1938. Even though Ickes warned Roosevelt of the likely uproar, on 15 March 1943 the president proclaimed 221,610 acres, including the tract that Rockefeller owned and more than 179,000 acres from the Grand Teton National Forest, as a national monument of historic and scientific significance.[3]

For the first time since the ad hoc creation of Mount Olympus in 1909, serious opposition appeared to uses of the immense discretionary power of the Antiquities Act. Jackson Hole was the consummate way-station monument, its creation inspired by Park Service desires to include an entire biota instead of just mountain peaks in Grand Teton National Park. Area residents, the Wyoming congressional delegation, and the Forest Service all objected to the establishment of the monument. At the height of the Second World War, executive discretion on the home front became a controversial issue.

Local and state interests immediately responded. Sen. Edward Robertson of Wyoming denounced the proclamation as a "foul, sneaking Pearl Harbor blow."[4] Other members of the legislative delegation, including Congressman Frank Barrett of the Jackson Hole district, were outraged. The *Jackson Hole Courier*, a traditional nemesis of the Park Service, vilified the proclamation, and newspapers across the state castigated the agency.

Opposition also took other forms. On 2 May 1943 local ranchers, headed by Hollywood actor Wallace Beery, a summer resident of the area, took on the NPS. Heavily armed and lacking the necessary permits, the men drove 550 yearlings across the monument to summer range higher in the mountains, defying the NPS to stop them. Superintendent Charles J. Smith of Grand Teton National Park refused to take the bait and ignored them, but because of Beery's presence, the incident attracted national attention for the burgeoning Jackson Hole controversy.[5]

On 18 May 1943 the state of Wyoming also got into the act, filing a civil suit in federal court against Superintendent Smith. The suit charged that the Jackson Hole proclamation was illegal because it was "not authorised by the provisions of law upon which it purports to be based." It also contended that Smith completely excluded state officials from decisions concerning the tract. The state asserted that it had an investment in the property, including highways, game animals, and birds, and contended that because Wyoming had "not given her consent to the acquisition of lands within Wyoming by the United States for monument purposes," the tract was "not a national monument or park, and there is no authority therefor," and that the Park Service had no right to receive donations of private land within the monument. Financial considerations also played an important role in the suit. State officials believed that they would lose important tax revenue, a share of the grazing fees collected in the portion of the monument that used to be a part of the Grand Teton National Forest, if the court upheld the monument proclamation.[6]

The suit also had serious implications for the future of the Antiquities Act. It charged that "the proclamation . . . has not declared any historic landmark, or any historic or prehistoric structure, or any other object of historic or scientific interest to be a national monument. . . . The said area itself, does not actually contain any historic landmark, or any historic or prehistoric structure, or any other object of historic or scientific interest."[7] After thirty-seven years of using the Antiquities Act to proclaim whatever it wanted, the Department of the Interior finally was asked to define the boundaries of the national monument category.

The question had never really been formally asked. After the furor surrounding the proclamation of Mount Olympus in 1909 had subsided, only Ralph Henry Cameron had spoken out against the Antiquities Act. He questioned the validity of the Grand Canyon National Monument in his lawsuits over mineral claims and property rights in the 1910s and 1920s. Other objections had been confined to public outcry, special interest lobbying, and congressional carping, mostly by western representatives.[8] The authority of the Antiquities Act had escaped substantive legal challenges until 1943. "A case of actual controversy exists as to the proper and correct interpretation of the Antiquities Act," the suit contended, and it further requested that the court hold the proclamation of the monument to be null and void.[9] In short, the state asked the federal judiciary to determine the limits of executive power under the Antiquities Act. The challenge attempted to define the limits of the Antiquities Act as well as to abolish the Jackson Hole National Monument. The attack contained broader implications that Deputy Attorney General John J. McIntyre, in charge of the case for the state of Wyoming, apparently did not recognize. The State of Wyoming narrowly perceived the issues, and the Park Service responded with a multifaceted interpretation.

Park Service officials held their ground and addressed the broader implications of the lawsuit. Initially, the agency answered the complaint by denying all charges of substance, including the contention that the agency prevented state officials and local residents from using the disputed area. Superintendent Smith cited his response to Beery and the other publicity-seeking "commandos." He had ignored their presence, making it difficult for the opposition to substantiate its charges.[10] The Office of the United States Attorney General offered assistance, and the agency began to develop the basis of its defense. It needed to define the historical and scientific values to which Roosevelt referred in the proclamation, and to show through precedent the many applications of the word *object* in the Antiquities Act.

The federal legal staff began to work on the defense. On 17 June 1943 Jackson E. Price offered suggestions for defense strategy. Price saw three available options. Citing *Colorado vs. Toll*, 268 U.S. 228, he suggested that the suit was an unauthorized challenge to federal authority "since [the] plaintiff seeks to control and interfere with the use and administration of federal property." In another vein, Price believed that the court would not review the "President's express determination" that the area contained significant historical landmarks or objects, nor his implied determination that the area fit the criteria of the Antiquities Act. Price also thought that numerous cases established that "a decision of a head of a Department on a question of fact, rendered in a matter within his jurisdiction, is final and conclusive, binding on the courts and not subject to review." Finally, Price debunked the idea that Jackson Hole represented a deviation from prior uses of the Antiquities Act. He cited the example of the second Zion and Grand Canyon national monuments as precedents for adjacent monuments that were later incorporated into existing national parks.[11] From the position of the Office of the Attorney General of the United States, the state of Wyoming had no real basis for its suit.

As a result, the Park Service requested a summary judgment to dismiss the case. Much to the chagrin of NPS officials, on 3 December 1943 the motion was denied.[12] The Park Service recognized the backlash against federal authority and believed that local politics influenced the decision. Agency officials worried that partisan stances would become a factor in the court case. There was no recourse. The state would have its opportunity to challenge the agency.

Immediately, Chief Historian Herbert Kahler began searching for experts to support the contention that the Jackson Hole area was historically significant. He settled on Dr. Leroy Hafen, the author of a number of books on the fur trade and the West, and chose Dr. Frederic Paxson, of the University of California, as an alternate. Park Service director Newton B. Drury, who replaced Cammerer in 1940, suggested noted scientist Olaus B. Murie as the appropriate person to testify on biological values, Dr. F. M. Fryxell for geological values, and Lawrence Merriam, the assistant director of Region II, which included the Jackson Hole region, on administrative issues.[13]

The Act offered the Park Service great leeway; its inherent ambiguity made it easy to defend in court. The Park Service only had to show that the establishment of Jackson Hole was not an unusual instance. In such an amorphous category, its size did not make it an anomaly. Although there were few nineteenth-century structures in the region, Jackson Hole had historic importance because of its significance for the fur trade. Its unique geological features and important kinds of scarce wildlife became the basis for its scientific value. From the perspective of the agency, both values made the establishment of Jackson Hole National Monument a legitimate use of the Antiquities Act. Agency witnesses sought to convince the court of the scientific and historical value of the region. Its case would be strengthened by evidence that Jackson Hole contained compound cultural and scientific value.

On 9 March 1944 the NPS settled on its expert witnesses, but confusion continued over how to make its case. The agency chose Fryxell, Hafen, and Murie, along with Merrill J. Mattes of the NPS historical staff. The search for a biologist and geologist outside the agency continued.[14] But the specialists took narrow view of their responsibilities, and someone had to develop a broadly based integrative approach.

The process of creating an historical justification produced tension within the agency. Mattes felt that the agency wavered on important historical questions. He advocated presenting Jackson Hole as an historic landmark, but contended that the NPS needed to assert conclusively that mountain men like John Colter, Jedediah Smith, and Jim Bridger traversed the Jackson Hole area. The agency was too tentative, Mattes wrote, asserting that its objective was "to win a lawsuit rather than to write an historical monograph. . . . [o]ur main job is to prove to the satisfaction of the court that *Jackson Hole does have special historical significance*. If I am wrong in this I am wondering what kind of a case for history we have left."[15] Mattes saw that accepting the pronouncements of historical professionals offered a tactical advantage. He wanted the agency to capitalize on it.

Presenting the comparable values of history and science became the crucial question in pretrial strategy. The agency had to decide which value offered a more credible argument for the court. Assistant Regional Director Howard Baker answered that question in a memo of 4 July 1944 to Director Drury. "It is our opinion," he wrote, "that all of the values contained in the Jackson Hole National Monument should be presented with equal importance, for the composite of all places the monument in the national [significance] category."[16] Baker argued that the most compelling way to make the case was to present Jackson Hole as an aggregation of values, equally justifiable historically or scientifically, and certainly secure together. The latitude in the Antiquities Act afforded the NPS that option.

It was sound policy: broaden the issues at stake and overwhelm the state in court. Between the twenty-first and twenty-fourth of August 1944, the case was heard in Federal District Court in Sheridan, Wyoming, and according to National Park Service accounts, the trial went exactly as the agency planned. The state tried to show that the creation of the Jackson Hole National Monument had been a political tactic to extend the boundaries of Grand Teton National Park. As a result, Attorney General McIntyre had to prove that there were no outstanding historic or scientific objects in the region. He presented a series of local and state residents and experts to support his claims.[17]

The Park Service countered by presenting its witnesses. Murie testified that Jackson Hole was unique because there were 120 different species of birds and forty species of mammals in the region. Dr. Harold E. Anthony of the American Museum of Natural History testified that the monument contained objects of interest to scientists and students of natural history, and that the region was "a unique ecological area." Mattes testified to the historical significance of the region, in Jackson Price's opinion, "adequately demonstrat[ing] the historical significance of the area." A geologist from the University of Illinois, Dr. Leland Horberg, and Dr. Rudolph Edmund of the Shell Oil Company "revealed the importance of the Jackson Hole valley as an outstanding example of a fault-trough, to be considered in connection with the fault-block comprising the Teton Range."[18] According to their testimony, the region also contained examples of three separate stages of glaciation, lending even more significance from a geological perspective.

The NPS succeeded in showing that the area had significance, and Price chose not to present evidence justifying the size of the national monument area. He thought such a tactic unnecessary. Wyoming failed to show that the size of the monument was inappropriate, and Price believed that the court record clearly showed that the Antiquities Act offered sufficient authority to establish the national monument. "Under the recognized authorities," Price wrote in his report of the trial, "the court may not substitute its judgement for that of the President in reviewing the propriety of the action."[19] Judge T. Blake Kennedy took the case under advisement at the close of the trial, and Price was confident that the judge planned to vindicate the creation of the monument.

The lawsuit challenged the nature of the proclamation as well as its constitutionality, but in the courtroom, the state emphasized the specifics of the case. The NPS counterattacked with a challenge to the right of the state of Wyoming to question the authority of the president. After this tactic, the state appeared to be on shaky ground, barring the kind of partisan judicial interpretation that the NPS officials indicated they feared when they discovered Judge Kennedy's close ties to the grazing industry and the local Republican party.[20]

Because Park Service strategists were able to construe the lawsuit as an attack on the Antiquities Act itself as well as on the monument, they built a defensible case. In the more than seventy previous instances that employed the Antiquities Act, no one had ever challenged the law itself. Even larger natural areas than Jackson Hole, including the original Grand Canyon, Mount Olympus, and Joshua Tree national monuments, were proclaimed under its auspices. The representative area monuments of the 1930s, such as Organ Pipe Cactus National Monument, established a precedent for including flora typical of an area. Proclaimed as scientific monuments, they were additional ammunition in favor of the Park Service.

Although the crucial issue appeared to be the limits of the Antiquities Act, Judge Kennedy avoided addressing it when he made his decision. Kennedy dismissed the case on the grounds that it was "a controversy between the legislative and executive branches of the

Government in which . . . the Court can not interfere."[21] By circumventing the larger issue, the judge refused to rule upon the discretionary power of the president. The establishment of the monument stood, a sizable victory for the agency. The only redress for the state of Wyoming lay in legislative initiative.

The battle over the Jackson Hole National Monument was the last of the first generation of conflicts between the interests of conservation/preservation and unregulated use of land. Wyoming pitted its rights as a sovereign state against those of the federal government— a battle not unlike the one Ralph Henry Cameron had fought against the Park Service at the Grand Canyon—and lost. Despite vindication of their position, Park Service officials recognized the importance of good relations with individual states. The agency had further objectives in the region and used the legal victory as a place from which to negotiate a compromise.

As a result, the court case served as an indirect prelude to the abrogation of the Antiquities Act. During the late 1930s and 1940s, other park projects created controversy in Congress. The Park Service lost much of its support in Congress as a result of weak leadership, attrition, and retirement. The need for the development and interpretation of new park areas made the Antiquities Act a less formidable tool for preservation. Coupled with the unfavorable coverage the entire Jackson Hole episode generated, congressional uproar and greater public expectations made agency officials reconsider its assumptions about further expansion of the national park system.

The discovery phase of American preservation ended before the beginning of the New Deal, and the Antiquities Act became an anachronism that recalled the Progressive-era values that shaped the early years of the agency. Between 1906 and 1944, the hegemony that invested the presidency with unlimited authority broke down. The rush also went out of the reservation of park areas. New additions were no longer established just ahead of bulldozers and dam builders. Money for developing areas other than national parks became available. As the Park Service realized the value of all its different categories of areas and developed the kinds of programs that built and sustained an infrastructure, it spread its resources more evenly among the park system. Cooperation with Congress became critical to the future of the system, and the appeal of the advantages of the Antiquities Act diminished. In an environment where the pronouncement of the establishment of an area meant less than its subsequent development, limits on uses of the Antiquities Act became inevitable.

Although in 1943 Earl Warren, then the governor of California, suggested to a conference of western governors that they work together to abolish the Antiquities Act and Wyoming senator Joseph O'Mahoney cosponsored a bill in the Senate to that end, the abrogation of the Antiquities Act came only in 1950. The heated exchanges of earlier years cooled considerably in the postwar climate, and the participants negotiated an amicable compromise. What the NPS and the president sacrificed to acquire the new and enlarged Grand Teton National Park, which included the disputed Jackson Hole National Monument, was the right to use the Antiquities Act within the boundaries of the state of Wyoming.[22]

The NPS gave up little in the compromise, for the role of the Antiquities Act had already diminished. After the division into regions in 1937, the Park Service gradually ceased to use the designation of an area to determine its value to the system. The manner in which an area entered the system became less important than its potential, and because most of the important areas in the public domain had long before been scrutinized for membership in the park system, the legal limits upon its use were no greater than the restrictions the agency placed upon itself.

Under this kind of integrated management, the monuments fared better than they ever had. The last vestiges of second-class status for the national monuments disappeared with the initiation of Mission 66, a ten-year capital improvement program designed to rejuvenate the park system in honor of the fiftieth anniversary of the Park Service in 1966. Mission 66 financed capital development programs in all categories of park areas. More than 2,000 miles of roads were built or improved, and the modern visitor centers that highlight many park areas were also developed.[23] Another ramification was the development of new criteria for assessing the needs of park areas. Designation ceased to be of paramount importance; instead, the popularity of an area with the public became a more accurate measure of its position within the system.

During and after Mission 66, distinction between categories of NPS areas became nearly indistinguishable. No longer were monuments slighted because they remained in the monument category; publicity, appropriation, and maintenance were determined more by need than by the nomenclature of an area. Yet later national monuments formed the basis for the creation of new national parks, as did the way-station monuments of the 1910s and 1920s. Older national monuments, such as the Petrified Forest and Arches, became national parks; other areas, such as Chaco Canyon, which went from national monument status to that of national historic park, also acquired new designations in the constant attempts of the Park Service to lend even a peripheral sense of cohesiveness to the elements that comprised the system. A plethora of categories were available and the title of national monument, when bestowed by a Congressional bill, was increasingly reserved for areas that showed something of pre-European physical or cultural life on this continent.[24]

The new additions to the system were different than their predecessors at the turn of the century. In the continental United States, new park areas were rarely undiscovered. Most often they represented a change in emphasis by the agency or Congress, or a reevaluation or recognition of the resource that the area contained. The excitement of urgency left the preservation process, and additions to the system became part of a process of choosing between similar alternatives. Particularly after the civil and women's rights movements of the 1960s and 1970s, areas that the Park Service would not have recognized as significant in 1920 became important additions to the system. As the message of the park system changed to fit the times, the areas added to it reflected new values. The process of determining appropriate new areas became more selective, yet somehow less critical to the survival of the system. The pressure was off the Park Service and it ceased to have to rely on the instincts of its leaders.

Yet more and more, the restrictions upon park areas came from outside the agency. The insistence of Congress on maintaining control through appropriations effectively prevented the Antiquities Act from being an important weapon in the preservation arsenal. The use of the Antiquities Act was no longer the primary way to preserve a worthy location; instead it became an emergency step used when all other means had failed. If the NPS was to receive funding for a monument authorized by the Antiquities Act, the Interior and Insular Affairs Committee of the U.S. House of Representatives often insisted that the agency request and receive its approval prior to the issuance of a proclamation. Only upon receiving committee approval would budgets for newly established areas be sanctioned. As a result, after 1950 most new national monuments were created by Congress and the Antiquities Act was invoked for their proclamation. Rare occasions saw presidents use the discretionary power that the Antiquities Act offered.

There were, however, a number of cases in which executive fiat made a mockery of any legislative attempts to control the establishment of new areas or even the type of park area labelled a national monument. During each of the Eisenhower, Johnson, and Carter administrations, the NPS and the Department of the Interior made at least one use of the Antiquities Act without the prior sanction of Congress, recalling vividly the administrations of Theodore Roosevelt and Franklin D. Roosevelt, as well as other presidents who regarded executive power over the public domain as an important part of their responsibility. Each attempt created problems, even with members of the president's own party.

Two of the most significant cases of executive proclamation, the establishment of the Chesapeake and Ohio (C & O) Canal in 1961 and the Marble Canyon in 1969, were lame-duck proclamations, following the tradition begun by Theodore Roosevelt with the Mount Olympus National Monument and elevated to an art form by Herbert Hoover after his defeat by Franklin D. Roosevelt in 1932.[25] Another group of important national monuments proclaimed without congressional approval since 1950, the "d-2" group established in Alaska in 1978, mirrored earlier cases where threats of exploitation loomed large. In all cases, at the request of the NPS and the Department of the Interior, the president proclaimed as national monuments areas Congress had considered but had not made national parks. These were maneuvers of the Jackson Hole National Monument variety, the establishment by fiat of areas that Congress would not otherwise reserve.

The establishment of the C & O Canal National Monument in 1961 ended nearly a decade of debate about the character of the park area for that locale. Initial NPS proposals were to develop a parkway, but due to citizen initiative led by Supreme Court Justice William O. Douglas, the canal was ultimately established as a walkway rather than as a road. After nearly seven years of discussion and with the inauguration of John F. Kennedy approaching, Dwight D. Eisenhower attempted to resolve the situation with the establishment of a national monument in the final hours of his administration.[26]

Congressman Wayne Aspinall, the chairman of the House Committee on Interior and Insular Affairs, disapproved of such bold executive action. Aspinall's position was that since Congress had to appropriate money for the upkeep of the C & O Canal, no matter how the law read, the legislative branch was entitled to input in the process. Aspinall took a hard-line position, stating that if the president was going to circumvent Congress, then he was going to have to pay for the activation and subsequent needs of any such area out of his own pocket.

Eisenhower's proclamation did not give the Park Service everything it wanted. As in many cases, the initial proclamation was a short-term solution designed to enable further development of the area. It began the process of transforming the C & O Canal to national historic park status, which required congressionally appropriated funds. Aspinall stuck to his position and throughout the 1960s refused to fund development of the park. In effect, the powerful congressman annulled most of the power that remained in the Antiquities Act; any future use of the act unsanctioned by Congress was sure to create controversy. Although rarely used during the prior decade, after the C & O Canal controversy, the Antiquities Act became a measure reserved for emergency or lame-duck situations.[27]

It took less than a decade for the legislative and executive branches to clash over the Antiquities Act once again. During the "lame-duck" portion of his term in 1969, Lyndon B. Johnson established the Marble Canyon National Monument as part of a program to leave a final legacy of his term. Secretary of the Interior Stewart Udall recommended the reservation of large areas of Alaska as well as the fifty-mile area between the Grand Canyon National Park and Glen Canyon National Recreation Area as additions to the National Park System. Johnson apparently was ready to use the Antiquities Act to proclaim nearly eight million acres of national monuments, but in what has been called a "series of excruciating coincidences," the original plan was altered and the one eventually enacted added less than half a million acres to the system.[28]

In December 1968, Richard Nixon announced his new Secretary of the Interior, Gov. Walter Hickel of Alaska. Like the West at the end of nineteenth century, Alaska had been a hotbed of anti-conservationism. Many Alaskans felt that there was too much government intervention in the affairs of their state, and Hickel would have to serve his constituency. His appointment put the sizable Alaskan part of the project in doubt. President Lyndon B. Johnson wondered whether the Governor would offer any support for the new parklands in his state and used this as a reason to delay the proclamation.

The NPS continued to prepare for the reservation of the lands that Udall recommended. Agency officials believed the President would go forward with the proposed proclamations on 19 December 1968 as a "conservation Christmas gift to the nation." One day before the scheduled proclamations, Johnson became ill with the flu. The proclamations were again postponed, but the NPS still had reason for hope. In his final State of the Union address on 14 January 1969, Johnson announced: "there is more [parkland] going to be set aside before this administration ends."[29]

But Udall had not cleared the project with all the pertinent people on Capitol Hill. The congressional delegations of the states involved received briefings. Senator Henry Jackson of Washington, Chairman of the Interior and Insular Affairs Committee in the Senate, pledged his support; his counterpart in the House of Representatives, Wayne Aspinall, had not been informed. Despite his stance on the Chesapeake and Ohio Canal, Aspinall had helped the Park Service in a number of situations; he was instrumental in preventing a compromise which would have allowed mining in Canyonlands National Park. But as the C & O Canal showed, he was also a staunch advocate of congressional jurisdiction over the establishment of areas that required funds from Congress. From Aspinall's point of view, the proclamation was an attempt to "by-pass Congress."[30]

The legislative and executive branches were prepared to do battle over the President's right to exercise power granted him by the Antiquities Act. From Udall's point of view, the proclamation offered the last chance for the addition of important lands to the Park System under a sympathetic administration, and the Antiquities Act was the only remaining tool that served the purpose. From Aspinall's perspective, it was an arrogant challenge to congressional authority and a blatant usurpation of the powers of the legislative branch. He objected on principle to the manner in which the lands were established, not to the reservation of the land itself. In essence, the battles of the early twentieth century were recast in the terms of the 1960s.

But even as a "lame duck," Lyndon Johnson could not afford to be as cavalier with Congress as could Theodore Roosevelt. As he threatened, Aspinall could prevent the appropriation of funds for as long as he remained in Congress. With control over that crucial element of the preservation process in the hands of an angry Congress, the new areas might have become nonexistent entities, similar to the national monuments before Frank Pinkley brought them to prominence. In the end, an unhappy compromise was reached. The Marble Canyon National Monument was established, and almost 350,000 acres were added to existing park areas in Alaska, but the additions fell far short of the nearly 8 million acres that Udall proposed. Among the costs of the endeavor was the creation of an adversarial relationship between the ex-president and his former secretary of the interior.[31]

Sixty-three years after its passage, the Antiquities Act remained a point of contention between the president and Congress. Its capricious powers continued to present adamant presidents and agency directors with a direct way to achieve desired goals. Its broad powers offered solutions in seemingly irresolvable situations. It remained a "court of last resort" in public domain matters so long as the president, the secretary of the interior, and the NPS were willing to face the consequences of an alienated and often furious Congress.

The most recent use of the Antiquities Act, the proclamation of large sections of Alaska as national monuments by Jimmy Carter in 1978, fit the pattern established for the use of aggressive executive power since 1950. Like the proclamation of Muir Woods and many other early national monuments, the establishment of the Alaskan national monuments was a response to the threat that lands reserved under the section 17 (d)(2) provision of the Alaska Native Claims Settlement Act of 1971 would revert to public domain or state control and eventually be sold for commercial purposes. Like the temporary withdrawals made by the GLO at the end of the nineteenth century, the d-2 lands were reserved so that they could be sorted into appropriate categories when Congress could agree on the proper way to complete the project.

The withdrawal in 1978 paved the way for "lame-duck" congressional establishment of what has been called the "Alaskan National

Park System" in 1980. More than a stopgap measure, Jimmy Carter's proclamations sprang from the same vision of governmental responsibility that motivated the decisions of Theodore Roosevelt, Herbert Hoover, and Franklin D. Roosevelt. Faced with the need for swift and decisive action in the national interest, Carter used the aggressive and arbitrary power willed him by an earlier generation of American leaders.

The Alaskan Native Claims Settlement Act of 18 December 1971 authorized the secretary of the interior to select up to 80 million acres of public land in Alaska for possible inclusion in federal land reservation systems. The law gave the secretary two years within which to make his recommendations and an additional five beyond the original two for Congress to act upon the suggestions. In 1973, Secretary Rogers C. B. Morton made his recommendations, which included 32.3 million acres for the national park system.

Bills for and against the proposal made little progress until the 1977-78 session of the 95th Congress, when Morris K. Udall introduced H.R. 39. A compromise version of Udall's bill passed the House on 18 May 1978, but Alaskan senators Mike Gravel and Ted Stevens prevented action on a similar bill in the Senate. With no successful action during the 95th Congress and 18 December 1978, the date upon which the withdrawn lands would revert to the public domain, approaching, the only remaining tool available to change the temporary withdrawals into permanent ones was the Antiquities Act. On 1 December 1978, Jimmy Carter proclaimed fifteen new national monuments, eleven under NPS jurisdiction and two each for the Forest Service and the Fish and Wildlife Service.[32]

In a situation recreating the urgent conditions for which it had been passed, the Antiquities Act once again became the most effective and expedient way to achieve preservation goals. Congressional disapproval was a smaller problem with areas in Alaska than it would have been elsewhere. Like the inaccessible monuments at the turn of the century, many of the "d-2" national monuments were remote enough to be insulated from the threats of depredation and vandalism. As were their counterparts eighty years earlier, the new Alaskan monuments were more susceptible to legal encroachment: land claims, energy exploration, or commercial exploitation of another kind. But once reserved, they could exist safely with minimal funding for maintenance and upkeep, a fact that put their creation beyond the control of Congress. The Alaskan national monuments were "pre-created" as protection against future growth and exploitation. They ensured the availability of parkland when it became necessary.

As did earlier "waystation" monuments, the Alaskan monuments became national parks during the "lame-duck" session following a president's ouster. Jimmy Carter's defeat in 1980 was the catalyst for the transformation. Alaskan senators had fought proposals every step of the way, and their efforts limited the chances of park bills. On 19 August 1979, a more limited conservation measure than earlier House bills passed the Senate. Feeling their power ebb after the election of Ronald Reagan, advocates orchestrated a compromise. Rather than risk an even less comprehensive piece of legislation under the incoming Reagan administration, House supporters accepted the more limited Senate bill on 12 November 1980. On 2 December, Jimmy Carter signed into law the Alaskan National Interest Lands Conservation Act [ANILCA]. Under its terms, a total of 47,080,730 acres were added to the national park system.[33]

Carter's use of the Antiquities Act in the Alaskan situation revealed that the law remained a viable way to achieve short-term preservation goals. It was available as a means to rapidly reserve threatened land; a sort of peacemaker, the Antiquities Act bought time for the National Park Service, the Department of the Interior, the president, and Congress. It permitted an intelligent decision to be made regarding the permanent status of the various lands, for it gave the conflicting parties the opportunity to work out the details to the satisfaction of most of the participants.

In many ways, the Alaskan national monument proclamation was in keeping with the uses of the Antiquities Act. Early uses of the act had made the diverse national park system of today possible; the more than 45 million-acre Alaskan reservation laid the basis for the national park system of the future. The same bold executive action that protected the Grand Canyon, Muir Woods, the Teton biota, and similar areas initiated the reservation of the inaccessible yet spectacular land in Alaska. The remote and forgotten monuments of the 1920s are on the visiting list of millions of American tourists today. In the coming decades, the Alaskan parks may be the salvation of the increasingly threatened park system.

Once again, the Antiquities Act has given the United States a new national park system into which to grow, much the way it provided the legal authorization for the system of today. Even when Congress passed the Archaeological Resources Protection Act of 1979, which rectified many of the shortcomings of the Antiquities Act, the section in the earlier law that authorized the president to proclaim national monuments remained unchanged. As it was designed to do in 1906, the Antiquities Act remains a way, albeit a controversial one, to put the interests of the general public ahead of those of any individual group of constituents.

In the rare cases in which it has been used by the president since 1950, the Antiquities Act has usually filled a gap much as it did at the turn of the century. The certainty of its powers and the speed with which it can reserve land in the public domain make it a unique piece of legislation from conservation and preservation perspectives. The Antiquities Act is a reminder of the executive discretion in the name of the greater good with which the United States once trusted its presidents; despite periodic uses rightly termed excessive, its legacy is generally one of placing the future of the nation over the present needs or desires of individuals. It is an important indication of the social obligation American leaders once felt to maintain the physical and cultural features in this country for the benefit of all Americans.

The unique category of park areas it established, the national monuments, have been poorly understood since their inception. Initially conceived to preserve archaeological ruins, the category grew to include the broadest range of areas ever reserved by a government for its people. Evolving into an integral part of the federal preservation of the natural and human past on this continent, the national monuments are truly monuments; their existence reminds Americans of the need to remember the past as well as of the necessity of preparing for a long-term future. Of aesthetic and cultural value, the national monuments are testimony to a vision of social responsibility shared by American leaders of an earlier time.

NOTES

1. Robert W. Righter, *Crucible for Conservation: The Creation of Grand Teton National Park* (Boulder: Colorado Associated University Press, 1982), 96–97; Sen. Henry Ashurst of Arizona stated during the 1933 hearings on the enlargement of Grand Teton National Park that "the other states are not going to put over on Wyoming something that her two Senators do not want."

2. Ibid., 105-6, 108.

3. Ibid., 108.

4. Ibid., 110-11.

5. Ibid., 114-15.

6. *State of Wyoming vs. Charles J. Smith et al.*, 18 May 1943, NA, RG 79, Series 7, Jackson Hole National Monument, file 201-06.

7. Ibid.

8. Solicitor Jackson E. Price informed the Attorney General of the United States that the validity of the Grand Canyon National Monument was an issue in *Cameron vs. U.S.*, 252 U.S. 450, on 17 June 1943. But Cameron only challenged the federal government's right to take title to land to which he had filed a claim (see NA, RG 79, Series 7, Jackson Hole National Monument file 201-06; Shankland, *Steve Mather*, 225-42; NA, RG 79, Series 6, Grand Canyon, file 12-5, and Series 17, Records of Horace M. Albright 1927-33, Grand Teton file).

9. *State of Wyoming vs. Charles J. Smith et al.*

10. Charles J. Smith memorandum for the Associate Director, 2 June 1943, NA, RG 79, Series 7, Jackson Hole National Monument, file 201-06.

11. Solicitor Jackson E. Price to Attorney General, 17 June 1943, NA, RG 79, Series 7, Jackson Hole National Monument, file 201- 06.

12. See letters following the 3 December 1943 decision in the National Archives, RG 79, Series 7, Jackson National Monument, file 201-06, particularly a confidential memo date 6 December 1943 from Regional Director Lawrence C. Merriam to superintendent Paul Franke, who replaced Smith as the superintendent of the Grand Teton National Park.

13. Newton B. Drury memo, 7 January 1944, NA, RG 79, Series 7, Jackson Hole National Monument, file 201-06.

14. Hillary A. Tolson, 13 March 1944, memo for the files, NA, RG 79, Series 7, Jackson Hole National Monument, file 201-06.

15. Merrill J. Mattes to Director, 30 June 1944, NA, RG 79, Series 7, Jackson Hole National Monument, file 201-06.

16. Howard Baker memo to Newton B. Drury, 4 July 1944, NA, RG 79, Series 7, Jackson Hole National Monument, file 201-06.

17. Jackson E. Price memo to Newton B. Drury, 30 August 1944, NA, RG 79, Series 7, Jackson Hole National Monument, file 201-06.

18. Ibid.

19. Ibid.

20. Paul Franke memo to Associate Director, 19 April 1944, NA, RG 79, Series 7, Jackson Hole National Monument, file 201-06.

21. Righter, *Crucible for Conservation*, 119.

22. Ibid., 113, 117.

23. Foresta, *America's National Parks and Their Keepers*, 54-55.

24. Barry Mackintosh, *The National Parks: Shaping The System* (Washington, DC: National Park Service, 1984), 9.

25. Among Hoover's lame-duck proclamations were the second Grand Canyon National Monument, proclaimed on 22 December 1932; White Sands, New Mexico, on 18 January 1933; Death Valley, on 11 February 1933; Saguaro, on 1 March 1933; and the Black Canyon of the Gunnison, on 2 March 1933. Albright, *Birth of the National Park Service*, 276-78, recounts Hoover's influence on the process.

26. William Everhart, *The National Park Service* (New York: Praeger Publishers, 1972), 196-98; see also April L. Young, "Saving the C & O Canal: Citizen Participation in Historic Preservation" (unpublished M.A. thesis, George Washington University, 1973). Young's thesis is on file at the National Park Service Record Center, Harper's Ferry, West Virginia.

27. Ibid., 196-98, 177; this was substantiated during an interview with Park Service historian Barry Mackintosh, 15 January 1985.

28. Everhart, *National Park Service*, 176.

29. Ibid., 176.

30. Ibid., 177.

31. Ibid., 178.

32. William Everhart, *The National Park Service* (Boulder: Westview Press, 1983), 128-32; Barry Mackintosh, *Shaping the System*, 100-106.

33. Mackintosh, *Shaping the System*, 100-106.

18. Dinosaur National Monument, established 4 October 1915. Photo courtesy of the National Archives.

19. Long House ruins in Frijoles Canyon, Bandelier National Monument, established 11 February 1916. Photo courtesy of the National Archives.

20. Casa Grande National Monument, established 3 August 1918. Photo courtesy of the National Park Service, Southwest Regional Office.

21. Scotts Bluff National Monument, established 12 December 1919. Photo courtesy of the National Park Service, photographer William Keller.

22. Cypress Swamp, Lehman Caves National Monument, established 24 January 1922. Photo courtesy of the National Park Service.

23. Castillo de San Marcos (originally Fort Marion), established 15 October 1924. Photo courtesy of the National Park Service, photographer Richard Frear.

24. Statue of Liberty National Monument, established 15 October 1924. Photo courtesy of the National Park Service, photographer Richard Frear.

25. Fort Matanzas National Monument, established 15 October 1924. Photo courtesy of the National Park Service, photographer Jack E. Boucher.

26. Black Falls group of ruins, Wupatki National Monument, established 9 December 1924. Photo courtesy of the National Archives.

27. George Washington Birthplace National Monument, established 23 January 1930. Photo courtesy of the National Park Service, photographer Richard Frear.

28. Colonial National Monument, established 3 July 1930. Photo courtesy of the National Park Service.

29. White House Ruins, Canyon de Chelley National Monument, established 1 April 1931. Photo courtesy of the National Archives.

30. White Sands National Monument, established 18 January 1933. Photo courtesy of the National Park Service, from a postcard in the collection of the author.

31. Fort Frederica National Monument, established 26 May 1936. Photo courtesy of the National Park Service, photographer Cecil W. Stoughton.

32. Joshua Tree National Monument, established 10 August 1936. Photo courtesy of the National Park Service, photographer Richard Frear.

33. Restored earth lodge, Ocmulgee National Monument, established 23 December 1936. Photo courtesy of the National Park Service, photographer Glenn W. Peart.

34. Sonoyata Valley, Organ Pipe Cactus National Monument, established 13 April 1937. Photo courtesy of the National Park Service.

35. Capitol Reef National Monument, established 2 August 1937. Photo courtesy of the National Park Service.

36. Chesapeake and Ohio Canal National Monument, established 18 January 1961. Photo courtesy of the National Park Service.

Appendix. Chronology of National Monument Establishment

Part 1. Monuments Established between 1906 and May 1944.
Source: *The National Monuments* (Washington, D.C.: Department of the Interior, 1944).

Site Name	Date Established	State	President	Total Federal Area[1]
Devils Tower	24 September 1906	Wyo.	T. Roosevelt	1,152.91
El Morro	8 December 1906	N.M.	T. Roosevelt	240.00
Montezuma Castle	8 December 1906	Ariz.	T. Roosevelt	520.00
Petrified Forest	8 December 1906	Ariz.	T. Roosevelt	84,597.1
Chaco Canyon	11 March 1907	N.M.	T. Roosevelt	17,636.73
Cinder Cone	6 May 1907	Calif.	T. Roosevelt	5,120.00[2]
Lassen Peak	6 May 1907 9 August 1916[3]	Calif.	T. Roosevelt	1,280.00
Gila Cliff Dwellings	16 November 1907	N.M.	T. Roosevelt	160.00
Tonto	19 December 1907	Ariz.	T. Roosevelt	1,120.00
Muir Woods	9 January 1908	Calif.	T. Roosevelt	424.56

[1] Figures indicate gross acreage in 1944 or at the time area was transferred to national park category or abolished.

[2] For monuments no longer in existence the gross area (not the Federal area) is given in this column.

[3] Lassen Volcanic National Park was created by the Act of 9 August 1916 (39 Stat. 442), including the lands formerly in Cinder Cone and Lassen Peak national monuments.

Site Name	Date Established	State	President	Total Federal Area[1]
Grand Canyon	11 January 1908 26 February 1919[4]	Ariz.	T. Roosevelt	806,400.00
Pinnacles	16 January 1908	Calif.	T. Roosevelt	12,817.65
Jewel Cave	7 February 1908	S.D.	T. Roosevelt	1,274.56
Natural Bridges	16 April 1908	Utah	T. Roosevelt	2,740.00
Lewis and Clark Cavern	11 May 1908 24 August 1937[5]	Mont.	T. Roosevelt	
Tumacacori	15 September 1908	Ariz.	T. Roosevelt	10.00
Wheeler	7 December 1908	Colo.	T. Roosevelt	300.00
Mount Olympus	2 March 1909 29 June 1938[6]	Wash.	T. Roosevelt	298,090.00
Navajo	20 March 1909[7] 14 March 1912[8]	Ariz.	Taft Taft	360.00
Oregon Caves	12 July 1909	Ore.	Taft	480.00
(Mukuntuweap) Zion	31 July 1909 19 November 1919[9]	Utah	Taft	76,800.00
Shoshone Cavern	21 September 1909	Wyo.	Taft	212.37
Gran Quivira	1 November 1909	N.M.	Taft	370.94
Sitka	23 March 1910	Alaska	Taft	57.00
Rainbow Bridge	30 May 1910	Utah	Taft	160.00
Big Hole Battlefield	23 June 1910		Taft	200.00
Colorado	24 May 1911	Colo.	Taft	16,763.39
Devils Postpile	6 July 1911	Calif.	Taft	800.00
Cabrillo	14 October 1913	Calif.	Wilson	0.50
Papago Saguaro	31 January 1914 7 April 1930[10]	Ariz.	Wilson	1,940.43

[4] Grand Canyon National Park was created by the Act of 26 February 1919 (40 Stat. 1175), including most of the land formerly in the monument.

[5] The monument was abolished by the Act of 24 August 1937 (50 Stat. 746), and the land transferred to the State of Montana.

[6] Olympic National Park was created by the Act of 29 June 1938 (52 Stat. 1241), including the land formerly in the monument.

[7] The proclamation did not specify a particular acreage, but included all of the ruins within a described area, with an area of forty acres around each ruin.

[8] The area was "reduced" to 360 acres.

[9] Zion National Park was created by the Act of 19 November 1919 (41 Stat. 356), including the land formerly in the monument.

[10] The Monument was abolished by the Act of 7 April 1930 (46 Stat. 142) and the land divided among state and local agencies.

Site Name	Date Established	State	President	Total Federal Area[1]
Dinosaur	4 October 1915	Utah	Wilson	183,221.56
Walnut Canyon	30 November 1915	Ariz.	Wilson	1,593.16
Bandelier	11 February 1916	N.M.	Wilson	25,972.79
	25 February 1932[11]		Hoover	
Sieur de Monts	8 July 1916	Maine	Wilson	5,000.00
	26 February 1919[12]			
Capulin Mountain	9 August 1916	N.M.	Wilson	680.37
Old Kasaan	25 October 1916	Alaska	Wilson	38.00
Verendrye	29 June 1917	N.D.	Wilson	253.04
Casa Grande	3 August 1918[13]	Ariz.	Wilson	472.50
Katmai	24 September 1918	Alaska	Wilson	2,697,590.00
Scotts Bluff	12 December 1919	Nebr.	Wilson	1,652.15
Yucca House	19 December 1919	Colo.	Wilson	9.60
Lehman Caves	24 January 1922	Nev.	Harding	639.31
Timpanogos Cave	14 October 1922	Utah	Harding	250.00
Fossil Cycad	21 October 1922	S.D.	Harding	320.00
Aztec Ruins	24 January 1923	N.M.	Harding	25.88
Hovenweep	2 March 1923	Utah and Colo.	Harding	285.80
Mound City Group	2 March 1923	Ohio	Harding	57.00
Pipe Spring	31 May 1923	Ariz.	Harding	40.00
Bryce Canyon	8 June 1923	Utah	Harding	7,440.00
	7 June 1924[14]			
Carlsbad Cave	25 October 1923	N.M.	Coolidge	719.22
	14 May 1930[15]			
Chiricahua	18 April 1924	Ariz.	Coolidge	10,529.80

[11] Transferred to NPS.

[12] Lafayette National Park (later changed to Acadia) was created by the Act of 26 February 1919 (40 Stat. 1178), including the lands formely in Sieur de Monts National Monument.

[13] The proclamation gave monument status to lands previously pursuant to the act of 2 March 1889 (25 Stat. 961).

[14] Utah National Park (later changed to Bryce Canyon) was created by the Act of 7 June 1924 (43 Stat. 593), including the land formerly in Bryce Canyon National Monument.

[15] Carlsbad Cavern National Park was created by the Act of 14 May 1930 (46 Stat. 279), including the land formerly in the Monument.

Site Name	Date Established	State	President	Total Federal Area[1]
Craters of the Moon	2 May 1924	Idaho	Coolidge	47,540.70
Castle Pinckney	15 October 1924	S.C.	Coolidge	3.50
Fort Marion	15 October 1924	Fla.	Coolidge	18.51
Fort Matanzas	15 October 1924	Fla.	Coolidge	18.34
	9 January 1935		F. D. Roosevelt	
Fort Pulaski	15 October 1924	Ga.	Coolidge	5,427.39
Statue of Liberty	15 October 1924	N.Y.	Coolidge	10.38
Wupatki	9 December 1924	Ariz.	Coolidge	34,680.89
Meriwether Lewis	6 February 1925	Tenn.	Coolidge	300.00
Glacier Bay	26 February 1925	Alaska	Coolidge	2,299,520.00
Father Millet Cross	5 September 1925	N.Y.	Coolidge	0.01
Lava Beds	21 November 1925	Calif.	Coolidge	45,727.00
Arches	12 April 1929	Utah	Hoover	33,360.00
	25 November 1938		F. D. Roosevelt	
Holy Cross	11 May 1929	Colo.	Hoover	1,392.00
George Washington Birthplace	23 January 1930[16]	Va.	Hoover	394.47
Sunset Crater	26 May 1930	Ariz.	Hoover	3,040.00
Colonial	3 July 1930	Va.	Hoover	9,430.00
Canyon de Chelly	1 April 1931[17]	Ariz.	Hoover	83,840.00
Great Sand Dunes	17 March 1932	Colo.	Hoover	43,769.19
Grand Canyon	22 December 1932	Ariz.	Hoover	196,531.00
White Sands	18 January 1933	N.M.	Hoover	135,085.15
Death Valley	11 February 1933	Calif.	Hoover	1,850,565.20
Saguaro	1 March 1933	Ariz.	Hoover	55,124.00
Black Canyon of the Gunnison	2 March 1933	Colo.	Hoover	12,723.46
Cedar Breaks	22 August 1933	Utah	F. D. Roosevelt	5,946.60
Fort Jefferson	4 January 1935	Fla.	F. D. Roosevelt	86.82
Fort Frederica	26 May 1936	Ga.	F. D. Roosevelt	94.30
Perry's Victory Memorial	6 July 1936	Ohio		14.25
Joshua Tree	10 August 1936	Calif.	F. D. Roosevelt	653,123.30

[16] The Monument was established by the Act of 23 January 1930 (46 Stat. 58).
[17] Pursuant to the Act of 14 February 1931 (46 Stat. 1161).

Site Name	Date Established	State	President	Total Federal Area[1]
Ocmulgee	23 December 1936[18]	Ga.		683.48
Zion	22 January 1937	Utah	F. D. Roosevelt	37,464.00
Organ Pipe Cactus	13 April 1937	Ariz.	F. D. Roosevelt	328,161.73
Capitol Reef	2 August 1937	Utah	F. D. Roosevelt	33,735.67
Pipestone	25 August 1937	Minn.		115.39
Channel Islands	26 April 1938	Calif.	F. D. Roosevelt	1,119.98
Fort Laramie	16 July 1938	Wyo.	F. D. Roosevelt	214.41
Ackia Battleground	25 October 1938	Miss.		49.15
Homestead	3 January 1939	Nebr.		160.82
Badlands	25 January 1939	S.D.		118,796.41
Santa Rosa Island	17 May 1939	Fla.	F. D. Roosevelt	9,500.00
Tuzigoot	25 July 1939	Ariz.	F. D. Roosevelt	42.67
Fort McHenry	11 August 1939[19]	Md.		47.64
Whitman	20 January 1940	Wash.		45.93
Appomattox Court House	10 April 1940	Va.		973.30
Andrew Johnson	27 April 1942	Tenn.		17.08
Jackson Hole	15 March 1943	Wyo.	F. D. Roosevelt	173,064.62

Part 2. Monuments Established between June 1944 and December 1981. Compiled by the author.

Site Name	Date Established	State	President
Harpers Ferry	30 June 1944[20]	W.Va., Md. and Va.	F. D. Roosevelt
Castle Clinton	12 August 1946	N.Y.	Truman
Fort Vancouver	19 June 1948[21]	Wash.	Truman

[18] Pursuant to the Act of 14 June 1934 (48 Stat. 958).
[19] Fort McHenry National Park was changed to Fort McHenry National Monument and Historic Shrine by an act of Congress.
[20] Redesignated a National Historic Park in 1963.
[21] Redesignated a National Historic Site in 1961.

238 Appendix

Site Name	Date Established	State	President
Fort Sumter	12 July 1948	S.C.	Truman
Saint Croix Island	8 June 1949[22]	Maine	Truman
Fort Union	28 June 1954	N.M.	Eisenhower
Booker T. Washington	2 April 1956	Va.	Eisenhower
Edison Laboratory	14 July 1956[23]	N.J.	Eisenhower
Chesapeake and Ohio Canal	18 January 1961[24]	District of Columbia and Md.	Eisenhower
Russell Cave	11 May 1961	Ala.	Kennedy
Buck Island Reef	28 December 1961	Virgin Islands	Kennedy
Agate Fossil Beds	5 June 1965	Neb.	L. B. Johnson
Pecos	28 June 1965	N.M.	L. B. Johnson
Biscayne	18 October 1968[25]	Fla.	L. B. Johnson
Marble Canyon	20 January 1969[26]	Ariz.	L. B. Johnson
Florissant Fossil Beds	20 August 1969	Colo.	Nixon
Hohokam-Pima	21 October 1972	Ariz.	Nixon
Fossil Butte	23 October 1972	Wyo.	Nixon
John Day Fossil Beds	26 October 1974	Ore.	
Congaree Swamp	18 October 1976	S.C.	Ford
Aniakchak	1 December 1978[27]	Alaska	Carter
Bering Land Bridge		Alaska[28]	Carter
Cape Krusenstern		Alaska	Carter
Denali		Alaska[29]	Carter
Gates of the Arctic		Alaska[30]	Carter
Glacier Bay		Alaska[31]	Carter

[22] Redesignated an international historic site in 1984.
[23] Incorporated in Edison National Historic Site in 1962.
[24] Authorization dated from 1938; became a national monument in 1961; incorporated in Cheasapeake and Ohio National Historic Park in 1971.
[25] Incorporated in Biscayne National Park in 1980.
[26] Incorporated in Grand Canyon National Park in 1975.
[27] Incorporated in legislated Aniakchak National Monument and National Preserve in 1980.
[28] Redesignated as a national preserve in 1980.
[29] Incorporated with Mount McKinley National Park in Denali National Park and National Preserve in 1980.
[30] Incorporated in Gates of the Arctic National Park and Preserve in 1980.
[31] Addition to existing monument; both incorporated in Glacier Bay National Park and National Preserve in 1980.

Site Name	Date Established	State	President
Katmai		Alaska[32]	Carter
Kenai Fjords		Alaska[33]	Carter
Kobuk Valley		Alaska[34]	Carter
Lake Clark		Alaska[35]	Carter
Noatak		Alaska[36]	Carter
Wrangell-St. Elias		Alaska[37]	Carter
Yukon-Charley		Alaska[38]	Carter
Salinas	19 December 1981[39]	N.M.	Reagan

[32] Addition to existing monument; both incorporated in Katmai National Park and National Preserve in 1980.

[33] Redesignated a national park in 1980.

[34] Redesignated a national park in 1980.

[35] Incorporated in Lake Clark National Park and National Preserve in 1980.

[36] Incorporated in Noatak National Preserve in 1980.

[37] Incorporated in Wrangell-St. Elias National Park and National Preserve in 1980.

[38] Redesignated Yukon-Charley Rivers National Preserve in 1980.

[39] Incorporated Gran Quivira, a national monument, and two state-designated areas, Salinas and Ato.

Bibliographic Essay

THE CONSERVATION MOVEMENT IN THE UNITED STATES has been the focus of a number of excellent studies in recent years. The best overall view of conservation during the Progressive era is Samuel P. Hays, *Conservation and the Gospel of Efficiency: The Progressive Conservation Movement 1890-1920* (Cambridge: Harvard University Press, 1959). Donald C. Swain, *Federal Conservation Policy 1921-1933* (Berkeley: University of California Press, 1963), covers the subsequent era until the start of the New Deal. On the history of the preservation impulse in the United States, Charles B. Hosmer, Jr., *Presence of the Past: A History of the Preservation Movement in the United States Before Williamsburg* (New York: G. P. Putnam's Sons, 1965) and *Preservation Comes of Age: From Williamsburg to the National Trust 1926-1949*, 2 vols. (Charlottesville: University of Virginia Press, 1981), set the standard by which all other works of preservation history are evaluated.

In recent years, scholarship about the National Park Service, its leaders, and its policies has proliferated. Alfred Runte's *National Parks: The American Experience*, 2d ed. (Lincoln: University of Nebraska Press, 1987), remains the top book in the field. This synthesis offers the most comprehensive look at the evolution of American attitudes about the national park system. Runte is at his best when he discusses the impact of changing values on the national parks. John Ise, *Our National Park Policy: A Critical History* (Baltimore: Johns Hopkins University Press, 1961), addresses the legislative history of the park system. Ise's book is marred by inconsistency in both the text and footnotes, and his interpretation often seems dated and subjective. Ronald Foresta, *America's National Parks and Their Keepers* (Washington, DC: Resources for the Future, 1984), is an ambitious book that focuses on Park Service policy during the last two decades. Although valuable as an assessment of the period after 1960, the book does not live up to its title. It is an account of the parks and their policymakers, not of their keepers, and the idiosyncratic perspective of the author often interferes with the presentation of the material. Foresta is not a historian, and his work reflects that fact. Donald C. Swain has published a number of articles that tell important pieces of the story of the park system. His "The National Park Service and the New Deal, 1933-1940," *Pacific Historical Review* 41 (August 1972), and "The Passage of the National Park Service Act of 1916," *Wisconsin Magazine of History* 50 (Autumn 1966), help present the broad outlines of the history of the agency.

The Park Service has also produced general studies of its history, of which the best example is Harlan D. Unrau and G. Frank Williss, *Administrative History: Expansion of the National Park Service in the 1930s* (Denver: Denver Service Center, 1983). This a helpful account of the growth of the system during the Great Depression. John C. Paige, *The Civilian Conservation Corps and the National Park Service, 1933-1942: An Administrative History* (National Park Service, 1985), looks closely at the impact of the CCC on the system. Both of these present much raw data, establish chronology, and provide the researcher with a valuable frame of reference.

Only one prior general study deals directly with the Antiquities Act. Ronald F. Lee, *The Antiquities Act of 1906* (Washington, DC: National Park Service, 1971) is a narrative account of the process that led to the passage of the act. Lee's work yielded many primary sources and served as an important starting point for this book.

In its early years, personality played a major role in the development of the Park Service. Biographies of the leading figures provide another way to monitor the evolution of the park system and the monuments. Donald C. Swain, *Wilderness Defender: Horace M. Albright and Conservation* (Chicago: University of Chicago Press, 1970), is an excellent if laudatory look at the second director of the Park Service. Donald C. Swain's "Harold Ickes, Horace Albright, and the Hundred Days: A Study in Conservation Administration," *Pacific Historical Review* 34

(November 1965): 455-465, is an outstanding analysis of Albright's maneuvering during the early days of the Roosevelt administration. Horace M. Albright as told to Robert Cahn, *The Birth of the National Park Service: The Founding Years, 1913-1933* (Salt Lake City: Howe Brothers, 1985), tells the story of the early years of the Park Service in Albright's own words. This interesting and informative account suffers from the problems that often plague oral histories. A check of documentary sources reveals that Albright's memory is often selective, and in many cases, he engages in inadvertent mythmaking and self-promotion at the expense of his co-workers. Robert Shankland, *Steve Mather of the National Parks*, 3d ed. (New York: Alfred A. Knopf, 1970), tells the story of the early years of the agency and the dynamic leader who brought the parks to the attention of the American public in an engaging fashion. Shankland makes Mather come alive on the pages; a reader truly feels the vigor of this driven man. Unfortunately, the Shankland book lacks footnotes.

The history of American archaeology and anthropology are other important components of the history of the Antiquities Act and the national monuments. The best overall study of American archaeology is Gordon R. Willey and Jeremy A. Sabloff, *A History of American Archaeology* 2d ed., (San Francisco: W. H. Freeman, 1980). Curtis Hinsley, Jr., *Scientists and Savages: The Smithsonian Institution and the Development of American Anthropology 1846-1910* (Washington, DC: Smithsonian Institution Press, 1981), establishes the context for an analysis of the state of American anthropology and archaeology at the turn of the twentieth century. Another recent book that includes historical information about southwestern archaeology is Robert H. Lister and Florence C. Lister, *Those Who Came Before* (Tucson: The University of Arizona Press, 1983).

Despite his importance as the leading archaeologist of the first two decades of the twentieth century, Edgar L. Hewett remains largely unstudied. Hewett's own writings, particularly *Ancient Life in the American Southwest* (Indianapolis: Bobbs-Merrill Company, 1930), give considerable insight into this volatile and influential figure. One study, which is not really a biography despite its title, Beatrice Chauvenet, *Hewett and Friends: A Biography of Santa Fe's Vibrant Era* (Santa Fe: Museum of New Mexico Press, 1983), falls far short of the mark. Derived strictly from Hewett's papers and almost completely devoid of any context or interpretation, it does not do justice to the complexity of Hewett, his time, or the early years of southwestern archaeology. Curtis M. Hinsley, Jr., "Edgar Lee Hewett and the School of American Research in Santa Fe, 1906-1912," in *American Archaeology Past and Future*, ed. David J. Meltzer, Don D. Fowler, and Jeremy A. Sabloff (Washington, DC: Smithsonian Institution Press, 1986), does a much better job, but his article covers only a small story within the larger picture. Hewett had an immense impact on every aspect of southwestern archaeology and nearly as great an impact on tourism; the scholarly record is far from complete.

The conflict between the Park Service and Forest Service has been the subject of an increasing amount of scholarship. Most authors have studied the conflicts from one side or the other, and as a result, scholars have not reached a consensus on the topic. The sources already cited contain the traditional perspective of the Park Service; the best examples of the point of view of the Forest Service are Harold K. Steen, *The United States Forest Service: A History* (Seattle: University of Washington Press, 1976), and Sally K. Fairfax and Samuel T. Dana, *Forest and Range Policy* (New York: McGraw-Hill, 1980). David A. Clary, *Timber in the Forest Service* (Lawrence: University of Kansas Press, 1986) is an important addition to the history of the field of forest history. In recent years, a number of efforts to synthesize the material on this issue have been published. Ben Twight, *Organizational Values and Political Power: The Forest Service Versus the Olympic National Park* (University Park: Pennsylvania State University Press, 1983), is an interesting start in this direction. Rather than follow the traditional stand of the USFS (that the NPS aggressively encroached on its domain), Twight posits that the values of the USFS and the kind of people attracted to a career in forestry gave the Forest Service a point of view that it found difficult to defend when faced with NPS arguments. Although Twight relies heavily on social science theory to make his point and does not really look at the actions of the NPS, his work has opened up new areas. Another study that builds on Twight's work is my own "Shaping the Nature of a Controversy: The Park Service, The Forest Service, and the Cedar Breaks National Monument" *Utah Historical Quarterly* 55 (Summer 1987). This piece explores the factors that led to the establishment of the Cedar Breaks National Monument from a tract of the Dixie National Forest, countering Twight by adding the

Park Service perspective. This is an area with plenty of room for future scholarship.

Primary sources played a major part in shaping this book. Park Service sources such as the annual reports of the directors of the agency and the proceedings of the various national parks conferences held by the agency helped build a framework from which to interpret the story of the national monuments. Record Group 79 of the National Archives, which is the records of the National Park Service, offered volumes of information. This series contains the records of each park unit as well as general records pertaining to the national parks and monuments from the period prior to 1949. In the reading room on the second floor of the National Archives I pieced together the story of the stone dish incident at Sequoia, and I began to sense Frank Pinkley's energy and commitment. For the scholar of any aspect of the history of the national park system, there is no more important source.

Index

Note on the Author

Hal K. Rothman is Associate Professor of History at the University of Nevada–Las Vegas where he edits *Environmental History Review*, the journal of the American Society for Environmental History. He is the author of *"I'll Never Fight Fire with My Bare Hands Again,"* a social history of early federal forestry (forthcoming), *On Rims and Ridges: The Los Alamos Area since 1880* (Lincoln, 1992), and histories of Bandelier, Navajo, and Pipestone national monuments. His articles have appeared in numerous journals, including *Western Historical Quarterly, Journal of the Southwest, Environmental History Review,* and *Public Historian.*